THE KEEPER OF THE FLAME

THE SUPREME COURT OPINIONS OF JUSTICE CLARENCE THOMAS
(1991 – 2005)

HENRY MARK HOLZER

OTHER BOOKS BY THE AUTHOR

The Gold Clause: What It Is And How To Use It Profitably (ed.)

Government's Money Monopoly: Its Origin, Scope,
And How To Fight It (ed.)

Sweet Land Of Liberty? The Supreme Court And Individual Rights

Speaking Freely: The Case Against Speech Codes (ed.)

The Layman's Guide To Tax Evasion

"Aid And Comfort": Jane Fonda In North Vietnam (with Erika Holzer)

Fake Warriors: Identifying, Exposing, And Punishing Those Who
Falsify Their Military Service (with Erika Holzer)

Why *Not* Call It Treason? Korea, Vietnam, Afghanistan, And Today

DEDICATION

To Clarence Thomas, Associate Justice,
Supreme Court of the United States,
the keeper of the flame ignited on
July 4, 1776,
September 17, 1787,
and
December 15, 1791.

ACKNOWLEDGEMENTS

Without the wisdom and courage of those who understood then-Judge Clarence Thomas's fundamental judicial philosophy and worked so diligently for his appointment as an associate justice of the Supreme Court of the United States, this book would never have been written. For their efforts, I am grateful, as should be this nation.

Nor would it have been written without a great service done me by William Madison, Esq., of Albuquerque, New Mexico, and Lance Gotko, Esq., of New York City. They appeared in the night of pessimism and brought with them the light of day.

I had practiced constitutional law from my admission to the bar in 1959 until 1972, and have done so from 1992 to the present. During the two decades in between, I not only practiced constitutional law, I taught it and related subjects at Brooklyn Law School. It was in the crucible of those countless hours of intellectual engagement in Socratic dialogue with my students that my own constitutional jurisprudence crystallized. To many of those students—especially those who disagreed with me—I am indebted. I may have been the hammer, but they were the (mostly) willing anvil.

As she has done with my previous books, my wife, Erika Holzer, lawyer and writer, edited this manuscript with her typical insight, skill, and dedication. It has been much improved by her ministrations, for which, as always, I am deeply indebted.

The manuscript was copy edited by the sharp-eyed, conscientious, and knowledgeable Shaynee Snider, and it has benefited greatly from her expertise.

Although I retired from Brooklyn Law School as professor emeritus in 1993, various courtesies continue to be extended to me by several members of the faculty and staff—especially by my former assistant, Deanna Handler—for which I am grateful.

And my thanks to Bill Gates and Microsoft for their Word software, that has liberated writers from our ancient foes: typographical errors and carbon paper.

The Congress, whenever two thirds of both Houses shall deem it necessary, shall propose Amendments to this Constitution, or, on the Application of the Legislatures of two thirds of the several States, shall call a convention for proposing Amendments, which, in either Case, shall be valid to all Intents and Purposes, as Part of this Constitution, when ratified by the Legislatures of three fourths of the several States, or by Conventions in three fourths thereof, as the one or the other Mode of Ratification may be proposed by the Congress . . . .

(Article V of the Constitution of the United States of America)

TABLE OF CONTENTS

INTRODUCTION

In his fourteen complete terms as an associate justice of the Supreme Court, Clarence Thomas has written 327 opinions.[1] Despite their consistency in showing him to be a formidable intellect and staunch defender of the Constitution, his reputation among laypersons is not commensurate with his achievements. Too many members of the public have uncritically accepted the professional character assassination visited upon Justice Thomas by the liberal professional and academic legal community. I cannot count the times that people who should have known better have, simply upon hearing Clarence Thomas's name, immediately responded with derogatory comments about his abilities as a justice—even though they have never read a single opinion of the hundreds Thomas has written.

In the summer of 2005, when Associate Justice Sandra Day O'Connor announced her retirement, liberals launched a preemptive attack against Thomas because of rumors about the possibility of his being appointed chief justice. Not only did the Thomas-haters disinter their ugly rhetoric from the early nineties, they also impugned his fourteen-term record on the Court. Their unwarranted criticism covered all areas of Supreme Court adjudication: federalism, separation of powers, judicial review—and worse, Justice Thomas's record in Bill of Rights and Fourteenth Amendment cases.[2]

Attacks on Justice Thomas have been unconscionable distortions of an unambiguous and distinguished record. Simple justice requires they be rebutted because his opinions, often eloquent, reveal him as a thoughtful conservative who understands the role of a Supreme Court justice, the methodology of proper constitutional and statutory adjudication, and the appropriate resolution of the many issues that have come to the Court during his tenure.

1

That is why I have written this book, the first to examine Clarence Thomas's entire body of Supreme Court opinions[3] — majority, concurring,[4] and dissenting.[5]

The Keeper of the Flame is not, however, a personal biography of Clarence Thomas, tracking his ascent from humble beginnings to the highest Court in the land. It is not a revisiting of the bruising confirmation battle that the Left turned into a deplorable spectacle. Nor is it a discourse on how liberals have retreated into the courts as the last bastion of furthering an agenda that is anathema to the majority of Americans, and thus can't be forced through unwilling legislatures. It is not a commentary on the typically uninformed, and sometimes deliberately distorted, hearsay accounts of Justice Thomas's opinions.

On the contrary, this book is about the jurisprudence of Associate Justice of the Supreme Court Clarence Thomas *as reflected to a considerable extent, but not exclusively, in his written dissents from, and concurrences with, majority opinions.* In this book, Thomas's jurisprudence will be gleaned extensively *from his own words*, not from what others—especially the liberals and their handmaiden media—have "reported" about what Thomas has written.

The cases and quotations I have selected for detailed examination in this book are those most illustrative of his jurisprudence. They have been culled from *every* opinion Justice Thomas has written during his tenure on the Supreme Court of the United States.

Thomas's words unequivocally reflect what he understands to be the appropriate role of a Supreme Court justice, his methodology for proper decision-making, and his position on fundamental constitutional questions, among them: separation of powers, federalism, judicial review, and such Bill of Rights issues as abortion, affirmative action, the death penalty, and the alleged rights of prisoners.

Many of those words have been written in dissent.

The Latin word for "dissent" is "dissentire," which in turn comes from "dis," meaning "apart," and "sentire," meaning "to feel, think."[6] It is Clarence Thomas's "thinking apart" that is the *subject* of this book. Its *theme* is that Thomas's opinions reveal him to be a judicial conservative's conservative.[7] His jurisprudence can best be described as "conservative" because of Thomas's commitment to "originalist" interpretation of the Constitution and federal statutes, to the Constitution's structural pillars of federalism and separation of powers, and to judicial restraint.[8]

To understand Justice Thomas's constitutional jurisprudence it is essential that the reader understand precisely what is meant by the concept of constitutional "originalism."

Although the principle of "originalism" had been around for quite some time, not until 1985 was it formally introduced to the organized bar. In July of that year, Attorney General of the United States Edwin Meese III delivered an historic speech to the American Bar Association at its meeting in Washington, D.C.[9] Meese's speech caused a constitutional explosion whose reverberations are still being felt, most notably in the recent appointments of John G. Roberts, Jr., to be chief justice of the Supreme Court of the United States and Samuel Alito to be an associate justice.[10]

In his address to the ABA, Meese reminded the assembled lawyers and judges of "the proper role of the Supreme Court in our constitutional system":

> The text of the document and the original
> intention of those who framed it would
> be the judicial standard in giving effect to
> the Constitution.

After surveying the Court's October 1984 term's decisions in three subject areas[11] —federalism, criminal law, and religion—Meese asked:

What, then, should a constitutional jurisprudence actually be? It should be a Jurisprudence of Original Intention. By seeking to judge policies in light of principles, rather than remold principles in light of policies, the Court could avoid both the charge of incoherence *and*[12] the charge of being either too conservative or too liberal.

A jurisprudence seriously aimed at the explication of original intention would produce defensible principles of government that would not be tainted by ideological predilection. This belief in a Jurisprudence of Original Intention also reflects a deeply rooted commitment to the idea of democracy. The Constitution represents the consent of the governed to the structures and powers of the government. The Constitution is the fundamental will of the people; that is why it is the fundamental law. To allow the courts to govern simply by what it views at the time as fair and decent, is a scheme of government no longer popular; the idea of democracy has suffered. The permanence of the Constitution has been weakened. A constitution that is viewed as only what the judges say it is, is no longer a constitution in the true sense.

Disabusing his audience of the notion that a Jurisprudence of Original Intention was some newfangled fad, merely an interpretive theory *du jour*, the Attorney General adverted to the words of legendary Supreme Court justice Joseph Story, written in the nineteenth century, which were applicable not only to the Constitution specifically but also to statutory interpretation in particular:

> In construing the Constitution of the
> United States, we are in the first instance
> to consider, what are its nature and
> objects, its scope and design, as apparent
> from the structure of the instrument,
> viewed as a whole and also viewed in its
> component parts. Where its words are
> plain, clear and determinate, they require
> no interpretation . . . . Where the words
> admit of two senses, each of which is
> conformable to general usage, that sense
> is to be adopted, which without departing
> from the literal import of the words, best
> harmonizes with the nature and objects,
> the scope and design of the instrument.

A few months later, the Attorney General elaborated his theme:

> In recent decades many have come to
> view the Constitution—more accurately,
> part of the Constitution, provisions of the
> Bill of Rights and the Fourteenth
> Amendment—as a charter for judicial
> activism on behalf of various
> constituencies. Those who hold this view
> often have lacked demonstrable textual or
> historical support for their conclusions.
> Instead they have "grounded" their
> rulings in appeals to social theories, to
> moral philosophies or personal notions of
> human dignity, or to "penumbras,"
> somehow emanating ghostlike from

various provisions—identified and not
identified—in the Bill of Rights.[13]

Meese was referring to the Supreme Court's liberal justices, and
their cohorts in academia and the legal profession, who worship at the
altar of a "Living Constitution." "One Supreme Court justice," he
noted, "identified the proper judicial standard as asking 'what's best for
this country.' Another said it is important to 'keep the Court out front'
of the general society. Various academic commentators have poured
rhetorical grease on this judicial fire, suggesting that constitutional
interpretation appropriately be guided by such standards as whether a
public policy 'personifies justice' or 'comports with the notion of moral
evolution' or confers 'an identity' upon our society or was consistent
with 'natural ethical law' or was consistent with some 'right of equal
citizenship'."

The Attorney General could have effectively
quoted the "Living Constitution's" high priest, the late
Supreme Court Associate Justice William J. Brennan, Jr.
"[T]he Constitution," according to Brennan,

> embodies the aspiration to social
> justice,[14] brotherhood, and human
> dignity that brought this nation into
> being. * * * Our amended Constitution is
> the lodestar for our aspirations. Like
> every text worth reading, it is not
> crystalline. The phrasing is broad and the
> limitations of its provisions are not
> clearly marked. Its majestic generalities
> and ennobling pronouncements are both
> luminous and obscure. * * * When
> Justices interpret the Constitution they
> speak for their community, not for
> themselves alone. The act of
> interpretation must be undertaken with

full consciousness that it is . . . the
community's interpretation that is sought.
* * * But the ultimate question must be,
what do the words of the text mean in our
time. For the genius of the Constitution
rests not in any static meaning it might
have had in a world that is dead and
gone, but in the adaptability of its great
principles to cope with current problems
and current needs. * * * Our
Constitution was not intended to preserve
a preexisting society but to make a new
one, to put in place new principles that
the prior political community had not
sufficiently recognized.[15]

Not content to loose this blather, Brennan, in a
not-so-veiled reproach to originalists, referred to

> those who find legitimacy in fidelity to
> what they call "the intentions of the
> Framers". In its most doctrinaire
> incarnation, this view demands that
> Justices discern exactly what the Framers
> thought about the question under
> consideration and simply follow that
> intention in resolving the case before
> them. It is a view that feigns self-
> effacing deference to the specific
> judgments of those who forged our
> original social compact. *But in truth it is
> little more than arrogance cloaked as
> humility.*[16]

Twenty years after Meese's remarks, in an article[17] for a leading
Internet website—www.frontpagemag.com—entitled "Originalism

Above All Else," Steven Geoffrey Gieseler[18] explained originalism
this way:

> Originalism alone produces a body of law
> evincing the will of America's citizenry.
> America has assented to the Constitution
> as the nation's supreme law, altered only
> by its own process of amendment. Every
> day that it remains unchanged, it is
> ratified again as our governing document.
> Any deviation from the Constitution that
> occurs outside of its own terms not only
> lacks the consent of the governed, but
> violates it. This includes deviation by
> judicial fiat. * * * An originalist judge's
> opinions are moored to the intent of the
> drafters of the Constitution and its
> amendments, not the faddish slogans of
> the day. His or her own predilections are
> subjugated to our nation's founding
> papers. This results in a coherent and
> consistent interpretation of laws. More
> importantly, originalism results in a
> canon blessed with America's consent
> via its adopted Constitution.

Robert H. Bork, former law professor, judge of the United
States Court of Appeals for the District of Columbia Circuit, and
defeated nominee for a seat on the Supreme Court of the United States,
recently wrote that:

> For the past 20 years conservatives have
> been articulating the philosophy of
> originalism, the only approach that can
> make judicial review democratically
> legitimate. Originalism simply means

> that the judge must discern from the
> relevant materials—debates at the
> Constitutional Convention, the Federalist
> Papers and Anti-Federalist Papers,
> newspaper accounts of the time, debates
> in the state ratifying conventions, and the
> like—the principles the ratifiers
> understood themselves to be enacting.
> The remainder of the task is to apply
> those principles to unforeseen
> circumstances, a task that law performs
> all the time. Any philosophy that does not
> confine judges to the original
> understanding inevitably makes the
> Constitution the plaything of willful
> judges.[19]

In other words, the concept of a "Living Constitution," so central to liberal jurisprudence and evident in so much Supreme Court adjudication, means no Constitution at all.

A "Living Constitution" is anti-democratic because it removes from the public forum and from those politically accountable, and thus from the electorate itself, important issues of social, economic, and other policy, and reposes those issues in nine unelected philosopher kings appointed for life.

There is no worse example of the "Living Constitution" in action than the case of *Griswold v. Connecticut*,[20] to which Attorney General Meese alluded when he spoke of "penumbras."

A Connecticut statute provided that "[a]ny person who uses any drug, medicinal article or instrument for the purpose of preventing contraception shall be fined not less than fifty dollars or imprisoned not less than sixty days nor more than one year or be both fined and imprisoned"—proving, once again, that in a democracy popularly elected legislators and governors can enact outrageous laws.

Because the federal Constitution does not prohibit the states from enacting outrageous laws—indeed, the Tenth Amendment expressly recognizes state power to enact laws, implicitly allowing them to affect public health, welfare, safety, and morals—the Warren Court had to find some other way to hold the Connecticut statute unconstitutional. The chief justice assigned the task to his chief smoke-and-mirrors associate justice, William O. Douglas, darling of America's liberals.

In a barely three-page opinion, Douglas prospected his way through the Constitution. Although what he found was fools' gold, it glittered enough to satisfy six of his colleagues.

According to Douglas, prior cases of the Supreme Court "suggested that specific guarantees in the Bill of Rights"—dealing with speech, press, association, quartering soldiers, search and seizure, self-incrimination, and the education of one's children—"have penumbras, formed by emanations from those guarantees that help give them life and substance." On the basis of these "penumbras" and "emanations"—but not a shred of constitutional precedent or other authority—the Warren Court gave birth to a constitutionally guaranteed "right of privacy."

For the seven-justice majority, Douglas wrote:

> We deal with a right of privacy older than
> the Bill of Rights—older than our
> political parties, older than our school
> system. Marriage [about which the
> Connecticut law said nothing] is a
> coming together for better or for worse,
> hopefully enduring, and intimate to the
> degree of being sacred [said the oft-

married Douglas]. It is an association
that promotes a way of life, not causes; a
harmony in living, not political faiths; a
bilateral loyalty, not commercial or social
projects. Yet it is an association for as
noble a purpose as any involved in our
prior decisions.

Despite this pretentious mumbo-jumbo, or perhaps because of
it, neither Douglas nor any of his six colleagues had an answer to a
simple question asked in Justice Stewart's dissent (in which Justice
Black joined): "*What provision of the Constitution . . . make[s] this
state law invalid?* The Court says it is the right of privacy 'created by
several fundamental constitutional guarantees.' With all deference, I
can find no such general right of privacy in the Bill of Rights, in any
other part of the Constitution, or in any case ever before decided by this
Court."[21]

Despite the clarity of Stewart's persuasive dissent—and because
the Warren Court majority wanted to rid Connecticut of what Stewart
rightly characterized an "uncommonly silly law"—the *Griswold*
majority invented an ersatz "right to privacy." This construct would
later be used in *Roe v. Wade* to justify invalidating the anti-abortion
laws of virtually every state. As a result, *Griswold*, the "Living
Constitution's" poster-case, provided—by a 7-2 vote in a barely three-
page opinion—a "constitutional" rationale for the destruction of
literally millions of the unborn. (Only three votes the other way would
have changed the case's outcome, and profoundly affected the
American culture for the better.)

Thus, the notion of a "Living Constitution," the opposite of
originalism, is not only an anti-democratic and intellectually dishonest
way to interpret our Constitution and federal statutes. It is also
demonstrably capable of manufacturing dangerous ersatz "rights" that
carry tremendous moral and social costs.

It is *Griswold*'s interpretive methodology—imposed by liberals on the basic Constitution, on the Bill of Rights, on the Fourteenth Amendment, and on federal statutes—and the invention and institutionalization of ersatz "rights," that has made possible the decades-long metastasis of the "Living Constitution's" malignant doctrines into most areas of constitutional law.

In the name of our Founding Fathers, Justice Clarence Thomas has consistently fought against this anti-constitutional disease during his fourteen terms as an associate justice of the Supreme Court. More than any other member of the Court in modern times he has kept the constitutional faith.

To understand the jurisprudence that drives Justice Thomas, it is necessary to understand first the genesis and genius of the Constitution of the United States of America and its amendments.[22]

ENDNOTES

[1] Appointed by President George H. W. Bush on October 16, 1991, Justice Thomas took his seat on the Supreme Court of the United States on October 23, 1991.

[2] The professional literature abounds with not only articles legitimately critical of Justice Thomas's jurisprudence, but also with those that are snide and insulting. See, for example: "Clarence Thomas, Victim? Perhaps, and Victimizer: Yes—A Study in Social and Racial Alienation from African-Americans" (48 St. Louis University Law Journal 327); "Using the Master's 'Tool' to Dismantle His House: Why Justice Clarence Thomas Makes the Case for Affirmative Action" (47 Arizona Law Review 113); "Clarence Thomas, Affirmative Action and the Treachery of Originalism" (21 Harvard Blackletter Law Journal 1); "Just Another Brother on the Supreme Court? What Justice Clarence Thomas Teaches Us About the Influence of Racial Identity" (90 Iowa

Law Review 931). Non-professional periodic literature, including editorial and op-ed writing, is no better.

[3] A comprehensive list of all of 327 Justice Thomas's opinions can be found in Appendix A.

Because many of the Supreme Court's cases involve interpretation of specific sections of federal statutes (and some administrative rules), and because Justice Thomas's approach to statutory interpretation has been consistent during his fourteen terms, only his more important statutory interpretation opinions will be discussed in the text. Others will be referred to in Endnotes. However, a list of all Justice Thomas's statutory interpretation opinions, some with selected language providing a flavor of his jurisprudence, will be found in Appendix B.

[4] A justice writes a concurring opinion when he agrees with the conclusion (or a part of it) reached by the majority but disagrees with some other aspect of the opinion (e.g., whether to reverse a lower court's decision outright, or to remand the case for further proceedings).

[5] One other category of "opinion" by Justice Thomas is included: his comments when the Supreme Court has denied a request for review, but he believed strongly either that the Court erred or that some explanation was required. Like his colleagues, Thomas has written his share of such "opinions." Usually, but not always, brief, and nearly always far from a comprehensive statement of his jurisprudence, these "opinions" are examined in this book only when they reveal an important aspect of Thomas's jurisprudence.

For example, in *Hoffman* v. *Harris*, 511 U.S. 1060, 114 S.Ct. 1631 (1994), the Court denied review of this question: are social workers entitled to absolute immunity from being sued under the federal civil rights act (42 United States Code, Section 1983)? Thomas "dissented" from the Court's *denial* of review because lower courts had found such immunity to exist, but he believed that "the federal courts do not have a license to establish immunities from Section 1983 in the interests of what [they] judge to be sound public policy."

In other words, according to Thomas, the Court should have granted review.

[6] *Webster's New World Dictionary of the American Language.*

[7] One label that has never been attached to Justice Thomas is "liberal." However, some have characterized him not so much as a conservative, but as more of a libertarian.

A conservative is popularly understood to be "reluctant to accept change; in favor of preserving the status quo and traditional values and customs, and against abrupt change." (*Encarta* dictionary).

"Libertarian thought represents a highly individualistic extension of classic liberalism into the 20th century. Libertarians explicitly embrace most of the assumptions of classical liberalism. * * * Libertarians emphasize very strongly the autonomy of the individual and the minimal role required of government. * * * Given that the rights of the individual are superior to all other political values, libertarians think that the individual should be free of government restraint in both economic and non-economic spheres. Property rights are central to individual rights; security and freedom in property transactions are prerequisites to individual development. * * * [I]t is also essential that the individual remain free of coercion in matters of religion, morality, conscience, and other purely private matters." (Madox and Lilie, *Beyond Liberal and Conservative: Reassessing the Political Spectrum*, 14 – 15.)

Conservatives, on the other hand, "see a need to use government power to guide and limit human behavior in the realm of individual morals, but at the same time oppose the use of government to restrict human behavior in the economic realm." (Madox and Lilie, *Beyond Liberal and Conservative: Reassessing the Political Spectrum*, 14 – 15.)

I leave to the reader's judgment which of these two labels—conservative or libertarian—best describes Justice Thomas's jurisprudence.

[8] No matter how consistent any judge's jurisprudence, one would expect there to be some anomalies in hundreds of decisions written over the course of fourteen years. In Justice Thomas's case, however, there are virtually none among his 327 majority, concurring, and dissenting opinions.

[9] That portion of Attorney General Meese's speech relating to originalism, as well as speeches on that subject by Supreme Court Justices William J. Brennan, Jr., and John Paul Stevens, Judge Robert Bork, and President Ronald Reagan, are collected in "The Great Debate: Interpreting Our Written Constitution," published by the Federalist Society as Occasional Paper No. 2 (1986).

[10] On August 17, 2005, the *New York Times* News Service wrote that:

> [i]n 1985, after the Supreme Court had just delivered several decisions that infuriated conservatives and reinforced President Ronald Reagan's resolve to steer the judiciary rightward, Attorney General Edwin Meese III gave what many say was the speech of his career. Helping lay the foundation for the judicial wars that continue today, he advocated in a speech to the American Bar Association a "jurisprudence of original intention."

[11] Meese said that "[a]s has been generally true in recent years, the 1984 term did not yield a coherent set of decisions. Rather, it seemed to produce . . . 'a jurisprudence of idiosyncracy. Taken as a whole, the work of the term defies analysis by any strict standard. It is neither

simply liberal nor simply conservative; neither simply activist nor simply restrained; neither simply principled nor simply partisan. The Court this term continued to roam at large in a veritable constitutional forest."

During the 1984 term, the Supreme Court consisted of Chief Justice Warren E. Burger and Associate Justices William J. Brennan, Jr., Byron R. White, Thurgood Marshall, Harry A. Blackmun, Lewis F. Powell, Jr., William H. Rehnquist, John Paul Stevens, and Sandra Day O'Connor. For years after Meese's speech, Reagan appointee O'Connor would swing 4-4 decisions one way or another, inventing supposed constitutional "tests" as she went along.

[12] Emphasis in original.

[13] Speech by Attorney General Edwin Meese III to the District of Columbia chapter of the Federalist Society Lawyers Division, November 15, 1985, Washington, D.C., reprinted in "The Great Debate: Interpreting Our Written Constitution," published by the Federalist Society as Occasional Paper No. 2 (1986).

[14] On August 1, 2005, Dr. Thomas Sowell wrote at www.townhall.com: "I never cease to be amazed at how often people throw around the lofty phrase 'social justice' without the slightest effort to define it. It cannot be defined because it is an attitude masquerading as a principle."

[15] Speech by Associate Justice of the Supreme Court William J. Brennan, Jr., to the Text and Teaching Symposium, Georgetown University, October 12, 1985, Washington, D.C., reprinted in "The Great Debate: Interpreting Our Written Constitution," published by the Federalist Society as Occasional Paper No. 2 (1986).

[16]*Ibid.* Emphasis added.

[17] The article appeared on July 15, 2005.

[18] When the article was written, Mr. Gieseler was an attorney with Pacific Legal Foundation's Atlantic Center. PLF opposes judicial action that substitutes a judge's personal policy preferences for the freedoms guaranteed by the Constitution.

[19] Opinion Journal, *Wall Street Journal*, October 19, 2005, www.wsj.com.

[20] 381 U.S. 479, 85 S.Ct.1678 (1965). "U.S." refers to the official reports of Supreme Court decisions; "S.Ct." refers to the unofficial reports, published by West Publishing Company. The number preceding the reference is to the report's volume; the number following is to the report's page. A few current citations lack a "U.S." citation because at the time this book appeared, the official report of the case had not yet been published.

[21] Emphasis added.

[22] It is also useful to have a general understanding of how the Supreme Court of the United States operates.

The Supreme Court sits atop the state and federal judicial systems and rules on whether their courts have properly interpreted the Constitution and laws of the United States (i.e., the federal government). An example is the 2004 – 2005 term's decision in *Kelo* v. *City of New London,* _U.S._, 125 S.Ct. 2611 (2005), where the Supreme Court reviewed a decision of *Connecticut's* highest court concerning the federal Constitution's Fifth Amendment Eminent Domain Clause. An example of the Court's function as it relates to *federal* laws is its decision in *Sabri* v. *U.S.*, 541 U.S. 600, 124 S.Ct. 1941 (2004) (also discussed later in this book), where the Court had to rule on a federal criminal statute.

How do cases reach the Supreme Court, and what happens once they get there? Under Article III of the Constitution, certain cases can begin in the Supreme Court, without having to wend their way up from lower state or federal courts. These "original jurisdiction" cases are few and far between.

Non-original jurisdiction cases reach the Supreme Court in either of two ways. Under certain federal statutes (see 28 *United States Code*, Section 1251), a litigant who loses in the last state or federal court where the case can be heard has an alleged right to appeal to the Supreme Court of the United States. (See 28 *United States Code*, Section 1253.) This supposed right is, in practice, ephemeral, because if at least four of the nine justices don't want to entertain the case, it will not be heard.

The second way, and by far the most prevalent, through which cases reach the Court, is by its granting petitions for review. (See 28 *United States Code*, Sections 1254 and 1255.) A party wishing to invoke this discretionary jurisdiction of the Supreme Court files a "Petition for a Writ of Certiorari." If the petition is granted, which requires the affirmative vote of at least four of the nine justices, the Supreme Court "lifts up" the case from the lower state or federal court.

Each term, the Supreme Court receives literally thousands of petitions but grants only a small percentage.

Within months of "cert" being granted, the parties file written briefs. Not long after, they orally argue their case, in public, before the entire bench of nine justices.

Soon after, the justices meet in private conference. They discuss the case and take a preliminary vote. If the chief justice is a member of the majority, he assigns himself or an associate justice to write the majority opinion; if he is not, the senior justice in the majority performs that task. The same process is followed if the chief justice is a member of the minority. Because no decision of the Court is final until it is officially filed with the clerk of the Court and announced, occasionally justices change sides after the initial assignments are made. However, the drafting assignments virtually always remain in place unless it is one of the designated authors who changes sides.

CHAPTER 1.

"We the People"

CONSTITUTION OF THE UNITED STATES

*We the People of the United States, in Order
to form a more perfect Union, establish
Justice, insure domestic Tranquility, provide
for the common defence, promote the
general Welfare, and secure the Blessings
of Liberty to ourselves
and our Posterity, do ordain and establish
this Constitution for the United States of
America.*[23]

The first permanent English colony in the New World was founded in Virginia in 1607. Twelve years later, the first Assembly of Virginia convened, marking the beginning of a rudimentary form of representative government. Ten years after that, the survivors of the *Mayflower* obtained the First Charter of Massachusetts. Other charters followed, in New Netherlands (New York), Maryland, Connecticut, Pennsylvania. And with them, increasing agitation for more political representation.

In 1765, the "Stamp Act Congress" convened in New York and informed the English king that only the colonial legislatures could levy taxes on His Majesty's subjects in America. Two years later, Massachusetts protested the Townshend Revenue Act based on the idea that the English parliament could not pass statutes contrary to "fundamental law"—an idea that would become an organizing principle of American constitutionalism.

With passage in 1774 of the "Intolerable Acts," the momentum toward independence gained strength. Discontent was rife, and in May of that year eighty-one members of the Virginia House of Burgesses met in Williamsburg. They recommended that delegates from the colonies meet in a "continental congress." Massachusetts soon did the same; among its delegates was John Adams. Virginia's delegates included George Washington and Patrick Henry.

The First Continental Congress met in Philadelphia in the fall of 1774, fifty-five delegates from twelve colonies in attendance. The assembly adopted the "Declaration and Resolves of the First Continental Congress," which embodied principles that would become bedrock for the nation-to-be[24]:

> That the inhabitants of the English
> colonies in North America, by the
> immutable laws of nature, the principles
> of the English constitution, and the
> several charters or compacts, have the
> following Rights:
>
> 1. That they are entitled to life, liberty,
>   and property, & they have never
>   ceded to any sovereign power
>   whatever, a right to dispose of either
>   without their consent.
>
> 4. That the foundation of English
>   liberty, and of all free government,
>   is a right in the people to participate
>   in their legislative council . . . .
>
> 5. That the respective colonies are
>   entitled to the common law of
>   England, and more especially to the
>   great and inestimable privilege of

being tried by their peers . . .
according to the course of that law.

8.   That they have a right peaceably to
assemble, consider of their
grievances, and petition the King;
and that all prosecutions, prohibitory
proclamations, and commitments for
the same, are illegal.

10.   It is indispensably necessary to good
government, and rendered essential
by the English constitution, that the
constituent branches of the
legislature be independent of each
other; that, therefore, the exercise of
legislative power in several colonies,
by a council appointed during
pleasure, by the crown, is
unconstitutional, dangerous, and
destructive to the freedom of
American legislation.[25]

In July 1775, the Continental Congress adopted the "Declaration of the Causes and Necessity of Taking Up Arms," prepared by a Virginian named Thomas Jefferson.

By spring 1776, a few colonies had declared themselves free of England. Virginia instructed her delegates to the Continental Congress to "declare the colonies free and independent states."

In June of 1776, a five-man committee was appointed to prepare a formal statement—a declaration.

Then, on the evening of July 4, 1776, there occurred the most profound moral-political explosion in the history of mankind. Mutually pledging to each other their lives, their fortunes, and their sacred honor, the delegates to the Second Continental Congress adopted the Declaration of Independence of the United States of America.

I repeat Jefferson's opening words not only because the Declaration's principles influenced the founding document that came next—the Constitution of the United States of America—but because, today, those words often influence the constitutional jurisprudence of Associate Justice Clarence Thomas.

> We hold these truths to be self-evident:
> that all men are created equal; that they
> are endowed by their Creator, with
> certain unalienable rights; that among
> these are life, liberty, and the pursuit of
> happiness. That to secure these rights,
> governments are instituted among men,
> deriving their just powers from the
> consent of the governed . . . .

These principles were virtually unknown in the history of man. Consider:

- Truths, let alone self-evident;

- Equality, as imperfect as it may have been;

- Rights, inalienable no less;

- Three enumerated rights from which another, property, could logically be inferred;

- Government, yes, but existing to protect rights;

- Government, certainly, but created by men, not by the divine right of kings;

- Government, surely, but possessing only limited, "just" powers, and those powers legitimized not by gift from the sovereign, but only from the consent of the governed.

This was a real revolution, with a capital "R"—a Revolution of principle, of ideology, of rights, of a political philosophy non-existent before and unequalled since.

But the Declaration—a statement of political/philosophical principles—then had to be implemented. Needed was a charter for the actual organization and operation of the new government.

Sixteen months later, the Continental Congress submitted Articles of Confederation to the states for their approval. By July 1778 they had been approved by enough states to become effective. But they didn't work. One major problem was lack of a chief executive. Another was that some states erected trade barriers against other states—a problem later sought to be cured by the Constitution, but which continues to cause Justice Thomas and his colleagues considerable difficulty.

After the war, ostensibly to cure the deficiencies in the Articles of Confederation, Congress approved the convening of a convention at Philadelphia "for the sole and express purpose of revising the Articles of Confederation and reporting to Congress and the several legislatures such alterations and provisions therein as shall when agreed to in Congress and confirmed by the States render the Federal Constitution adequate to the exigencies of government and the preservation of the Union."

Though the stated purpose of the Constitutional Convention of 1787 was to revise the Articles of Confederation, after the delegates finished their work in Philadelphia that summer they reported to Congress a Constitution for an entirely new form of government. Even with its faults, some of which were major (and still plague Justice

Thomas and his colleagues), the Constitution written by men Jefferson called "demigods" has never been equaled as an attempt at the practical implementation of the principle of individual rights propounded by the Declaration of Independence.

If one regards the Constitution in its essentials—without, for example, details like the electoral college and organization of the House of Representatives—it is immediately apparent that the document masterfully reduced to fundamentals the complex machinery of a representative republic.

It is not without reason that the Preamble begins with "We the People of the United States." Remember the words of the Declaration of Independence: "Governments are instituted among Men, deriving their just Powers from the Consent of the governed."

It is not without reason that the stated objects of the government-in-creation were "to form a more perfect Union, establish Justice, insure domestic Tranquility, provide for the common defence, promote the general Welfare, and secure the Blessings of liberty to ourselves and our Posterity . . . ." Remember the words of the Declaration of Independence: "that all Men are created equal, that they are endowed . . . with certain unalienable Rights, that among these are Life, Liberty, and the Pursuit of Happiness."

To accomplish these objects by creating a national government possessed of only delegated powers, the Constitution contains a mere six articles.

The first three—legislative, executive, and judicial—contain specific delegations of power to the federal government and establish its working machinery.

The fourth deals with the relationship of the states to the federal government.

The fifth provides the process for amendment.

The sixth establishes the supremacy of the federal government over the states.

No one can reasonably read the Constitution as doing anything but creating a federal system consisting of a national government and constituent states, delegating power to that national government, making it supreme in its sphere, and providing for the Constitution's amendment.

To restrain the power delegated to the federal government, the Constitution created a system of "checks and balances" by dividing power "horizontally" among the three branches—and in the very nature of the federal system itself, by dividing power "vertically" between the federal government and the states. It would be the courts, and ultimately the Supreme Court of the United States, that would interpret the laws and resolve constitutional questions.[26] Thus, in Professor Corwin's words, American constitutionalism rests on three pillars: separation of powers, federalism, and judicial review—principles that Justice Thomas respects, understands, and consistently attempts to implement.

The Continental Congress submitted the proposed Constitution to the states for ratification, and the battle was immediately joined. So jealously did the colonists cherish their hard-won freedom from the crown that some of them opposed ratification because they believed the Framers had not gone far enough.

A major concern, aggravated by a diffuse uneasiness about the strong central government being created, was the absence of a bill of rights. Even though only power was being delegated to the new federal government—and nowhere in the Constitution was there even a suggestion that individual *rights* were being surrendered—still, opposition to it was fierce. George Clinton, governor of New York, a crucial state in the battle for ratification, engaged in a war of letters with Alexander Hamilton, and from the Convention's end through 1788 most of the ablest men in America exchanged countless letters attacking and defending its proposal.

It was Hamilton, soon after the Convention, who "conceived the idea of composing a series of essays analyzing the Constitution systematically, dispassionately, and at length. Thus . . . he addressed the 'People of the State of New York' in the first 'Publius' or *Federalist* paper . . . ."[27]

> I propose . . . to discuss the following interesting particulars—The *utility of the UNION to your political prosperity—The insufficiency of the present Confederation to preserve that Union—The necessity of a government at least equally energetic with the one proposed, to the attainment of this object—The conformity of the proposed Constitution to the true principles of republican government—Its analogy to your own state constitution— and lastly, the additional security which its adoption will afford to the preservation of that species of government to liberty, and to property.*[28]

For the next seven months, Hamilton and James Madison (assisted at the beginning by John Jay) "engineered the construction of the most famous political commentary in American history."[29]

Close to the end of their Herculean labors, Hamilton produced *Federalist No. 84*, containing his classic argument against a bill of rights. Because of that essay's impact on ratification of the Constitution, on Madison's later argument in Congress when introducing the Bill of Rights, and on how it affects constitutional adjudication and Justice Thomas's jurisprudence today, the essence of *Federalist No. 84* is reproduced here.

> It has been several times truly remarked that bills of rights are, in their origin, stipulations between kings and their subjects, abridgements of prerogative in favor of privilege, reservations of rights not surrendered to the prince. Such was Magna Charta, obtained by the barons, sword in hand, from King John. * * * It is evident, therefore, that, according to their primitive signification, they have no application to constitutions, professedly founded upon the power of the people, and executed by their immediate representatives and servants. Here, in strictness, the people surrender nothing; and as they retain every thing they have no need of particular reservations. "We, THE PEOPLE of the United States, to secure the blessings of liberty to ourselves and our posterity, do *ordain* and *establish* this Constitution for the United States of America." Here is a better recognition of popular rights than volumes of aphorisms which make the principal figure in several of our State bills of rights, and which would sound much better in a treatise of ethics than in a constitution of government.

> *   *   *

> I go further, and affirm that bills of rights, in the sense and to the extent in

29

which they are contended for, are not
only unnecessary in the proposed
Constitution, but would even be
dangerous. They would contain various
exceptions to powers not granted; and, on
this very account, would afford a
colorable pretext to claim more than were
granted. For why declare that things shall
not be done which there is no power to
do? Why, for instance should it be said
that the liberty of the press shall not be
restrained, when no power is given by
which restrictions may be imposed? I
will not contend that such a provision
would confer a regulating power; but it is
evident that it would furnish, to men
disposed to usurp, a plausible pretence
for claiming that power. They might
urge with a semblance of reason, that the
Constitution ought not to be charged with
the absurdity of providing against the
abuse of an authority which was not
given, and that the provision against
restraining the liberty of the press
afforded a clear implication, that a power
to prescribe proper regulations
concerning it was intended to be vested
in the national government.

Referring to all eighty-five of the *Federalist* papers, Jefferson
would write to Madison soon after the last essay was written that they
were "the best commentary on the principles of government . . . ever
written."[30] George Washington agreed:

When the transient circumstances and
fugitive performances which attended this

Crisis shall have disappeared, That Work
will merit the Notice of Posterity;
because in it are candidly and ably
discussed the principles of freedom and
the topics of government, which will be
always interesting to mankind so long as
they shall be connected in Civil Society.[31]

By July 1788, with the Constitution's approval by the requisite nine states, Hamilton and his federalists had won the ratification battle. Some states, however, had ratified only because of explicit assurances from Washington and other Founders that a bill of rights would be forthcoming.

ENDNOTES

[23] Preamble, Constitution of the United States of America.

[24] Paragraphs 2, 3, 6, 7, and 9 have been omitted.

[25] *Journals of the Continental Congress* (W.C. Ford, ed.).

[26] *Marbury* v. *Madison*, 5 U.S. (I Cranch) 137 (1803).

[27] Fairfield (ed.), *The Federalist Papers: A Collection of Essays Written in Support of the Constitution of the United States*, viii.

[28] *Federalist No. 1.* Emphasis in original.

[29] Fairfield (ed.), *The Federalist Papers: A Collection of Essays Written in Support of the Constitution of the United States*, ix.

[30] Fairfield (ed.), *The Federalist Papers: A Collection of Essays Written in Support of the Constitution of the United States*, 281, n. 24.

---

[31] Fairfield (ed.), *The Federalist Papers: A Collection of Essays Written in Support of the Constitution of the United States*, 281, n. 25. Emphasis in original.

CHAPTER 2.

"Further declaratory and restrictive clauses"

BILL OF RIGHTS

THE Conventions of a number of the States, having at the time of their adopting the Constitution, expressed a desire, in order to prevent misconstruction or abuse of its powers, that further declaratory and restrictive clauses should be added: And as extending the ground of public confidence in the Government, will best ensure the beneficent ends of its institution:

RESOLVED . . . that the following Articles be proposed to the Legislatures of the several States, as Amendments to the Constitution of the United States . . . .[32]

In September 1788, the Continental Congress resolved that the Constitution had become effective. By mid-April 1789, both houses of Congress had organized themselves, the electoral votes were counted, and George Washington and John Adams had been elected president and vice president, respectively.

To make good on the promises by many of the Constitution's proponents, James Madison, at the first session of the first Congress, introduced a set of amendments to the Constitution—a Bill of Rights. As the Supreme Court of the United States would later note, Madison's purpose was "to quiet the apprehension of many, that without some such declaration of rights, the government would assume and might be held to possess the power to trespass upon those rights of persons and property which by the Declaration of Independence were affirmed to be unalienable."

> On June 8, 1789, James Madison moved
> that the House [of Representatives] go
> into Committee of the Whole to receive
> some constitutional amendments which
> he hoped would be unanimously
> approved. Hours of debate followed—
> some members calling for reference to a
> select committee, others urging delay;
> some opposing all amendments, others
> concealing a desire for drastic alterations
> in the Constitution. Shifting ground,
> Madison moved for a select committee.
> Former advocates of it switched to
> Committee of the Whole. Madison then
> stymied the opposition by simply moving
> the adoption of his resolutions. Both
> sides joined in sending them to
> Committee of the Whole. The situation
> was not really bad. Dullards on civil
> rights had temporarily united with
> intriguers for a second constitutional
> convention.[33]

Much has been written about how the "dullards" and "intriguers," under Madison's deft hand, won the day, so suffice to say merely that "[o]f the ten amendments thus adopted, not one was reduced in force from the form in which Madison introduced them."[34]

Effective December 15, 1791, the first ten amendments were officially ratified. The first nine amendments, guaranteeing the protection of individual rights against infringement by the federal government, are:

Amendment I. Congress shall make no law respecting an establishment of religion, or prohibiting the free exercise thereof; or abridging the freedom of speech, or of the press; or the right of the people peaceably to assemble, and to petition the Government for a redress of grievances.

Amendment II. A well regulated Militia, being necessary to the security of a free State, the right of the people to keep and bear Arms, shall not be infringed.

Amendment III. No Soldier shall, in time of peace be quartered in any house, without the consent of the Owner, nor in time of war, but in a manner to be prescribed by law.

Amendment IV. The right of the people to be secure in their persons, houses, papers, and effects, against unreasonable searches and seizures, shall not be violated, and no Warrants shall issue, but upon probable cause, supported by Oath or affirmation, and particularly describing the place to be searched, and the persons or things to be seized.

Amendment V. No person shall be held to answer for a capital, or otherwise infamous crime, unless on a presentment or indictment of a Grand Jury, except in cases arising in the land or naval forces, or in the Militia, when in actual service in time of War or public danger; nor shall any person be subject for the same offence to be twice put in jeopardy of life or limb; nor shall be compelled in any criminal case to be a witness against himself, nor be deprived of life, liberty, or property, without due process of law[35]; nor shall private property be taken for public use, without just compensation.

Amendment VI. In all criminal prosecutions, the accused shall enjoy the right to a speedy and public trial, by an impartial jury of the State and district wherein the crime shall have been committed, which district shall have been previously ascertained by law, and to be informed of the nature and cause of the accusation; to be confronted with the witnesses against him; to have compulsory process for obtaining witnesses in his favor, and to have the Assistance of Counsel for his defence.

Amendment VII. In Suits at common law, where the value in controversy shall exceed twenty dollars, the right of trial by jury shall be preserved, and no fact tried by a jury, shall be otherwise re-examined in any Court of the United States, than according to the rules of the common law.

> **Amendment VIII.** Excessive bail shall not be required, nor excessive fines imposed, nor cruel and unusual punishments inflicted.

> **Amendment IX.** The enumeration in the Constitution of certain rights shall not be construed to deny or disparage others retained by the people.

I have separated the first nine amendments from the tenth because there is a fundamental difference between the former and the latter.

> **Amendment X.** The powers not delegated to the United States by the Constitution, nor prohibited by it to the States, are reserved to the States, respectively, or to the people.

Though an integral part of the Bill of Rights, the Tenth Amendment is a reiteration of the *federal* nature of the American Union, not, like the Ninth Amendment, a direct acknowledgement of *individual rights*.

Unlike the other nine amendments, the tenth expressly deals with *state* (and *people*) *power*, not *individual rights*. The nature of that power "reserved" to the states and to the people from the Constitution's grant of power to the federal government—to legislate regarding the public health, safety, welfare, and morals (the common law "police power")—is such that in modern times it has often been exercised in a manner and to a degree antithetical to individual rights.

One need only consider the extent of state regulation of citizens' lives—control that has provided considerable grist for the Supreme Court's (and Justice Thomas's) mill.

From 1791 to 1992, the Constitution has been amended only seventeen times.[36] Of those amendments, the most constitutionally important has been the fourteenth,[37] which early in its history became a favorite tool of the proponents of the "Living Constitution." It is the Fourteenth Amendment that has given rise to thousands of supposed "Bill of Rights" cases because of the pernicious "Incorporation Doctrine"—a judicial construct at which the Founders, federalist and anti-federalist alike, would doubtless have scoffed.

An examination of the Incorporation Doctrine begins with an undeniably valid premise: *The Bill of Rights was intended by Madison who introduced it, by the Congress that approved it, and by the states that ratified it, to apply only to actions by the federal government.* Indeed, the First Amendment begins by reciting that "*Congress* shall make no law . . . ." [38]

Never was a political intent, nor a legal statement, clearer. Even those who would have it otherwise cannot ignore that in the early days of the Supreme Court of the United States it ruled squarely that the Bill of Rights was *not* applicable to the states.[39] Eminent constitutional law scholars have had no choice but to recognize that "[t]his holding was correct historically because the drafters of the Bill of Rights designed the amendments as a check on the new national government."[40]

How, then, has the Supreme Court been able to hold unconstitutional *under the federal Constitution* acts of the *states* violating such rights as free speech, protection against double jeopardy, and many other guarantees found in the *federal* Bill of Rights?

The answer lies in the Incorporation Doctrine and the Due Process Clause of the Fourteenth Amendment: "[N]or shall any State deprive any person of life, liberty, or property, without due process of law."

Even though the federal Bill of Rights contains at least thirty specific rights-guarantees—one of which is the Fifth Amendment's own Due Process Clause—in a series of cases beginning with *Gitlow v. New York*[41] the Supreme Court ruled that the Fourteenth Amendment's Due Process Clause, as the centerpiece of the "Living Constitution," "incorporates" many of those guarantees, thus making them applicable to state action.

In other words, "due process" of the Fourteenth Amendment, according to years of Supreme Court decisions, tests the legitimacy of state laws and official conduct affecting religion, speech, press, assembly, petition (First Amendment); search and seizure (Fourth Amendment); double jeopardy, self-incrimination, eminent domain, due process (Fifth Amendment); speedy and public trial, impartial jury, confrontation, compulsory process, assistance of counsel (Sixth Amendment); and excessive bail, excessive fines, and cruel and unusual punishments (Eighth Amendment).

An example of the "Living Constitution's" Incorporation Doctrine at work is the Warren Court's decision in *Mapp v. Ohio*.[42]

Police illegally searched the residence of Dollree Mapp, where they found obscene material, for the possession of which she was tried and convicted. Had the officers been FBI agents and the prosecution in a *federal* court, the incriminating evidence would have been suppressed for having been obtained in violation of the federal Constitution's Fourth Amendment.

However, Mapp was prosecuted in an *Ohio* court, where, presumably, the *Fourth* Amendment *didn't* apply. Because the *Fourteenth* Amendment *did*, the Supreme Court held that the illegally obtained evidence should be suppressed, because the police had violated Mapp's "due process" rights.[43] Writing for the 6-3 majority (Warren, Brennan, Black, Douglas, Stewart), Justice Clark ruled that "all evidence obtained by searches and seizures in violation of the

Constitution [the Fifth Amendment] is, by that same authority [the Fourteenth Amendment], inadmissible in a state court."

The Incorporation Doctrine also explains how the Supreme Court was able to rule unconstitutional "separate but equal" District of Columbia public schools in *Bolling v. Sharpe*.[44] The Fourteenth Amendment ("[N]or shall any *state* . . . deny . . . equal protection of the laws")[45] does not, and cannot, apply to the District of Columbia, a *federal* jurisdiction. Although the Fifth Amendment *does* apply to the District of Columbia, that amendment contains *no* equal protection clause. To deal with the problem, the Supreme Court simply ruled that the concept of "due process" in the federal Fifth Amendment—though silent about equal protection—contained equal protection "content."[46]

Thus does the Incorporation Doctrine explain how the Supreme Court was able to invalidate Connecticut's anti-contraceptive statute in *Griswold v. Connecticut*. As I said in the Introduction, according to Douglas prior cases of the Supreme Court (all incorporation cases) "suggested" that specific guarantees in the Bill of Rights—dealing with speech, press, association, quartering soldiers, search and seizure, self-incrimination, and the education of one's children—have "penumbras, formed by emanations" from those guarantees that help give them life and substance. As a result of these so-called penumbras and emanations—*but not a shred of constitutional precedent or other authority*—the Warren Court gave birth to a constitutionally guaranteed "right of privacy."

For now, the fight over incorporation has been lost, with *Griswold*, its ancestors, and its progeny (e.g., *Roe v. Wade*) having institutionalized in scores of Fourteenth Amendment precedents the jurisprudential principle of a "Living Constitution."

But the final word has not yet been written.

For fourteen terms, Justice Thomas, while having to accept the principle and consequences of incorporation, has respected and endeavored to uphold Professor Corwin's three pillars of American constitutionalism—separation of powers, federalism, and judicial review—as his majority, concurring, and dissenting opinions eloquently demonstrate.

ENDNOTES

[32] September 25, 1989, Resolution of Transmittal of the proposed amendments to the states, by the Speaker of the House of Representatives (Frederick Augustus Muhlenberg) and the Vice President of the United States and President of the Senate (John Adams).

[33] Brant, *The Fourth President: A Life of James Madison*, 231.

[34] Brant, *The Fourth President: A Life of James Madison*, 231.

[35] The Due Process Clause of the Fourteenth Amendment provides that "[N]or shall any State deprive any person of life, liberty, or property, without due process of law . . . . " Because Supreme Court decisions under the Fourteenth Amendment's Due Process Clause have eclipsed those under the Fifth Amendment's in number and impact, this book's discussion of due process will concentrate on the former unless otherwise indicated.

[36] The Eleventh Amendment (1795) prevented states from being sued in a federal court. The Twelfth Amendment (1804) dealt with the electoral college. The Thirteenth Amendment (1865) abolished slavery. The Fourteenth Amendment (1868)—which would give rise to thousands of cases for the Supreme Court—embedded the concepts of "due process" and "equal protection" in American constitutional law. The Fifteenth Amendment (1870) gave the vote to former slaves. The Sixteenth Amendment (1913) constitutionalized the income tax. The Seventeenth Amendment (1913) provided for direct election of senators. The Eighteenth Amendment (1919) created prohibition. The

Nineteenth Amendment (1920) granted women the vote. The Twentieth Amendment (1933) addressed presidential succession. The Twenty-First Amendment (1933) repealed the Eighteenth Amendment. The Twenty-Second Amendment (1951) limited the president to two terms. The Twenty-Third Amendment (1961) granted the District of Columbia power to choose presidential and vice presidential electors. The Twenty-Fourth Amendment (1964) eliminated poll taxes. The Twenty-Fifth Amendment (1967) provided for presidential succession and disability. The Twenty-Sixth Amendment (1971) lowered the voting age to eighteen. The Twenty-Seventh Amendment (1992) dealt with congressional compensation.

[37] The Fourteenth Amendment was ratified on July 9, 1868.

[38] Emphasis added.

[39] *Barron* v. *Mayor and City Council of Baltimore*, 32 U.S. (7 Pet.) 243 (1833).

[40] Nowak and Rotunda, *Constitutional Law* (fourth edition), 332.

[41] 268 U.S. 652, 45 S.Ct. 625 (1925).

[42] 367 U.S. 643, 81 S.Ct. 1684 (1961).

[43] Chapter 8 examines the "tests" the Supreme Court has developed to determine whether "due process" rights have been violated.

[44] 347 U.S. 497, 74 S.Ct. 693 (1954).

[45] Emphasis added.

[46] That "legally" segregated public schools in federal jurisdictions, an obscenely intolerable wrong and an ugly blemish on our nation, should have been declared unconstitutional was not debatable by reasonable people.

Whether that result should have been achieved by the Warren Court's inventing an indefensible "equal protection" component of the Fifth Amendment's Due Process Clause is, however, another matter entirely—especially when at least one other specific provision of the federal Bill of Rights was available: the Ninth Amendment:

> *The enumeration in the Constitution of certain rights shall not be construed to deny or disparage others retained by the people.*

Surely, it should be a federally protected constitutional right that American citizens not be discriminated against by their government on the basis of their race.

CHAPTER 3.

"Shall be vested in"

SEPARATION OF POWERS

All legislative Powers herein granted shall be vested in a Congress of the United States.[47]

The executive Power shall be vested in a President of the United States of America.[48] *The President shall be Commander in Chief of the Army and Navy of the United States.*[49]

The judicial Power of the United States, shall be vested in one supreme Court, and in Such inferior courts as Congress may from time to time ordain and establish.[50]

It has been truly said that "[p]erhaps no principle of American constitutionalism has attracted more attention than that of separation of powers. It has in fact come to define the very character of the American political system."[51] Indeed, James Madison deemed separation of powers to be "a first principle of free government,"[52] as does Justice Thomas.

Madison's views were very much evident in an important 1983 separation of powers case, *Immigration and Naturalization Service v. Chadha.*[53] In that case, Supreme Court Justice Lewis Powell made the separation of powers principle the fundamental premise of his concurring opinion:

The Framers perceived that "[t]he accumulation of all powers legislative, executive and judiciary in the same hands, whether of one, a few or many, and whether hereditary, self appointed, or elective, may justly be pronounced the very definition of tyranny." *The Federalist No. 47*, p. 324 (J. Cooke ed. 1961) (J. Madison). Theirs was not a baseless fear. * * * During the Confederation, the States reacted by removing power from the executive and placing it in the hands of elected legislators. But many legislators proved to be little better than the Crown.

One abuse that was prevalent during the Confederation was the exercise of judicial power by the state legislatures. * * * Jefferson observed that members of the General Assembly in his native Virginia had not been prevented from assuming judicial power, and "[t]hey have accordingly *in many* instances *decided rights* which should have been left to *judiciary controversy*." *The Federalist No. 48*, p. 336 (J. Cooke ed. 1961) (emphasis in original) (quoting T. Jefferson, *Notes on the State of Virginia* 196 (London edition 1787)). * * * It was to prevent the recurrence of such abuses that the Framers vested the executive, legislative, and judicial powers in separate branches.

Too often, the separation of powers doctrine is thought to operate only "horizontally," by erecting a functional wall between the legislative, executive, and judicial branches of government. But there is also another aspect of separation of powers, one that operates "vertically." As Supreme Court Justice Anthony Kennedy explained, concurring in *Clinton v. City of New York*[54] :

> Separation of powers helps to ensure the ability of each branch to be vigorous in asserting its proper authority. In this respect the device operates on a horizontal axis to secure a proper balance of legislative, executive, and judicial authority. Separation of powers operates on a vertical axis as well, between each branch and the citizens in whose interest powers must be exercised. The citizen has a vital interest in the regularity of the exercise of governmental power. If this point was not clear before *Chadha*, it should have been so afterwards. * * * By [Congress] increasing the power of the President beyond what the Framers envisioned, the statute compromises the political liberty of our citizens, liberty which the separation of powers seeks to secure.

Given the doctrinal and historical roots of the separation of powers principle, it comes as no surprise that Justice Thomas's strong view on the subject reflects those of the Founders. For example, although Thomas's dissent in *Musick, Peeler & Garrett v. Employers Ins. of Wausau*[55] involved interpretation of a federal statute (and a rule of the Securities and Exchange Commission), at the core of his opinion there was a more fundamental principle.[56]

In a previous case, the Supreme Court had ruled that a private party injured by another person's violation of the SEC statute and rule could sue the wrongdoer for damages. In effect, the Court had ruled that allegedly injured parties could sue for a *securities tort* (a civil wrong) under the securities laws just as one can sue for a more traditional "*normal*" *tort* (e.g., assault and battery, false imprisonment, defamation, negligence).

In tort law generally, defendants who are found liable and who compensate the plaintiff can seek contribution from others who committed a tortious act against the plaintiff ("joint tortfeasors") in the same event, but who haven't paid anything or have paid less than their conduct warranted.

In *Musick*, the question for the Supreme Court was whether *under the federal securities* laws one tortfeasor could seek contribution from a joint tortfeasor. To answer that question, it was necessary for the Court to interpret the securities laws.

Although the Court held that a defendant *could* seek contribution, the ruling itself is not nearly as important as *why* Thomas dissented.

He began by noting that it was one thing for the Court in the earlier case to have recognized a private tort action under Section 10(b) of the Securities Exchange Act of 1934 and SEC Rule 10b-5 (a ruling he accepted, but of which he disapproved). But it was something else entirely for the Court to *extend* that interpretation of the securities laws to include an entirely *new* claim for joint tortfeasor contribution.

According to Thomas, the only appropriate way a new right to contribution could come into existence is if, expressly or at least by strong implication, *Congress manifested an intent* to *create one*.

As we will see again and again, Thomas's starting place in statutory interpretation is with the text of a statute itself.[57] In *Musick*, he could find nothing in the words of Section 10 or Rule 10b-5 expressly providing, or even implying, that joint tortfeasors had a *right* of contribution. Moreover, he noted that Section 10 and Rule 10b-5's strictness concerning the conduct of buyers and sellers of securities cut against the notion that Congress intended one wrongdoer to recover from another, thereby ameliorating the former's culpability.[58] In other words, Thomas found the language of the statute and rule clear.

Thomas added, from a precedential perspective, that because in an earlier case the Court had ruled "only *actual* purchasers and sellers of securities are entitled to press private 1-b-5 suits,"[59] for the Court now to judicially create a right of joint tortfeasor contribution would be to *extend* the law's reach well beyond the persons who were actual parties to the securities transaction. Examples would be accountants or lawyers who were not buyers or sellers but were somehow involved in the transaction.

As Thomas said:

> The rule adopted today thus undermines
> not only the discernable intent of
> Congress and the SEC, but also our own
> elaboration of this regulatory scheme.
> Such are the risks that inhere in the
> hazardous enterprise of recognizing a
> private right of action [to contribution]
> *despite congressional silence.*[60]

On the statutory interpretation issue, then, Thomas's *Musick* dissent is entirely consistent with the originalist approach we will see in every one of his other statutory interpretation opinions. *His inquiry begins with the text of the law.*

More important, however, is that congressional silence on a given point is nothing more than congressional silence, and thus, according to Thomas, "[c]ourts should not treat legislative and administrative [in this case, SEC] silence as a tacit license to accomplish what Congress and the SEC are unable or unwilling to do."

For Thomas, the conclusion in *Musick* was inescapable: "In their current condition, Section 10(b) and Rule 10b-5 afford no right to contribution. Congress has been, and remains, free to alter this state of affairs."

In so stating, Thomas was going beyond interpretation of the statute and rule and reaffirming the fundamental principle of separation of powers: Congress legislates, courts interpret. Though he wrote as a powerful associate justice of the Supreme Court of the United States, accountable to no one, Thomas understood the necessity for himself and his colleagues to yield to the structural constitutional difference between the power of Congress under Article I and the power of the Court under Article III.[61]

In that understanding, and his implementation of it in Supreme Court decisions, Thomas has kept the faith with Madison and his founding colleagues. He has done the same in cases presenting issues of federalism.

ENDNOTES

[47] Article I, Section 1, Constitution of the United States of America.

[48] Article II, Section 1, Constitution of the United States of America.

[49] Article II, Section 2, Constitution of the United States of America.

[50] Article III, Section 1, Constitution of the United States of America.

[51] Wood, *The Creation of the American Republic, 1776-1787*, 151. The author, writing in 1969, added in a footnote that "[t]he literature on separation of powers is enormous."

---

[52] Wood, *The Creation of the American Republic, 1776-1787,* 152.

[53] 462 U.S. 919, 103 U.S. 2764 (1983).

[54] 524 U.S. 417, 118 S.Ct. 2091 (1998).

[55] 508 U.S. 286, 113 S.Ct. 2085 (1993).

[56] During his fourteen complete terms on the Court, Justice Thomas has had few occasions to write explicitly about separation of powers, although other of his opinions, especially those concerning federalism and the scope of judicial review, implicitly deal with that doctrine. The *Musick* case is the best example of Thomas's explicit discussion of separation of powers.

[57] See Appendix B for a list of Justice Thomas's principal statutory interpretation opinions.

[58] Thomas also observed that Congress had expressly allowed contribution under other sections of the Act, and that Congress had at least five opportunities to expressly allow contribution under Section 10 but had never done so.

[59] Emphasis added.

[60] Emphasis added.

[61] An interesting twist on separation of powers doctrine is found in *Loving* v. *United States,* 517 U.S. 748, 116 S.Ct. 1737 (1996). An army court-martial convicted a soldier of two murders and other offenses, and imposed the death penalty due to the existence of three aggravating factors. Because those aggravating factors were established by the president, who was authorized to do so by Congress, Loving claimed that such "delegation" of power was unconstitutional. The majority disagreed, ruling that "[t]here is nothing in the constitutional scheme or our traditions to prohibit Congress from

delegating the prudent and proper implementation of the [military] capital murder statute to the President acting as Commander in Chief."

Justice Thomas agreed, but wrote separately:

> In light of Congress' express constitutional authority to regulate the Armed Forces and the unique nature of the military's mission, we have afforded an unparalleled degree of discretion to congressional action governing the military. * * * This heightened deference extends not only to congressional action *but also to executive action by the President who by virtue of his constitutional role as Commander in Chief . . . possesses shared authority over military discipline."* (Emphasis added.)

While the majority based its conclusion solely on an acceptable delegation of power from Congress to the President—in effect, a *combining* of Article I and Article II powers— Thomas saw no need for a delegation at all, essentially rooting the President's power to establish aggravating circumstances for military capital murder solely in Article II of the Constitution. His view would resurface several years later when the Court would rule on the "rights" of enemy combatants.

CHAPTER 4.

"The powers not delegated"

FEDERALISM

*The powers not delegated to the United
States by the Constitution, nor prohibited by
it to the States, are reserved to the States,
respectively, or to the people.*[62]

*The Congress shall have Power To . . .
regulate Commerce with foreign Nations,
and among the several States, and with the
Indian tribes.*[63]

Tenth Amendment

The Constitution of the *United* (i.e., combined into one federal union) States expressly affirms the existence of reserved powers in the states and in the people, respectively. Just as the first nine amendments are an assurance that individual rights were to be protected from the newly formed federal government, the Tenth Amendment is a guarantee that states and their citizens will retain their powers as against the national government (e.g., state regulation of liquor licenses)—except as to powers expressly granted in the Constitution to the federal government, or expressly denied to the states.[64]

Of all the opinions Justice Thomas has written—majority, concurring, and dissenting—few better reveal his sophisticated federalism jurisprudence than his dissent in *U.S. Term Limits, Inc. v. Thornton.*[65]

Sixty percent of the Arkansas voters approved an amendment to the state constitution imposing a type of term limit on members of Congress from that state.[66]   In a 5-4 vote, the Supreme Court ruled that the amendment was *unconstitutional* because a state lacked the power under the Tenth Amendment to impose qualifications for election to the House or Senate beyond those expressly provided for in the Constitution.

Justice Thomas dissented.

Thomas's dissent covered some seventy-five pages in the official reports. It articulates a view of the American Constitution rarely seen anywhere, let alone in opinions of the Supreme Court of the United States. *"Because the people of the several States are the only true source of power,"* he wrote, ". . . the Federal Government enjoys no authority beyond what the Constitution confers: *The Federal Government's powers are limited and enumerated."*[67]

On the other hand, Thomas observed:

> In each State, the remainder of the people's powers—'[t]he powers not delegated to the United States by the Constitution, nor prohibited by it to the States,' Amdt. 10—are either delegated to the state government or retained by the people. The Federal Constitution does not specify which of these two possibilities obtains; *it is up to the various state constitutions to declare which powers the people of each state have delegated to their state government.*[68]

Thomas's was saying that while the Tenth Amendment takes sides about *whether* the states and the people have power reserved as against the national government (they do), it does not take sides *between the two* about *where* that power resides—in the states themselves or in their citizens. The appropriate division of that power is for the citizens of each state to sort out for themselves—which, via the term limit constitutional amendment, the people of Arkansas did, and should have been allowed to do.

Thomas addressed the Tenth Amendment two years later, when the Court confronted the Brady Act, a comprehensive *federal* statutory scheme for gun control enacted by Congress—supposedly pursuant to its power to regulate interstate commerce.

The law required *state* law enforcement personnel to perform certain administrative tasks in connection with the *intra*state purchase of handguns. Challenged in *Printz v. United States*[69] as violative of the Tenth Amendment, the law was ruled unconstitutional by the Supreme Court.

Thomas voted with the majority, but wrote a separate concurring opinion. He used the occasion not to reiterate the majority's reasoning but "to emphasize that the Tenth Amendment affirms the undeniable notion that under our Constitution, *the Federal Government is one of enumerated, hence limited, powers.*"[70] Thus, the Interstate Commerce Clause's reach was not, in his view, sufficient "to extend to the regulation of wholly *intra* state, point-of-sale transactions" such as the in-state gun sales sought to be regulated by the Brady Act.[71]

From Justice Thomas's *Thornton* dissent and his *Printz* concurrence, at least two of his jurisprudential premises emerge: that the people of the several states delegated only limited powers to the federal government—a principle codified in the Tenth Amendment—and that the amendment should restrain Congress if it invades the states' (or the people's) reserved powers.

Although *Thornton* arose out of a state constitutional amendment, and *Printz* out of a congressional statute, Tenth

Amendment issues can also arise in the context of state criminal law. A good example is *Riggins v. Nevada.*[72]

Although the Supreme Court majority considered the case as involving an issue of compulsory process/due process, Justice Thomas viewed the case as presenting a clear- cut issue of Tenth Amendment federalism.

David Riggins, while awaiting trial for murder and robbery, complained that he was hearing voices and couldn't sleep. A psychiatrist prescribed an antipsychotic drug. Found competent to stand trial, and apparently appearing normal because of the drug, Riggins made an unusual request of the trial judge: allow him to suspend his medication during the trial, so the jury could see how psychotic he was when off the drug (i.e., at the time of the murder and robbery). The trial judge denied his request.

During the trial Riggins was taking his medication and was apparently sane enough to mount an insanity defense. It didn't work— he was convicted, and sentenced to death. The Supreme Court took the case "to decide whether *forced*[73] administration of antipsychotic medication during trial violated rights guaranteed by the Sixth and Fourteenth Amendments." In a 7-2 decision, the Court ruled that it did.

Justice Thomas dissented. He began by identifying what Riggins was complaining about: that the state trial judge would not allow the defendant to appear before the jury in an *unmedicated* state. In other words, that Riggins had been prevented from presenting relevant evidence of his *demeanor* when he killed the deceased (by stabbing him thirty-two times with a knife).

Thomas then posited a basic principle of federal-state relations:

> This Court has no power to decide
> questions concerning the admissibility of
> evidence under Nevada law. * * *

> Except in cases involving a violation of a
> specific *constitutional* provision such as
> the Confrontation Clause[74] . . . this
> Court may not reverse a state "trial
> judge's action in the admission of
> evidence" unless the evidentiary ruling
> "so infuse[s] the trial with unfairness as
> to deny due process of law."[75]

Thomas was making an important point. Because of the Tenth Amendment, the Court was obliged to defer to state rules of evidence (a pure statement of the federalism principle), unless there was a deprivation of due process or some other constitutional right.

Although the principle of "due process of law" is discussed in Chapter 8, a preview here in the context of the *Riggins* case will be useful—especially since Thomas's view of the due process aspect of the case circles back to his federalism jurisprudence.

He focused on Nevada's right to run its criminal trials as that state saw fit—in this case, subject only to Riggins's federal constitutional rights. Thus, the only question for Thomas was whether Riggins's due process rights (i.e., was the trial "so infused with unfairness"?) had been violated by the Nevada trial judge's refusal to admit the proffered demeanor evidence (i.e., his unmedicated condition).

Thomas found no constitutional violation, primarily because the trial judge *had* allowed Riggins to present evidence of his mental state when he committed the murder. This Riggins had accomplished in several ways, including through his own testimony.   Since state trial judges have considerable leeway in allowing or disallowing evidence in general, and demeanor evidence in particular, and since Riggins directly and indirectly presented to the jury his mental state at the time of the killing, in no sense was the trial "infused with unfairness," let alone to the extent of violating Riggins's constitutional right to due process.

That being the case, the Tenth Amendment's reservation of certain powers to the states required that Nevada's rules of evidence, not the Supreme Court of the United States, be the arbiter of what was appropriate in the functioning of the state's criminal justice system.

Federalism at work!

Commerce Clause

Federalism issues arise not only in cases involving reserved state power under the Tenth Amendment, but also in those that involve power under the Interstate Commerce Clause.

In response to a rash of shootings and other gun-related incidents in schools, Congress enacted the Gun-Free School Zones Act of 1990.[76] The law prohibited the possession of guns within 1,000 feet of a school. The question for the Supreme Court in *United States v. Lopez*[77] was whether the legislation, having only a local impact and in no measurable way affecting interstate commerce, could be justified as a legitimate exercise of congressional power under the Commerce Clause. The Court, 6-3, ruled that it could not. Justice Thomas voted with the majority but wrote separately.

In his concurring opinion, Thomas quickly agreed that "[t]he Court today properly concludes that the Commerce Clause does not grant Congress the authority to prohibit gun possession within 1,000 feet of a school . . . ." However, he took the occasion "to observe that [the Court's] case law has drifted far from the original understanding of the Commerce Clause." "My goal" in writing separately, he said, "is simply to show how far we have departed from the original understanding and to demonstrate that the result we reach today is by no means 'radical' [as Justice Stevens's dissent asserted] . . . ."

There followed a detailed analysis of the Commerce Clause's history, the many Commerce Clause cases decided by the Court over the years, and the *compelling logic* that if Congress can "regulate not only 'Commerce' . . . but also anything that has a 'substantial effect' on such commerce" the national legislature has a "blank check" with no local or state activity safe from federal control.

This said, Justice Thomas was not unmindful of another consideration pulling in a different direction (one I'll examine in Chapter 5, judicial review): "Although I might be willing," Thomas wrote, "to return to the original understanding [of the Commerce Clause], I recognize that many believe that it is too late in the day to undertake a fundamental reexamination of the past 60 years. Consideration of *stare decisis* and reliance interests may convince us that we cannot wipe the slate clean."

Maybe not. But Thomas's concurrence in *Lopez* made it quite clear that he would try to cancel that "blank check" whenever he could.[78]

Justice Thomas continued his fight for a balanced federalism and a rational Commerce Clause jurisprudence in *United States v. Morrison*.[79] There, the Supreme Court held unconstitutional under the Commerce Clause a provision of the federal Violence Against Women Act that provided a civil remedy for victims of *intra*state rape. While Thomas voted with the majority, once again he wrote a separate concurrence.

Although he agreed that in *Morrison* the majority had correctly applied *Lopez*, he objected to the perpetuation of a "substantial effects" test by which to measure Congress's power under the Commerce Clause—that is, how much does the congressionally regulated activity affect Interstate Commerce? "[T]he very notion," he wrote, "is inconsistent with the original understanding of Congress' powers and with this Court's early Commerce Clause cases. By continuing to apply this rootless and malleable standard, however circumscribed, the

Court has encouraged the Federal Government to persist in its view that the Commerce Clause has virtually no limits. *Until this Court replaces its Commerce Clause jurisprudence with a standard more consistent with the original understanding, we will continue to see Congress appropriating state . . . powers under the guise of regulating commerce.*"[80]

Justice Thomas stepped up his efforts to restrain the Commerce Clause and restore a proper federalism balance two years later in *Camps Newfound/Owatonna, Inc. v. Town of Harrison, Maine,*[81] one of his most important dissents. The case involved a state statute that imposed a higher real estate and personal property tax on a camp that served mostly *nonresidents,* as compared to a camp that limited its services primarily to *residents.*

The majority invalidated the state tax statute, and Thomas dissented. To understand his dissent, it is necessary first to understand something about the Supreme Court's Commerce Clause jurisprudence.

Article I, Section 8, Paragraph 3 of the Constitution provides that "The *Congress* shall have Power . . . To regulate Commerce . . . among the several States . . . ." The nature, though perhaps not the scope, of this power is textually very clear: *Congress* "regulates" interstate commerce.

Equally clear is that the Interstate Commerce Clause is silent about how far *state* legislation can go if it has an *effect* on interstate commerce. Despite this silence, there have been many Supreme Court cases dealing with the so-called "dormant" or "negative" Commerce Clause—cases deciding whether state legislation goes "too far" in its effect on interstate commerce.

In his *Camps Newfound/Owatonna* dissent, Thomas stated, without serious contradiction, that "[t]he negative Commerce Clause has no basis in the text of the Constitution, makes little sense, and has proved virtually unworkable. * * * In one fashion or another, every

Member of the current Court[82] and a goodly number of our predecessors have at least recognized these problems, if not been troubled by them." Worse, he noted, was that the majority ruling actually *expanded* negative Commerce Clause jurisprudence. Accordingly, he thought it "worth revisiting the underlying justifications for our involvement in the negative aspects of the Commerce Clause, and the compelling arguments demonstrating why those justifications are illusory."

Thomas was challenging decades of decisions that considered, and often invalidated, state legislation that had "some" effect on interstate commerce. If he had been a clergyman, his suggestion to "revisit" some of the Court's earlier decisions would have been apostasy.

"I believe," he wrote,

> that the improper expansion undertaken [by the majority] is possible only because our negative Commerce Clause jurisprudence, developed primarily to invalidate discriminatory state taxation of interstate commerce, was already overbroad and unnecessary. It was overbroad because, unmoored from any constitutional text, it brought within the supervisory authority of the federal courts state action far afield from the discriminatory taxes it was primarily designed to check.

As evidence that Thomas scrutinized *every* provision of the Constitution, not just the trendy ones, he continued: "It was unnecessary because the Constitution would seem to provide an express[83] check on the States' power to levy certain discriminatory taxes on the commerce of other States—not in the judicially created negative Commerce Clause, but in the Article I, Section 10, Import-Export Clause . . . ."

The point is not whether Thomas was correct or incorrect about the relatively obscure Import-Export Clause saving the Maine tax statute—though he makes a well-reasoned, historically thorough, and persuasive argument—but rather that he was willing to take on (and demolish) decades of Supreme Court negative Commerce Clause decisions. As he wrote, ". . . neither of the Court's proffered theoretical justifications—exclusivity or preemption-by-silence—currently supports our negative Commerce Clause jurisprudence, if either ever did."

In a nod to what is always a serious concern of his, separation of powers, Thomas noted that the Supreme Court has

> used the [Commerce] Clause to make policy-laden judgments that we are ill equipped and arguably unauthorized to make. In so doing, we have developed multifactor tests in order to assess the perceived "effect" any particular state tax or regulation has on interstate commerce. * * * And in an unabashedly legislative manner, we have "balanced" that "effect" against the perceived interests of the taxing or regulating State . . . .
>
> * * * Any test . . . surely invites us, if not compels us, to function more as legislators than as judges. * * * In my view, none of this policy-laden decision making is proper. Rather, the Court should confine itself to interpreting the text of the Constitution, which itself seems to prohibit in plain terms certain of

> the more egregious state taxes on
> interstate commerce . . . and leaves to
> Congress the policy choices necessary for
> any further regulation of interstate
> commerce.[84]

If the Supreme Court's Tenth Amendment and Commerce Clause decisions have tilted heavily toward federal power, so too have its decisions under the Necessary and Proper Clause.

Necessary and Proper Clause

Gonzales v. Raich[85] pitted a California law legalizing medical marijuana[86] against a federal law, the Controlled Substances Act (CSA), proscribing that use. Relying on Congress's enumerated power to regulate interstate commerce (even though the marijuana was home-grown for personal use), the Supreme Court majority ruled that the federal law trumped the state law. Justice Scalia was with the majority.

But Scalia's frequent ally, Justice Thomas, dissented.

As columnist (and physician) Charles Krauthammer noted, "[t]he Scalia-Thomas argument was not about concern for cancer patients, the utility of medical marijuana or the latitude individuals should have regarding what they ingest."[87]

Their disagreement was, fundamentally, about the role of precedent in judicial decision-making and the methodology of constitutional interpretation.

Scalia, as a typical conservative jurist, relied on a long string of Supreme Court precedents (especially one from the New Deal involving home-grown wheat for personal consumption) that had engorged Congress's power under the Commerce Clause.[88]

Thomas, however, employing his trademark "originalist" approach, adverted to the Founders' understanding of "commerce"—

"trade or exchange"—and concluded that, despite the precedents, the federal prohibition on intra-state, home-grown marijuana could not be justified by the Commerce Clause. The first paragraph of Thomas's dissenting opinion summed up not only his overall view of the case but, more important, his overarching federalism jurisprudence:

> Respondents Diane Monson and Angel Raich use marijuana that has never been bought or sold, that has never crossed state lines, and that has had no demonstrable effect on the national market for marijuana. If Congress can regulate this under the Commerce Clause, then it can regulate virtually anything— and the Federal Government is no longer one of limited and enumerated powers.

In these two sentences Justice Thomas was denying the two premises upon which the government and the Court majority rested its case that the California law was unconstitutional: that growing the marijuana at home for personal use was somehow part of "commerce," and that the substance somehow moved "interstate."

Thomas, convinced by the Commerce Clause's "text, structure, and history," by the meaning of "commerce" at the time of the founding, and by his opinion in *Lopez*, concluded that Congress lacked the power to regulate the purely intra-state production and use of marijuana by people who were doing so in conformity with the California statute.

Thomas turned to yet another question:

> More difficult, however, is whether the CSA is a valid exercise of Congress' power to enact laws that are "necessary and proper for carrying into Execution"

its power to regulate interstate commerce.
Art. I, § 8, cl. 18. The Necessary and
Proper Clause is not a warrant to
Congress to enact any law that bears
some conceivable connection to the
exercise of an enumerated power. Nor is
it, however, a command to Congress to
enact only laws that are absolutely
indispensable to the exercise of an
enumerated power.[89]

The Necessary and Proper Clause had already been discussed
by Justice Thomas in a previous term. In *Sabri v. United States,*[90]
Thomas had an opportunity to explain more fully his views on the
clause—a sacred cow of liberals everywhere, and one that is
infrequently the basis of Supreme Court decisions.

At issue in *Sabri* was a statute making certain types of bribery a
federal crime. Jurisdiction was based *solely* on the defendant's receipt
of federal grants, contracts, subsidies, loans, guarantees, insurance, or
any other form of federal assistance—even though they had no
connection whatsoever with the bribery.

Because of the doctrine of *stare decisis*, Justice Thomas had to
acquiesce in the Court's ruling that the statute was constitutional.
However, he took the occasion to "doubt that we have correctly
interpreted the Commerce Clause. * * * But until this Court
reconsiders its precedents, and because neither party requests us to do
so here, our prior case law controls the outcome of this case."

Then Thomas turned to the sacred cow. The final paragraph of
the Constitution's Article I, Section 8, provides that Congress shall
have the power "[t]o make all Laws which shall be necessary and
proper for carrying into Execution the foregoing Powers, and all other
Powers vested by this Constitution in the Government of the United
States, or in any Department or Officer thereof." Many constitutional

scholars have, appropriately, read this paragraph as a mere *implementing* power, requiring for its exercise a specifically delegated Article I power which is to be "carr[ied] into Execution."

In *Sabri*, Thomas wrote that he found

> questionable the scope the Court gives to the Necessary and Proper Clause as applied to Congress's authority to spend. In particular, the Court appears to hold that the Necessary and Proper Clause authorizes the exercise of any power that is no more than a "rational means" to effectuate one of Congress' enumerated powers. * * * This conclusion derives from the Court's characterization of the seminal case *McCulloch v. Maryland*, 17 U.S. 316, 4 Wheat. 316, 4 L. Ed. 579 (1819), as having established a "means-ends rationality" test . . . a characterization that I am not certain is correct.

In *McCulloch*, decided in the early days of the nineteenth century, the legendary Chief Justice John Marshall, had formulated the classic test by which to measure the functional scope of the Necessary and Proper Clause:

> Let the end be legitimate, let it be within the scope of the constitution, and all means which are *appropriate*, which are *plainly adapted* to that end, which are not prohibited, but consist with the letter and spirit of the constitution, are constitutional.[91]

The federal statute at issue in *Sabri* provided that, for any "organization, government, or agency [that] receives, in any one year period, benefits in excess of $10,000 under a Federal program . . . any person who

> corruptly gives, offers, or agrees to give anything of value to any person, with intent to influence or reward an agent of [such] organization or of [such] State, local or Indian tribal government, or any agency thereof, in connection with any business, transaction, or series of transactions of such organization, government, or agency involving anything of value of $5,000 or more,"

commits a federal crime.

All that is necessary for the statute to apply is that the organization, government, or agency in question receives more than $10,000 in federal benefits of any kind, and that a representative of the entity (e.g., a company treasurer) is bribed regarding a substantial *state-based* transaction of that entity. No connection whatsoever between the *state-based* corrupt transaction (the bribe) and the federal benefits need be shown.

Thomas found this attenuation unacceptable under the Spending and the Necessary and Proper Clauses of the Constitution, stating that:

> The Court does a not-wholly-unconvincing job of tying the broad scope of [the statute] to a federal interest in federal funds and programs. * * * But simply noting that "[m]oney is fungible" . . . for instance, does not explain how there could be any federal interest in "prosecut[ing] a bribe paid to a city's meat inspector in connection with a substantial transaction just because the

city's parks department had received a
federal grant of $10,000" .... It would
be difficult to describe the chain of
inferences and assumptions in which the
Court would have to indulge to connect
such a bribe to a federal interest in any
federal funds or programs as being
"plainly adapted" to their protection.
And, this is just one example of many in
which any federal interest in protecting
federal funds is equally attenuated, and
yet the bribe is covered by the expansive
language of [the statute]. Overall, then,
[the statute] appears to be no more
plainly adapted to protecting federal
funds or federally funded programs than
a hypothetical federal statute
criminalizing fraud of any kind
perpetrated on any individual who
happens to receive federal welfare
benefits.

Thomas then concluded that because he would decide the case
on "the Court's Commerce Clause jurisprudence," it was unnecessary to
decide whether "Congress' power to spend combined with the
Necessary and Proper Clause could authorize the enactment of [the
statute]." But as to the latter, he made it very clear that "the Court's
approach seems to greatly and improperly expand the reach of
Congress' power under the Necessary and Proper Clause."

Which brings us back to *Gonzales v. Raich*, the California
marijuana case.

"The question," said Thomas, "is thus whether the *intrastate*
ban is 'necessary and proper' as applied to medical marijuana users
like" Monson and Raich. Thomas thought not:

> [N]either in enacting the CSA nor in
> defending its application to [the two
> women] has the Government offered any
> obvious reason why banning medical
> marijuana use is necessary to stem the
> tide of interstate drug trafficking.
> Congress' goal of curtailing the interstate
> drug trade would not plainly be thwarted
> if it could not apply the CSA to patients
> like Monson and Raich. That is, unless
> Congress' aim is really to exercise police
> power of the sort reserved to the States in
> order to eliminate even the *intrastate*
> possession and use of marijuana.[92]

This conclusion, however, did not end Thomas's analysis of the Necessary and Proper Clause as it applied (or didn't) to California's medical marijuana law. "Even assuming," he wrote, that "the CSA's ban on locally cultivated and consumed marijuana is 'necessary,' that does not mean it is also 'proper.' The means selected by Congress to regulate interstate commerce cannot be 'prohibited' by, or inconsistent with the "letter and spirit' of, the Constitution." (Citing *McCulloch*.)

Continuing, he returned to his opinion in *Lopez*—where he had argued that "allowing Congress to regulate intrastate, noncommercial activity under the Commerce Clause would confer on Congress a general 'police power' over the Nation"—and related that case to *Gonzales*:

> This is no less the case if Congress ties
> its power to the Necessary and Proper
> Clause rather than the Commerce Clause.
> When agents from the Drug Enforcement
> Administration raided Monson's home,
> they seized six cannabis plants. If the
> Federal Government can regulate

69

growing a half-dozen cannabis plants for personal consumption (not because it is interstate commerce, but because it is inextricably bound up with interstate commerce), then Congress' Article I powers—as expanded by the Necessary and Proper Clause—have no meaningful limits. Whether Congress aims at the possession of drugs, guns, or any number of other items, it may continue to "appropria[te] state police powers under the guise of regulating commerce." (*United States v. Morrison* (Thomas, J., concurring).)

Apparently unable to resist resorting to a *reductio ad absurdum*, Thomas suggested that "[i]f the majority is to be taken seriously, the Federal Government may now regulate quilting bees, clothes drives, and potluck suppers throughout the 50 States. This makes a mockery of Madison's assurance to the people of New York that the 'powers delegated' to the Federal Government are 'few and defined,' while those of the States are 'numerous and indefinite.' The Federalist No. 45, at 313 (J. Madison)."

The balance of Justice Thomas's *Gonzales* dissent is a ballad to federalism:

- "Federal power expands, but never contracts, with each new locution. The majority is not interpreting the Commerce Clause, but rewriting it."

- "The majority's rewriting of the Commerce Clause seems to be rooted in the belief that, unless the Commerce Clause covers the entire web of human activity, Congress will be left powerless to regulate the national economy effectively."

- "The Framers understood what the majority does not appear to fully appreciate: There is a danger to concentrating too much, as well as too little, power in the Federal Government."

- "This Court has carefully avoided stripping Congress of its ability to regulate *inter*state commerce, but it has casually allowed the Federal Government to strip States of their ability to regulate *intra*state commerce—not to mention a host of local activities, like mere drug possession, that are not commercial." [93]

- "One searches the Court's opinion in vain for any hint of what aspect of American life is reserved to the States. Yet this Court knows that '[t]he Constitution created a Federal Government of limited powers'."

- "That is why today's decision will add no measure of stability to our Commerce Clause jurisprudence: This Court is willing neither to enforce limits on federal power, nor to declare the Tenth Amendment a dead letter."

- The majority's rush to embrace federal power "is especially unfortunate given the importance of showing respect for the sovereign States that comprise our Federal Union."

In concluding with the statement in *Gonzales v. Raich* that "[o]ur federalist system, properly understood, allows California and a growing number of other States to decide for themselves how to safeguard the health and welfare of their citizens," Justice Thomas proved that he fully understands and respects the federalism pillar of American constitutionalism. So, too, do his opinions in *Thornton,*

71

Printz, Riggins, Lopez, Morrison, Camps Newfound, Sabri, and many others.

That understanding is also manifested in his opinions that present issues of judicial review.

ENDNOTES

[62] Amendment X, Constitution of the United States of America.

[63] Article I, Section 8, Paragraph 3, Constitution of the United States of America.

[64] For example, Art. I, Sec. 10, Par. 1, provides that "No state shall . . . pass any Bill of Attainder, ex post facto law, or Law impairing the Obligation of Contracts . . . ."

[65] 514 U.S. 779, 115 S.Ct. 1842 (1995). This dissent is a fine example also of Thomas's statutory interpretation methodology, which will become apparent in the following discussion of his federalism jurisprudence.

[66] The name of an otherwise qualified candidate for Congress could not appear on the general election ballot if he or she had already served three terms in the House or two terms in the Senate. However, one could avoid this disqualification by succeeding as a write-in candidate.

[67] Emphasis added.

[68] Emphasis added.

[69] 521 U.S. 898, 117 S.Ct. 2365 (1997).

[70] Emphasis added.

[71] It is noteworthy that Justice Thomas raised an imaginative issue not addressed by the parties, and thus one unnecessary for the Court to have considered. "If," he wrote, "the Second Amendment is read to confer a *personal* right [like freedom of speech] to 'keep and bear arms,' a colorable argument exists that the Federal Government's regulatory scheme [in the Brady Act], at least as it pertains to the purely intrastate sale or possession of firearms, runs afoul of that Amendment's protections." (Emphasis in original.)

There is no need to wonder whether Thomas was extending a not-too-subtle invitation to the Second Amendment's supporters, because he concluded his concurring opinion by wondering whether "[p]erhaps, at some future date, this Court will have the opportunity to determine whether Justice Story was correct when he wrote that the right to bear arms 'has justly been considered, as the palladium of the liberties of a republic.' * * * In the meantime," he wrote, "I join the Court's opinion striking down the challenged provisions of the Brady Act as inconsistent with the Tenth Amendment."

[72] 504 U.S. 127, 112 S.Ct. 1810 (1992). *Riggins* was decided three years before *U.S. Term Limits, Inc.*

[73] Emphasis added.

[74] The Confrontation Clause of the Sixth Amendment provides that "In all criminal prosecutions, the accused shall . . . be confronted with the witnesses against him . . . ."

[75] Emphasis added.

[76] 18 United States Code, Section 922 (q)(1)(A) (1988 ed., supp V).

[77] 514 U.S. 549, 115 S.Ct. 1624 (1995).

[78] An opportunity arose in the next term in a case entitled *Cargill, Incorporated* v. *United States,* 516 U.S. 955, 116 S.Ct. 407 (1995), in

which the petition for certiorari presented the question "whether the Army Corps of Engineers . . . can, under the [federal] Clean Water Act, constitutionally assert jurisdiction over private property based solely on the actual or potential presence of migratory birds that cross state lines."

The Court denied certiorari, and Justice Thomas dissented based on the *Lopez* precedent: that possession of a firearm in a school zone did not substantially affect interstate commerce so as to justify the exercise of federal legislative power.

> The basis asserted to create federal jurisdiction in this case seems to me to be even more farfetched than that offered, and rejected, in *Lopez*. At least in *Lopez* the government could assert that the presence of weapons in and around schools may result in violent crime that affects education and, hence, the economy.

Farfetched or not, certiorari was denied, and the lower courts' ruling stood: the presence of migratory birds sufficed to justify application of the federal Clean Water Act.

[79] 529 U.S. 598, 120 S.Ct. 1740 (2000).

[80] Emphasis added.

[81] 520 U.S. 564, 117 S.Ct. 1590 (1997).

[82] Here, Thomas quoted his colleagues. *O'Connor*: "The scope of the dormant Commerce Clause is a judicial creation." *Stevens* (for a *unanimous* Court): The Commerce Clause "says nothing about the protection of interstate commerce in the absence of any action by Congress." *Scalia*: "describing the 'negative Commerce Clause' as 'nontextual.'" *Rehnquist*: "The jurisprudence of the 'negative side' of the Commerce Clause remains 'hopelessly confused.'" *Souter* (joining

---

Stevens, Kennedy, Ginsburg, and *Breyer*): "The Constitution is clearly silent on the subject of state legislation that discriminates against interstate commerce."

[83] Emphasis in original.

[84] In *Hillside Dairy, Inc.* v. *Lyons*, 539 U.S. 59, 123 S.Ct. 2142 (2003), Justice Thomas took another swipe at the "dormant Commerce Clause," because, he wrote, "the negative Commerce Clause has no basis in the text of the Constitution, makes little sense, and has proved virtually unworkable in application"—citing his dissent in *Camps Newfound/Owatonna, Inc.*, "and, consequently, cannot serve as a basis for striking down a state statute."

He made the same point in almost identical words in *American Trucking Associations, Inc.* v. *Michigan Public Service Commission*, 125 S.Ct. (2005): "[T]he negative Commerce Clause has no basis in the text of the Constitution, makes little sense, and has proved virtually unworkable in application . . . and, consequently, cannot serve as a basis for striking down a state statute."

[85] 125 S.Ct. 2195 (2005).

[86] In 1996, California voters passed the Compassionate Use Act, a "medical marijuana" law. According to the Supreme Court, "[t]he Act creates an exemption from criminal prosecution for physicians, as well as for patients and primary caregivers who possess or cultivate marijuana for medicinal purposes with the recommendation or approval of a physician. A 'primary caregiver' is a person who has consistently assumed responsibility for the housing, health, or safety of the patient."

[87] See Charles Krauthammer, "Thomas' originalism," www.townhall.com, June 10, 3005.

[88] Krauthammer wrote: "The position represented by Scalia's argument . . . is less 'conservative.' It recognizes that decades of precedent . . . become so ingrained in the life of the country, and so accepted as part of the understanding of the modern Constitution, that it is simply too revolutionary, too legally and societally disruptive, to return to an original understanding long abandoned." *Ibid.*

[89] Footnotes omitted.

[90] 541 U.S. 600, 124 S.Ct. 1941 (2004).

[91] Emphasis added.

[92] Emphasis added. Justice Scalia voted with the majority because he believed that "Congress could reasonably conclude that its objective of prohibiting marijuana from the interstate market could be undercut if those activities were excepted from its general scheme of regulation."

[93] Emphasis in original.

CHAPTER 5.

"One Supreme Court"

JUDICIAL REVIEW

*The judicial power of the United States,
shall be vested in one supreme Court, and in
such inferior Courts as the Congress may
from time to time ordain and establish.*[94]

*The judicial Power of the United States
shall extend to all Cases, in Law and Equity,
arising under this Constitution, the Laws of
the United States, and Treaties made, or
which shall be made, under their authority .
. . .*[95]

In the seminal case of *Marbury v. Madison*,[96] the legendary Chief Justice John Marshall established judicial supremacy by ruling that a federal court possesses power both to interpret the Constitution *and* to invalidate legislation deemed to be unconstitutional.

However, the *existence* of that power does not necessarily ensure that it will always be used.

Judicial Restraint

In addition to the Supreme Court hearing cases from state appellate courts regarding the federal Constitution, and from federal courts of appeal regarding the federal Constitution and federal statutes, the Court also has an "original jurisdiction"—meaning that a small number of controversies can begin in the High Court, without the need to wend their way up from state courts and lower federal courts.

Cases invoking the original jurisdiction of the Supreme Court of the United States do not arise very often, but in Justice Thomas's first term *Wyoming v. Oklahoma*[97] provided the new justice an opportunity to counsel his colleagues about judicial restraint.

An Oklahoma statute required "Oklahoma coal-fired electric generating plants producing power for sale in Oklahoma to burn a mixture of coal containing at least 10% Oklahoma-mined [local] coal." As a result, private companies mining coal in Wyoming sold less coal to Oklahoma, and the state of Wyoming thus collected fewer "extraction fees" from their own state's coal companies.

Accordingly, Wyoming sued Oklahoma, contending that the statute violated the Constitution's Interstate Commerce Clause because the ten-percent requirement "burdened" that commerce. The Supreme Court agreed, and held the Oklahoma statute unconstitutional.

Reminding the majority that in the past the Court had "exercised discretion in declining to hear cases that fall within the literal terms of our original jurisdiction," and that "[i]n determining which cases merit the exercise of original jurisdiction, the Court has typically focused on two considerations: [1] the nature of the claims involved and [2] the availability of alternate forums where they can be addressed," Justice Thomas wrote his first Supreme Court dissent.[98]

As to the "nature of the claims involved," he correctly saw that the real dispute was between the *Wyoming coal-mining companies* ("hardly bashful litigants," Thomas noted) who sold less coal to Oklahoma, and the state of Oklahoma—not between two states.

As to "the availability of alternate forums," Thomas observed that the coal-mining companies could sue Oklahoma either in lower federal courts or in state courts.

The factual context of the case, the precedent's two-part test, and Thomas's application of that test were more than adequate to justify his conclusion that the Court should decline to review the case: original jurisdiction (states suing sister states) is a serious matter, the Court has discretion to hear a case or not, Wyoming was really fronting for private companies in leap-frogging directly into the Supreme Court, and suit could have been brought in other courts (with possible review later in the Supreme Court).

Thomas then went beyond his admonition that the Court exercise judicial restraint:

> The implications of the Court's novel theory that tax-collection injury alone justifies exercise of original jurisdiction are, in my view, both sweeping and troubling. An economic burden imposed by one State on another state's taxpayers will frequently affect the other State's fisc.[99] * * * Under today's opinion, a State that can show *any*[100] loss in tax Revenue—even a [minor] loss . . . —that can be traced (albeit loosely) to the action of another State can apparently proceed directly to this Court to challenge that action.

Thomas was attempting to pull the majority back from the slippery slope that it had started down by "having extended the [Supreme Court's] original jurisdiction to one State's claim based on its tax-collector status." Having taken that step, he feared that in other cases invoking original jurisdiction "the Court cannot, in the exercise of discretion, refuse to entertain future disputes based on the same theory." That, he wrote, "would be the exercise not of discretion, but of caprice."[101]

As we shall see, the concept of "judicial restraint" is not unknown even to members of the Court who do not share Thomas's deeply held view of its wisdom and necessity. Indeed, under the rubric of Article III's "cases" and "controversies" restriction, the Court has from its earliest days exercised some measure of self-restraint, both as a constitutional requirement and as a prudential consideration.[102]

Ripeness

A question of "ripeness" arises when a dispute, between private parties themselves, or between them and the government (or even between states), is deemed by the Court to be not yet ready for judicial determination.

Most often, this occurs in cases involving administrative action, when the agency has not yet come far enough in its processes to warrant judicial intervention.

In *National Park Hospitality Association v. Department of the Interior*,[103] Justice Thomas explained the ripeness doctrine this way:

> Ripeness is a justiciability doctrine designed "to prevent the courts, through avoidance of premature adjudication, from entangling themselves in abstract disagreements over administrative policies, and also to protect the agencies from judicial interference until an administrative decision has been formalized and its effects felt in a concrete way by the challenging parties. * * * The ripeness doctrine is drawn both from Article III limitations on judicial power and from prudential reasons for refusing to exercise jurisdiction" . . . but, even in a case raising only prudential concerns, the question of ripeness may be considered on a court's own motion.

The issue in *National Park Hospitality Association* involved a dispute between an association representing concessionaires in national parks and the National Park Service. Because it is a fundamental principle of administrative law that *"agencies* do agency business"— not the courts, except that they eventually review the legality of agency decisions—the judicial ripeness decision is based on an evaluation of "(1) the fitness of the issues for judicial decision and (2) the hardship to the parties of withholding court consideration."

As Justice Thomas wrote in *National Park Hospitality Association,* "[a]bsent [a statutory provision providing for immediate judicial review], a regulation is not ordinarily considered the type of agency action 'ripe' for judicial review under the [Administrative Procedure Act (APA)] until the scope of the controversy has been reduced to more manageable proportions, and its factual components fleshed out, by some concrete action applying the regulation to the claimant's situation in a fashion that harms or threatens to harm him. (The major exception, of course, is a substantive rule which as a practical matter requires the plaintiff to adjust his conduct immediately . . . .)"

Based on that standard, under the rather complicated facts of the case, Thomas ruled for the Court that it was not ripe for adjudication. In so doing, he was applying settled legal principles of judicial restraint, rather than accepting the invitation of Justices O'Connor and Breyer that would have wasted the Court's time and resources by intervening in the administrative process before its action was an appropriate subject for judicial review. As Thomas saw the matter, implicit in the power of judicial review is the concomitant responsibility, when appropriate, of judicial restraint.

Standing to Sue

It is obvious that the Article III system of judicial review could not work if *no one* could sue over alleged grievances. Nor could it work if *everyone* could sue. Hence, some criteria must exist by which the federal judicial system regulates access to the courts. Those criteria are found in the doctrine of "standing to sue."

The city of Jacksonville, Florida, enacted an ordinance giving preference in the awarding of municipal contracts to certain minority-owned businesses. In Northeastern *Florida Chapter of the Associated General Contractors of America v. City of Jacksonville*,[104] the chapter itself, most of whose member-businesses were not minority-owned,[105] challenged the ordinance as a violation of equal protection of the law.

Justice Thomas wrote the 7-2 majority opinion,[106] identifying the criteria employed by the Court to determine standing to sue.

> It has been established by a long line of cases that a party seeking to invoke a federal court's jurisdiction must demonstrate three things: (1) "injury in fact," by which we mean an invasion of a legally protected interest that is (a) "concrete and particularized, and (b) actual or imminent, not conjectural or hypothetical" . . . ; (2) a causal relationship between the injury and the challenged conduct, by which we mean that the injury "fairly can be traced to the challenged action of the defendant," and has not resulted "from the independent action of some third party not before the court" . . . ; and (3) a likelihood that the injury will be redressed by a favorable decision, by which we mean that the "prospect of obtaining relief from the injury as a result of a favorable ruling" is not too speculative.

Based on the facts of the case, and these legal principles, Thomas had no difficulty finding that the plaintiff *had* standing to sue:

> When the government erects a barrier
> that makes it more difficult for members
> of one group to obtain a benefit than it is
> for members of another group, a member

> of the former group seeking to challenge
> the barrier need not allege that he would
> have obtained the benefit but for the
> barrier in order to establish standing. * *
> * And in the context of a challenge to a
> set-aside program, the "injury in fact" is
> the inability to compete on an equal
> footing in the bidding process, not the
> loss of a contract.

Although Thomas's opinion rested on Supreme Court precedent because the contractors satisfied the standing test—indeed, every other justice agreed with him about that—he drew lines when it came to *extending* the standing doctrine, explaining his position at some length in *Kowalski v. Tesmer*.[107]

In that case, the Court ruled on a challenge to Michigan's system of appointing appeal lawyers for defendants who pled guilty. The case had been brought by lawyers as third parties, on behalf of hypothetical clients. The Court denied them standing, and Justice Thomas took the occasion to question many of the Court's earlier precedents that had granted third-party standing to sue:

> That this case is even remotely close
> demonstrates that our third-party standing
> cases have gone far astray. We have
> granted third-party standing in a number
> of cases to litigants whose relationships
> with the directly affected individuals
> were at best remote. We have held, for
> instance, that beer vendors have standing
> to raise the rights of their prospective
> young male customers . . . ; that criminal
> defendants have standing to raise the
> rights of jurors excluded from service . . ;
> that sellers of mail-order contraceptives

have standing to assert the rights of
potential customers . . . ; that distributors
of contraceptives to unmarried persons
have standing to litigate the rights of the
potential recipients . . . ; and that white
sellers of land have standing to litigate
the constitutional rights of potential black
purchasers . . . . I agree with the Court
that "[t]he attorneys before us do not
have a 'close relationship' with their
alleged 'clients'; indeed, they have no
relationship at all." * * * The Court of
Appeals understandably could have
thought otherwise, given how generously
our precedents have awarded third-party
standing.

From the specifics of how far astray the Supreme Court's
standing to sue jurisprudence had gone, Justice Thomas moved on to
the more general principle involved:

It is doubtful whether a party who has no
personal constitutional right at stake in a
case should ever be allowed to litigate the
constitutional rights of others. Before
Truax v. Raich . . . and *Pierce v. Society
of Sisters* . . . this Court adhered to the
rule that "[a] court will not listen to an
objection made to the constitutionality of
an act by a party whose rights it does not
affect and who has therefore no interest
in defeating it." * * * This made sense.
Litigants who have no personal right at
stake may have very different interests
from the individuals whose rights they
are raising. Moreover, absent a personal

right, a litigant has no cause of action (or
defense), and thus no right to relief. It
may be too late in the day to return to this
traditional view. But even assuming it
makes sense to grant litigants third-party
standing in at least some cases, it is more
doubtful still whether third-party standing
should sweep as broadly as our cases
have held that it does.

Political Questions

Professors Nowak and Rotunda have correctly observed that
"[t]he political question doctrine—which holds that certain matters are
really political in nature and best resolved by the body politic rather
than suitable for judicial review—is a misnomer. It should more
properly be called the doctrine of nonjusticiability, that is, a holding
that the subject matter is inappropriate for judicial consideration."[108]

Cases presenting the "political question" issue do not frequently
reach the Supreme Court because the "rule of four" effectively keeps
them out.[109] However, occasionally there will be an opportunity for a
justice to address the subject.

One such occasion arose in a case entitled *Haitian Refugee
Center, Inc. v. Baker*,[110] involving Haitian "boat people." The
petitioners had lost in the court of appeals and sought a stay of
proceedings and a writ of certiorari so their case could be heard in the
Supreme Court.

Notwithstanding Justice Blackmun's lament—"The world has
followed with great concern the fate of thousands of individuals who
fled Haiti in the wake of that country's September 1991 military coup.
* * * Each of the issues presented . . . is difficult and susceptible to
competing interpretations"—there were not four votes on the Court to
grant certiorari.

But of the other eight justices, including Blackmun, only Justice Thomas bothered to explain *why* certiorari was denied:

> The affidavits filed throughout this litigation have sought to describe the conditions in Haiti and the treatment the returnees have received there. I am deeply concerned about these allegations. However, this matter must be addressed by the political branches, for *our role is limited to questions of law.* Because none of the legal issues presented in this petition [for certiorari] provides a basis for review, I join the Court's denial of certiorari.[111]

Empathy, sympathy, concern for the refugees—certainly. But as Thomas alone observed, dealing with the moral and immigration problems regarding the Haitian "boat people" is within the constitutional jurisdiction of the executive branch, not the judiciary— let alone the Supreme Court of the United States.

In Justice Thomas's view, the same can be said about certain aspects of national security.

On June 28, 2004, the Supreme Court decided three cases whose holdings and implications bode ill for the security of the United States. In only one of them, *Hamdi v. Rumsfeld,*[112] did Justice Thomas write.

When the clerk of the Supreme Court published the *Hamdi* decision, he should have provided a scorecard: There was a four-justice opinion written by Justice O'Connor, joined by Chief Justice Rehnquist and Justices Kennedy and Breyer. Justice Thomas, though writing in dissent supporting the government on another issue, provided the crucial fifth vote for the proposition that *the president could legally designate Hamdi and others similarly situated (American citizens and non-citizens alike) as "enemy combatants" who can be held without criminal charges being laid, and without being tried, until an armed conflict is ended, whenever that occurs.*

The opinion of the four-justice plurality, plus Thomas, relied on the World War II Supreme Court precedent of *Ex parte Quirin*, in which a *unanimous* Court held that the president could hold Nazi saboteurs (at least one of whom was an American citizen) for the duration of the war. (Indeed, after trial before a military tribunal, some of the *Quirin* spies were put to death.)

For the second part of the opinion, another voting lineup formed. It consisted of the original plurality (O'Connor, Rehnquist, Kennedy, and Breyer), plus Souter and Ginsburg (six votes), but without Thomas.

Although Souter and Ginsburg would have preferred that Padilla go free entirely unless the government charged him with a criminal act, they went along with the O'Connor-Rehnquist-Kennedy-Breyer ruling: *"We hold that . . . due process demands that a citizen held in the United States as an enemy combatant be given a meaningful opportunity to contest the factual basis for that detention before a neutral decision maker. . . . Plainly, the 'process' Hamdi has received is not that to which he is entitled under the Due Process Clause."* [113]

In the face of the O'Connor-Rehnquist-Kennedy-Breyer-Souter-Ginsburg opinion, and the strange-bedfellow dissent of Scalia and Stevens, [114] only Justice Clarence Thomas understood the real issue in Hamdi and enunciated a consistently principled position: *The power to designate captured Americans as enemy combatants lay with the president, and the courts had no role except to ascertain whether he had made a good-faith determination.*

The Executive Branch, acting pursuant to
the powers vested in the President by the

Constitution and with explicit congressional approval, has determined that Yaser Hamdi is an enemy combatant and should be detained. This detention falls squarely within the Federal Government's war powers, and we lack the expertise and capacity to second-guess that decision. As such, petitioners' habeas challenge should fail . . . . The plurality reaches a contrary conclusion by failing adequately to consider basic principles of the constitutional structure as it relates to national security and foreign affairs and by using the balancing scheme of *Mathews v. Eldridge* . . . . *I do not think that the Federal Government's war powers can be balanced away by this Court.* Arguably, Congress could provide for additional procedural protections, but until it does, we have no right to insist upon them. But even if I were to agree with the general approach the plurality takes, I could not accept the particulars. The plurality utterly fails to account for the Government's compelling interests and for our own institutional inability to weigh competing concerns correctly.[115]

Justice Thomas then invoked Supreme Court precedent, and Alexander Hamilton in the *Federalist*, for the proposition that there is no more compelling governmental interest than the nation's security. Indeed, the Preamble of the Constitution expressly provides that the purpose of union is "to provide for the common defence."

He cited Chief Justice John Marshall for the proposition that the president has primacy as "the sole organ of the nation in its external relations, and its sole representative with foreign nations," which is why Article II, Section 1, provides that he "shall be Commander in Chief" of the armed forces and "places in him the power to recognize foreign governments."

Citations of Supreme Court cases followed, all reiterating that the combination of the national interest and the president's constitutional power vests in him substantial power apart from and beyond that of Congress in matters of national security.

> Several points, made forcefully by [former Supreme Court] Justice Jackson, are worth emphasizing. First, with respect to certain decisions relating to national security and foreign affairs, the courts simply lack the relevant information and expertise to second-guess determinations made by the President based on information properly withheld. Second, even if the courts could compel the Executive to produce the necessary information, such decisions are simply not amenable to judicial determination because "[t]hey are delicate, complex, and involve large elements of prophecy." * * * Third, the Court in *Chicago & Southern Air Lines* and elsewhere has correctly recognized the primacy of the political branches in the foreign-affairs and national-security contexts.
>
> For these institutional reasons and because "Congress cannot anticipate and legislate with regard to every possible action the President may find it necessary

to take or every possible situation in which he might act," it should come as no surprise that "[s]uch failure of Congress ... does not, 'especially ... in the areas of foreign policy and national security,' imply 'congressional disapproval' of action taken by the Executive." * * * Rather in these domains, the fact that Congress has provided the President with broad authorities does not imply—and the Judicial Branch should not infer—that Congress intended to deprive him of particular powers not specifically enumerated. * * *

As far as the courts are concerned, "the enactment of legislation closely related to the question of the President's authority in a particular case which evinces legislative intent to accord the President broad discretion may be considered to invite measures on independent presidential responsibility."[116]

After considerable discussion about the relative powers of the president and the Court, the transcending importance of national security, and detailed consideration of historical and judicial precedents, Thomas's unwavering conclusion was "that the Government's detention of Hamdi as an enemy combatant does not violate the Constitution. By detaining Hamdi, the President, in the prosecution of a war and authorized by Congress, has acted well within his authority."

Statutory Interpretation

Molzof v. United States [117] appears to be the first majority
opinion Clarence Thomas wrote as an associate justice of the Supreme
Court. The opinion, written for a unanimous Court, is significant
because, like Thomas's position in *Musick*, it foreshadowed his
methodology in later statutory interpretation cases.

In partially waiving the government's sovereign immunity for
tortious conduct by its employees, the Federal Tort Claims Act—a civil
rather than a criminal statute— prohibits the award of "punitive
damages." Mrs. Molzof's husband had been rendered irreversibly
brain-dead in a VA hospital, and the government argued that the
damages she sought were not compensatory but punitive, and thus
barred under the FTCA.

In defining the statutory term "punitive damages," Thomas
began with the words themselves, rejecting the government's tortured
paraphrase ("damage awards that may have a punitive effect").
Relying on the statute's words, and "a widely accepted common-law
meaning," and "the concept of 'punitive damages' [having] a long
pedigree in the law," and "legal dictionaries in existence when the
FTCA was drafted," and Supreme Court precedents involving the
concept of punitive damages, and on "a cardinal rule of statutory
construction," Thomas concluded that "[a]s a general rule, the common
law recognizes that damages intended to *compensate* the plaintiff are
different in kind from 'punitive damages.'" [118]

Nowhere in Thomas's *Molzof* opinion are there trendy
references to "changing definitional norms," "modern understandings
of archaic nomenclature," or any other subjective method of defining
an important term in a federal statute. He resolved the case by
objective criteria applied in an objective manner. [119]

Later in the term, Thomas applied the same methodology to a
federal criminal statute.

In an FBI sting operation, a county commissioner took $7,000 in cash and a $1,000 contribution to his political campaign after being badgered, for seventeen months and in some thirty-three conversations, for help with a rezoning. Although there was no evidence that the commissioner had solicited or otherwise sought the money in return for the hoped-for rezoning, he was indicted for extortion under the federal Hobbs Act, which criminalizes "the obtaining of property from another . . . under color of official right." The commissioner was convicted.

The court of appeals affirmed the councilman's conviction, ruling that "passive acceptance of a benefit by a public official is sufficient to form the basis of a Hobbs Act violation if the official knows that he is being offered the payment in exchange for a specific requested exercise of his official power. *The official need not take any specific action to induce the offering of the benefit.*"[120]

The Supreme Court took the case, and the question to be decided was "whether an affirmative act of *inducement* by a public official, such as a demand, is an element of the offense of extortion . . . ."[121]

It's important to understand that in the Supreme Court the question was *not* whether there should be a Hobbs Act, whether extortion should be a crime, whether public officials should be punished for taking bribes, or any other legitimate *policy* issues that are grist for a *legislative* mill. On the contrary, there was only one *legal* question: whether the Hobbs Act, silent on its face about whether inducement was an element of extortion, did or did not require federal prosecutors to prove "inducement."

In a 6-3 vote the Supreme Court majority concluded that inducement was *not* an element of extortion because "of the common-law definition of extortion, which we believe Congress intended to adopt [in the Hobbs Act] . . . ." The councilman's conviction was affirmed.

Justice Thomas dissented, and his dissent provides a classic example of his approach to statutory interpretation.

First, he brushed aside the majority's reliance on a single law review article which discussed *English* common-law cases dealing with extortion. That alleged authority was "beside the point here—the critical inquiry for our purposes is *the American understanding at the time the Hobbs Act was passed in 1946.*"[122]

Next, surveying nineteenth- and early-twentieth-century *American* cases, Thomas concluded that they supported the requirement of an inducement.

More important, however, was what came next:

> As serious as the [majority's] disregard
> for history, is its disregard for well-
> established principles of statutory
> construction. The Court chooses not only
> the harshest interpretation of a criminal
> statute, but also the interpretation that
> maximizes federal criminal jurisdiction
> over state and local officials.

As we shall see, these two sentences speak volumes about Thomas's jurisprudence. (They also show that the councilman became a convicted felon because of a comma.)

"Extortion," as defined in the Hobbs Act, is "the obtaining of property from another, with his consent, *induced*[123]] by wrongful use of actual or threatened force, violence, or fear, or under color of official right." Note the comma. Its underlining and boldfacing are not typographical errors. They are meant to emphasize the *punctuation.* Based on the comma's placement, the Court majority read the statute as saying that the requirement of "induced" applied only to the first, pre-comma part of the sentence, "wrongful use," but not the second, "under color of official right." On that reading, the councilman would have been properly convicted because he did receive the money in his official capacity, no "inducement" being necessary.

Thomas agreed that such a reading was "conceivable," but offered an alternative interpretation: the statutory term "induced" applies to *both* types of extortion.[124]

Even laymen can see that his proffered construction is conceivable. With this foundation of equally plausible interpretations of the statute, Thomas turned to precedent:

> Our duty in construing this criminal statute, then, is clear: "The Court has often stated that when there are two rational readings of a criminal statute, one harsher than the other, we are to choose the harsher only when Congress has spoken in clear and definite language."

This is called the "rule of lenity."[125] Applying it in the councilman's case, by interpreting the statute to require inducement for a "color of official right" conviction, would not only prevent certain Hobbs Act defendants from going to prison over a wayward comma, *it would also restrain, albeit only slightly, the federal government's appetite to criminalize more and more conduct in violation of the spirit of the Tenth Amendment.*[126]

We see the same statutory interpretation methodology at work in another first- term Thomas dissent, *Rowland v. California Men's Colony*.[127]

An association of California prison inmates sued state correctional officers under the federal civil rights law and asked the trial judge for permission to proceed under a federal statute that allows a "person" who swears "he" is unable to pay court costs to sue "for free." It is called suing *in forma pauperis.*

Another federal statute[128] provides that "[i]n determining the meaning of any Act of Congress, *unless the context indicates otherwise*[129]—the wor[d] 'person' . . . include[s] corporations, companies, *associations,*[130] firms, partnerships, societies, and joint stock companies, as well as individuals." Seizing on the words "context" and "indicates," the 5-4 Supreme Court majority ruled that only natural persons, not the association of inmates, could sue *in forma pauperis.* The majority's reasoning is discussed in Justice Thomas's dissent.

While Justice Thomas shared the Court's understanding of the word "context," he did not agree with the majority's definition of the word "indicates": The Court's "gloss on that word apparently permits (and perhaps even requires) courts to look beyond the words of a statute and to consider the policy judgments on which those words may or may not be based."

Thus did Thomas establish his distance from the majority. Indeed, early in his dissent he flatly stated that the case could be dealt with in short order:

> Section 1915(a) [of the *in forma pauperis* statute] . . . contemplates that the "person" who is entitled to the benefits of the provision will have three characteristics: He will have the capacity to sue or be sued, to make an affidavit, and to be unable to pay court costs. An association clearly has the capacity to do each of these things, and that in my view, should be the end of the matter.

Declining to let it go at that, Justice Thomas dissected the majority's tactic of reading out of the statute the term "associations." The exact manner in which Thomas did so is less important than *that* he did, because in his criticism of the majority's approach to interpretation of the *in forma pauperis* statute, we see in bold relief his own typically restrained approach:

> The Court suggests that a reading of Section 1915 under which an artificial entity is entitled to in forma pauperis status would force it to confront "difficult issues of policy and administration." * * * Far from *avoiding* policy determinations, however, the Court effectively *engages* in policy-making by refusing to credit the legislative judgments that are implicit in the statutory language. Any reading of the phrase "unless the context indicates otherwise" that permits courts to override congressional policy judgments is in my view too broad. Congress has spoken, and we should give effect to its words.[131]

Before *Rowland* was decided, knee-jerk reactions by many of Justice Thomas's critics would likely have been that he was "anti-prisoner" and would have ruled that the inmates in *Rowland* should *not* be allowed to sue *in forma pauperis*. But as his rationale in *Rowland* makes clear, *judicial* policy considerations have no place in statutory interpretation. What matters are the words of the statute, and what the *legislature* intended, not what members of the Supreme Court deem desireable. In the last sentence of his *Rowland* dissent, Thomas drove home his point: "While it might make sense as a matter of policy to exclude associations and other artificial entities from the benefits of the *in forma pauperis* statute, I do not believe that *Congress* has done so."[132]

Stare Decisis

Georgia v. McCollum[133] raised a Fourteenth Amendment equal protection question: "whether the Constitution prohibits a criminal defendant from engaging in purposeful racial discrimination in the exercise of peremptory challenges."[134] Justice Thomas concurred with the majority, but his opinion stands for a wider, more structural principle of constitutional law.

Whites were charged with assaulting blacks. The defendants' lawyers made no secret of their intention to use their peremptory challenges to exclude as many blacks from the jury as they could, even if the result was that no black jurors would be seated. The trial judge ruled that the defense could use their peremptory challenges in that manner, and the Supreme Court of Georgia affirmed, 4-3. The Supreme Court of the United States granted certiorari.

Having ruled the year before in *Edmonson v. Leesville Concrete Company, Inc.*[135] that racially discriminatory exercise of peremptory challenges by a *civil* litigant violates the Equal Protection Clause of the Fourteenth Amendment, the Supreme Court reversed the conviction in *McCollum*, ruling that "the exercise of a peremptory challenge must not be based on the race of the juror or the racial stereotypes held by the party [exercising the challenge]."

Justice Thomas—though he believed that *Edmonson* had been wrongly decided—concurred with the majority *because the precedent was only one year old*, and his respect for the principle of *stare decisis*[136] dictated that it be followed.

In addition to providing yet another example of his belief that conservative adjudication normally requires respect for precedent, Justice Thomas took the occasion to "express [his] general dissatisfaction with [the Supreme Court's] continuing attempts to use the Constitution to regulate preemptory challenges." In light of the Court's seemingly anti-discrimination decisions in *Edmonson* and then

McCollum, one might think that Thomas's opposition to those decisions smacked of racial prejudice, or at least reflected a tolerance of racially motivated juror exclusion. Actually, his concerns were just the opposite:

> I am certain that black criminal defendants will rue the day that this Court ventured down the road that inexorably will lead to the elimination of peremptory strikes. * * * Today's decision, while protecting jurors, leaves defendants with less means of protecting themselves. * * * In effect, we have exalted the right of citizens to sit on juries over the rights of the criminal defendant, even though it is the defendant, not the jurors, who faces imprisonment or even death.

But Thomas's disagreement with the Court's entry into the business of deciding the constitutionality of various aspects of peremptory challenges did not end with his incisive recognition of the imbalance of values.

Once again, as in *Wyoming v. Oklahoma*, he saw the Supreme Court starting down the slippery slope:

> Today we decide only that white defendants may not strike black [potential jurors] on the basis of race. Eventually, we will have to decide whether black defendants may strike white [potential jurors].[137] * * * Next will come the question whether defendants may exercise peremptories on the basis of sex. * * * But whatever the

benefits were that this Court [in an 1880
case] perceived in a criminal defendant
having members of his class on the jury . .
. . they have evaporated.

Although Justice Scalia nodded obliquely to Thomas's
observations about race, in the end it was only Thomas who expressed
concern about the impact of *McCollum* upon black criminal defendants:

In the interest of promoting the
supposedly greater good of race relations
in the society as a whole (. . . that is what
underlies all of this)[138], we use the
Constitution to destroy the ages-old right
of criminal defendants to exercise
peremptory challenges as they wish, to
secure a jury that they consider fair.

Yet, despite Thomas's substantial concerns for the *McCollum*
decision's impact on black defendants, for him the jurisprudential
principle of *stare decisis* argued more strongly that he join the Court's
majority.[139]

Another example of Justice Thomas's adherence to the principle
of stare decisis, but where he went a step further, is the case of *City of
Indianapolis v. Edmond*.[140] The majority invalidated, on Fourth
Amendment grounds, a city drug-interdiction program using random
vehicle stops. Thomas dissented, but with a "kicker."

Taken together, our decisions in . . . *Sitz* . . . and . . .
Martinez-Fuerte . . . stand for the proposition that
suspicionless roadblock seizures are constitutionally
permissible if conducted according to a plan that limits
the discretion of the officers conducting the stops. I am
not convinced that *Sitz* and *Martinez-Fuerte* were
correctly decided. Indeed, I rather doubt that the

Framers of the Fourth Amendment would have considered "reasonable" a program of indiscriminate stops of individuals not suspected of wrongdoing.

[The defendants] did not, however, advocate the overruling of *Sitz* and *Martinez-Fuerte*, and I am reluctant to consider such a step without the benefit of briefing and argument.

Edmond is only one example of a case where Thomas has invited litigants, and the Court itself, to reconsider earlier decisions and overrule them if necessary.[141]

Thomas and Scalia

Both of these justices are strong believers in the jurisprudential principle of *stare decisis*. The case of *Mitchell v. United States*[142] is a good example of their similarities as well as their differences.

The questions for the Supreme Court were "whether, in the federal criminal system, a guilty plea waives the privilege [against self-incrimination] in the sentencing phase of the case . . . ." and "whether, in determining facts about the crime which bear upon the severity of the sentence, a trial court may draw an adverse inference from the defendant's silence." The majority, purportedly based on an earlier case, *Griffin v. California*,[143] ruled that there was no waiver, and that no adverse inferences could be drawn.

Scalia and Thomas dissented. Scalia wrote an opinion demonstrating conclusively that *Griffin* and its progeny were wrongly decided, and that *Mitchell* should not *extend* their rulings beyond the trial itself into the sentencing phase. However, Scalia observed, it may be true as the majority noted that because the *Griffin* rule has become "an essential feature of our legal tradition," there was "adequate reason not to overrule [those] cases."

Thomas, on the other hand, though also respecting *stare decisis*, was willing to go further: "Given their indefensible foundations," Thomas wrote, "I would be willing to reconsider *Griffin* and *Carter* in the appropriate case."

The Scalia-Thomas axis has been the subject of considerable discussion. It has been said that:

> Scalia describes himself as an "originalist," meaning he would defer to a text in terms of its objective meaning at the time of its enactment. Thomas is also an originalist, but takes a natural-law approach in discerning the meaning of the Constitution.

> There are other differences between Scalia and Thomas, not least that of whether to adhere to original meaning when doing so would lead to rulings sharply at odds with the Court's precedents. Scalia would not always so adhere and has called himself a "faint-hearted originalist," while Thomas seems quite willing to follow his arguments where they may lead.[144]

As we shall see when considering Thomas's Bill of Rights and Fourteenth Amendment opinions, his jurisprudence follows the path of the Founders.

ENDNOTES

[94] Article III, Section 1, Constitution of the United States of America.

[95] Article. III., Section. 2, Constitution of the United States of America.

[96] 5 U.S. (1 Cranch) 137 (1803).

[97] 502 U.S. 437, 112 S.Ct. 789 (1992).

[98] Justice Thomas took office on October 23, 1991. *Wyoming* v. *Oklahoma* was argued on November 4, 1991, and decided on January 22, 1992. Thus, it appears that this case is his first dissent.

[99] "Fisc" is a word often used by courts in place of the more common term "treasury."

[100] Emphasis in original.

[101] Three years later, Thomas made the same point in his dissent in the original jurisdiction case of *Nebraska* v. *Wyoming*, 515 U.S. 1, 115 S.Ct. 1933 (1995).

[102] Certain Article III "case" and "controversy" limits on the Court's jurisdiction do not involve separation of powers, while others, like "political questions," do.

Other "case" and "controversy" limits on the Supreme Court's jurisdiction, about which Justice Thomas has not expressly written, include "advisory opinions," "moot questions," "finality," "constitutional avoidance," "adequate and independent state grounds," and "abstention."

[103] 538 U.S. 803, 123 S.Ct. 2026 (2003).

[104] 508 U.S. 656, 113 S.Ct. 2297 (1993).

[105] "Minority" under the ordinance meant black- and female-owned businesses.

---

[106] Chief Justice Rehnquist was in the majority, and thus it was his prerogative to assign the writing of the Court's opinion.

[107] _U.S._, 125 S.Ct. 564 (2004).

[108] Nowak and Rotunda, *Constitutional Law,* 104.

[109] See Introduction, Endnote 22.

[110] 502 U.S. 1122, 112 S.Ct. 1245 (1992).

[111] Emphasis added.

[112] 542 U.S. 507, 124 S.Ct. 2633 (2004).

[113] Emphasis added,

[114] Scalia and Stevens rejected entirely the "enemy combatant" concept and argued instead that, absent congressional suspension of *habeas corpus,* captured Americans should be charged as criminals.

[115] Emphasis added.

[116] Citations and internal quotation marks omitted.

[117] 502 U.S. 301, 112 S.Ct. 711 (1992).

[118] Emphasis added.

[119] During Justice Thomas's fourteen terms on the Court, he has written a host of majority opinions requiring the interpretation of statutes (and some agency rules). Those opinions reflect the same methodology he employed in the *Molzof* case. See Appendix B for a list of those opinions, some of which contain representative quotations from Justice Thomas.

---

[120] Emphasis added.

[121] *Evans* v. *United States*, 504 U.S. 255, 112 S.Ct. 1881 (1992). Emphasis added.

[122] Emphasis added.

[123] Emphasis added.

[124] Grammarians may be interested to know that Thomas did not simply make the assertion and let it go at that. He explained at some length the grammatical mistake the majority was making: "[I]t sets up an unnatural and ungrammatical parallel between the *verb* 'induced' and the *preposition* 'under.' The more natural construction is that the verb 'induced' applies to *both* types of extortion described in the statute. * * * This construction comports with correct grammar and standard usage by setting up a parallel between two prepositional phrases, the first beginning with 'by'; the second with 'under'."

[125] In *United States* v. *R.L.C.*, 503 U.S. 291, 112 S.Ct. 1329 (1992), Thomas had occasion to agree with Justice Scalia in a federal homicide case involving a juvenile that "the use of legislative history to construe an otherwise ambiguous penal statute [as the majority did] against a criminal defendant is difficult to reconcile with the rule of lenity."

[126] This is, of course, a federalism point. Justice Thomas added: "The Court's construction of the Hobbs Act is repugnant not only to the basic tenets of criminal justice reflected in the rule of lenity, but also to *basic tenets of federalism.* Over the past 20 years, the Hobbs Act has served as the engine *for a stunning expansion of federal criminal jurisdiction into a field traditionally policed by state and local laws—* acts of public corruption by state and local officials." (Emphasis added.)

[127] 506 U.S. 194, 113 S.Ct. 716 (1993).

[128] The Dictionary Act, 1 United States Code, Section 1.

[129] Emphasis added.

[130] Emphasis added.

[131] Emphasis in original.

[132] Emphasis added. In *United Dominion Industries, Inc.* v. *United States*, 532 U.S. 822, 121 S.Ct. 1934 (2001), Thomas concurred separately because he disagreed "with the dissent's suggestion that, when a provision of the [Internal Revenue] Code and the corresponding regulations are ambiguous, this Court should defer to the Government's interpretation. * * * At a bare minimum, in cases such as this one, in which the complex statutory and regulatory scheme lends itself to any number of interpretations, we should be inclined to rely on the traditional canon that construes revenue-raising laws against their drafter."

[133] 505 U.S. 42, 112 S.Ct. 2348 (1992).

[134] A peremptory challenge in civil and criminal trials enables lawyers for both sides to remove potential jurors without giving any reason. The number of peremptory challenges is limited by statute in both the state and federal judicial systems.

[135] 500 U.S. 614, 111 S.Ct. 2077 (1991).

[136] The full Latin expression is "*Stare decisis et non quieta movere*," defined by *Black's Law Dictionary,* fifth edition, as "to adhere to precedents and not to unsettle things which are established."

[137] Here, Justice Thomas inserted the following footnote: "The NAACP Legal Defense and Education Fund, Inc., has submitted a brief arguing, in all sincerity, that 'whether white defendants can use peremptory challenges to purge minority jurors presents quite different issues from

whether a minority defendant can strike majority jurors'. * * *
Although I suppose that this issue technically remains open, it is
difficult to see how the result could be different if the defendants here
were black."

[138] Parenthetical statement in original.

[139] Another example of Justice Thomas's respect for *stare decisis* is
found in his concurring opinion in the following term's *Richmond* v.
Lewis, 506 U.S. 40, 113 S.Ct. 528 (1992). The majority ruled that
based on a Supreme Court precedent, a death sentence had been tainted
by an Eighth Amendment error made by the trial judge in sentencing.
Thomas had *dissented* in that earlier case and at the time of the
Richmond decision persisted in that view. However, he *concurred* in
Richmond because of the earlier precedent.

[140] 531 U.S. 32, 121 S.Ct. 447 (2000).

[141] For example, *Whitman* v. *American Trucking Associations*, 531 U.S.
457, 121 S.Ct. 903 (2000), involved the delegation of power from
Congress to an administrative agency—something long ago validated
by the Supreme Court so long as the delegation does not go "too far."

Justice Thomas concurred, focusing on "a genuine constitutional
problem . . . which the parties did not address." He continued:

> The parties to these cases who briefed the constitutional issue
> wrangled over constitutional doctrine with barely a nod to the
> text of the Constitution. Although this Court since 1928 has
> treated the "intelligible principle" [sufficient congressional
> guidance for the agency's exercise of its discretion] requirement
> as the only constitutional limit on congressional grants of power
> to administrative agencies . . . the Constitution does not speak
> of "intelligible principles." Rather, it speaks in much simpler
> terms: '*All* legislative Powers herein granted shall be vested in a

Congress.' * * * I am not convinced that the intelligible principle doctrine serves to prevent all cessions of legislative power. I believe that there are cases in which the principle is intelligible and yet the significance of the delegated decision is simply too great for the decision to be called anything other than "legislative." (Emphasis in original.)

Another example of Thomas's willingness, in an appropriate case, to consider the doctrine of *stare decisis* as not carved in stone is found in *Tennard* v. *Dretke*, 542 U.S. 274, 124 S. Ct. 2562 (2004), where he wrote in dissent:

Petitioner must rely on *Penry v. Lynaugh*, 492 U.S. 302 . . . 109 S.Ct. 2934 (1989), to argue that Texas' special issues framework unconstitutionally limited the discretion of his sentencing jury. I have long maintained, however, that *Penry* did so much violence to so many of this Court's settled precedents in an area of fundamental constitutional law, [that] it cannot command the force of *stare decisis*. * * * I therefore agree with Justice Scalia that a certificate of appealability cannot be issued based upon an "insubstantial right . . . derive[d] from case law in which this Court has long left the Constitution behind and embraced contradiction."

[142] 526 U.S. 314, 119 S.Ct. 1307 (1999).

[143] 380 U.S. 609, 85 S.Ct 1229 (1965).

[144] Terry Eastland, "Farewell to the Chief," *The Weekly Standard*, September 19, 2005, 12.

Professor David N. Mayer of Capital University has written that "[w]hen Thomas parts company with the conservative justices, especially Scalia, he reveals a jurisprudence that seems more libertarian than conservative" (David Mayer, "The Next Chief Justice," *The New Individualist*, June 2005, 9).

In his 2006 William Howard Taft Lecture at the University of Cincinnati School of Law, Boston University law professor Randy E. Barnett persuasively argued that Justice Scalia has "prove[d] unfaithful to the original meaning of the [constitutional] text in three distinct ways," that from Justice Scalia's 1988 Taft Lecture "and his behavior on the Court . . . [he] is simply not an originalist," and that "if any current justice can fairly be described as a committed originalist, it is Justice Thomas and not Justice Scalia." Professor Barnett also states that "Justice Scalia has been quoted as saying that Justice Thomas 'doesn't believe in *stare decisis*, period. . . . if a constitutional authority is wrong, [Thomas] would say, "let's get it right." I would not do that.' As quoted by Ken Foskett in Douglas T. Kendall, *A Big Question About Clarence Thomas*, WASHINGTON POST, Thursday, October 14, 2004, p.A31." Professor Barnett's Taft Lecture, entitled "Scalia's Infidelity: A Critique of 'Faint-Hearted' Originalism," can be downloaded without charge at The Boston University School of Law Working Paper Series Index: http://www.bu.edu./law/faculty/papers and The Social Science Research Network Electronic Paper Collection: http://www.ssrn.com/abstract=880112.

CHAPTER 6.

"Congress shall make no law"

FIRST AMENDMENT

Congress shall make no law respecting an establishment of religion, or prohibiting the free exercise thereof; or abridging the freedom of speech, or of the press, or the right of the people peaceably to assemble, and to petition the Government for a redress of grievances.[145]

Establishment of Religion[146]

Few provisions of the United States Constitution have been more troublesome jurisprudentially than the first clause of the First Amendment.

In our examination of Justice Thomas's Establishment Clause jurisprudence, we begin with *Zelman* v. *Simmons-Harris*,[147] a case with three prongs—religion, race, and federalism.

Ohio had a school voucher program which impacted on religious schools. Inevitably, the program was challenged on Establishment Clause grounds, and the Supreme Court ruled that there was no constitutional violation.

As we saw in Chapter 2, the Establishment Clause, the First Amendment in which it appears, and the entire Bill of Rights *were intended to apply to the federal government. Allegedly unconstitutional state conduct is measured by the Due Process and Equal Protection Clauses of the Fourteenth Amendment.* Thus, when we say that the Ohio school voucher program was challenged under the "establishment clause," that's merely shorthand for saying that the challenge was based on whatever "establishment" content may be found in the Due Process Clause of the Fourteenth Amendment. The importance of this distinction will be apparent in a moment.

Justice Thomas concurred in the *Zelman* case. He opened with a quotation from the renowned Frederick Douglass: "Education . . . means emancipation. It means light and liberty. It means the uplifting of the soul of man into the glorious light by which men can only be made free."

Thomas then noted that although *Brown v. Board of Education*[148] —the legendary case that ruled unconstitutional racial segregation in public education—had enshrined the importance of public education for minority students, nearly a half century later too many school systems still failed those pupils. He wrote:

> These [school voucher] cases present an example of such failures. Besieged by escalating financial problems and declining academic achievement, the Cleveland City School District was in the midst of an academic emergency when Ohio enacted its scholarship program.
>
> The dissents and [those attacking the program] wish to invoke the Establishment Clause of the First Amendment, *as incorporated through the Fourteenth,* to constrain a State's neutral efforts to provide greater educational opportunity for underprivileged minority students. Today's decision properly upholds the program as constitutional, and I join it in full.[149]

Why, then, did Thomas not simply vote with the majority to uphold the school voucher program? Why did he write a separate concurring opinion?

In the answer to these questions, we learn something about his jurisprudence that sets him apart from every other justice on the Supreme Court with whom he has served, and virtually every one that has *ever* served since ratification of the Fourteenth Amendment in 1868.

The Court's opinion was written by Chief Justice Rehnquist, whose opening paragraph stated that "[t]he question presented is whether this program offends the Establishment Clause of the United States Constitution." This was constitutional shorthand. Rehnquist really meant due process of the Fourteenth Amendment.

After weighing in on the constitutionality of the Ohio program, Thomas made a profound jurisprudential statement: "*as a matter of first principles, I question whether this* [Supreme Court's Establishment Clause] *test should be applied to the States.*"

Given that "incorporation" was at that time an entrenched dogma of Supreme Court jurisprudence, and countless decisions rested on the doctrine, *with this one sentence Thomas was potentially challenging the premise underlying nearly a century of precedents involving the applicability to the states of virtually every provision of the federal Bill of Rights*—from the Establishment Clause of the First Amendment to the Cruel and Unusual Punishments Clause of the Eighth.

His words deserve to speak for themselves:

> The Establishment Clause originally protected *States*, and by extension their citizens, from the imposition of an established religion by the Federal

Government.[150] *Whether and how this Clause should constrain state action under the Fourteenth Amendment is a more difficult question.*[151]

Thomas continued:

Consequently, in the context of the Establishment Clause, *it may well be that state action should be evaluated on different terms than similar action by the Federal Government.* * * * By considering the particular religious liberty right alleged to be invaded by a State, federal courts can strike a proper balance between the demands of the Fourteenth Amendment on the one hand and the federalism prerogatives of States on the other.[152]

Whatever the textual and historical merits of incorporating the Establishment Clause, I can accept that the Fourteenth Amendment protects religious liberty rights.[153]

But that protection is, as a matter of due process of law, not because the Establishment Clause itself operates against the states.

Indeed, as Thomas said earlier in his opinion, "[w]hen rights are incorporated against the States through the Fourteenth Amendment they should advance, not constrain, individual rights." By extension, Thomas was saying that "due process" may, and probably should, mean something *different* from establishment, free exercise, speech, press, assembly, petition, and the other "incorporated" provisions of the Bill of Rights.

This is why Thomas, in his words, could not "accept [the Fourteenth Amendment's] use to oppose neutral programs of school choice through the incorporation of the Establishment Clause. There would be a tragic irony in converting the Fourteenth Amendment's guarantee of individual liberty into a prohibition on the exercise of educational choice."

In other words, even if the meaning of the Establishment Clause was appropriately "incorporated" against the states via the Due Process Clause of the Fourteenth Amendment, the former cannot be used to subvert the very rights (in this case educational choice in the form of school vouchers) that the amendment was enacted to protect.

Thomas further spelled out his point this way: "[The program's opponents] advocate using the Fourteenth Amendment to handcuff the State's ability to experiment with education. But without education one can hardly exercise the civic, political, and personal freedoms conferred by the Fourteenth Amendment." In this statement, Thomas was adverting to Frederick Douglass, and he ended his opinion by returning to the words of the ex-slave:

> These [Ohio] programs address the root of the problem with failing urban public schools that disproportionately affect minority students. Society's other solution to these educational failures is often to provide racial preferences in higher education. Such preferences, however, run afoul of the Fourteenth Amendment's prohibition against distinctions based on race. * * * By contrast, school choice programs that involve religious schools appear unconstitutional only to those who would twist the Fourteenth Amendment against itself by expansively incorporating the

Establishment Clause. *Converting the Fourteenth Amendment from a guarantee of opportunity to an obstacle against education reform distorts our constitutional values and disserves those in the greatest need.*

As Frederick Douglass poignantly noted, "no greater benefit can be bestowed upon a long benighted people, than giving to them, as we are here earnestly this day endeavoring to do, the means of an education."[154]

Justice Thomas propounded the same theme once again in *Cutter v. Wilkinson.*[155]

A federal statute provides that "[n]o government shall impose a substantial burden on the religious exercise of a person residing in or confined to an institution . . . even if the burden results from a rule of general applicability, unless the government demonstrates that imposition of the burden on that person," first, "furthers a compelling governmental interest," and second, "is the least restrictive means of furthering that compelling governmental interest."[156]

The Supreme Court upheld the law's constitutionality against an Establishment Clause challenge.

Justice Thomas concurred, providing a clear statement of his Establishment Clause jurisprudence.

On its face . . . [the statute] is not a law "respecting an establishment of religion." This provision does not prohibit or interfere with state establishments, since no State has established (or

constitutionally could establish . . .) a
religion. Nor does the provision require a
State to establish a religion: It does not
force a State to coerce religious
observance or payment of taxes
supporting clergy, or require a State to
prefer one religious sect over another. *It
is a law respecting religion, but not one
respecting an establishment of
religion.*[157]

In short, the view that the Establishment
Clause precludes Congress from
legislating respecting religion lacks
historical provenance, at least based on
the history of which I am aware. Even
when enacting laws that bind the States
pursuant to valid exercises of its
enumerated powers, Congress need not
observe strict separation between church
and state, or steer clear of the subject of
religion. It need only refrain from making
laws "respecting an establishment of
religion"; it must not interfere with a
state establishment of religion. For
example, Congress presumably could not
require a State to establish a religion any
more than it could preclude a State from
establishing a religion.

Close on the heels of *Cutter* was one of the two last decisions
handed down by the Court in its 2004 – 2005 term, an Establishment
Clause case entitled *Van Orden v. Perry*[158] that caused a media frenzy.
The question for the Court was "whether the Establishment Clause of
the First Amendment allows the display of a monument inscribed with
the Ten Commandments on the Texas State Capitol grounds." The

Court ruled that it did. Thomas was with the majority, but, not untypically, he went his own way in a concurring opinion.

First, he noted that the case would be easier "if the Court were willing to abandon the inconsistent guideposts it has adopted for addressing Establishment Clause challenges and return to the original meaning of the Clause. * * * *The Framers understood an establishment 'necessarily* [*to*] *involve actual legal coercion'*." [159]

On that understanding, since there was no coercion involved in the religious display, its presence was not violative of the Establishment Clause.

As Justice Thomas put it: "In no sense does Texas compel petitioner Van Orden to do anything. The only injury to him is that he takes offense at seeing the monument as he passes it on his way to the Texas Supreme Court Library. He need not stop to read it or even to look at it, let alone to express support for it or adopt the Commandments as guides for his life. The mere presence of the monument along his path involves no coercion and thus does not violate the Establishment Clause."

Thomas then turned to what amounted to an indictment of the Court's previous Establishment Clause jurisprudence:

> Returning to the original meaning would do more than simplify our task. It also would avoid the pitfalls present in the Court's current approach to such challenges. This Court's precedent elevates the trivial to the proverbial "federal case," by making benign signs and postings subject to challenge. Yet even as it does so, the Court's precedent attempts to avoid declaring all religious symbols and words of longstanding

tradition unconstitutional, by counterfactually declaring them of little religious significance. Even when the Court's cases recognize that such symbols have religious meaning, they adopt an unhappy compromise that fails fully to account for either the adherent's or the non-adherent's beliefs, and provides no principled way to choose between them. Even worse, *the incoherence of the Court's decisions in this area renders the Establishment Clause impenetrable and incapable of consistent application. All told, this Court's jurisprudence leaves courts, governments, and believers and nonbelievers alike confused*—an observation that is hardly new.[160]

In concluding, Justice Thomas returned to a theme that pervades his opinions, and that explains much about his constitutional jurisprudence.

The unintelligibility of this Court's precedent raises the further concern that, either in appearance or in fact, adjudication of Establishment Clause challenges turns on judicial predilections. * * * *The outcome of constitutional cases ought to rest on firmer grounds than the personal preferences of judges.*[161]

What, then, is the solution to the problems created by Establishment Clause cases?

For Justice Thomas, the answer seems to be self-evidently clear:

> Much, if not all, of this would be avoided
> *if the Court would return to the views of
> the Framers* and adopt *coercion* as the
> touchstone for our Establishment Clause
> inquiry. Every acknowledgment of
> religion would not give rise to an
> Establishment Clause claim. *Courts
> would not act as theological
> commissions*, judging the meaning of
> religious matters. Most important, our
> precedent would be capable of consistent
> and coherent application. While the Court
> correctly rejects the challenge to the Ten
> Commandments monument on the Texas
> Capitol grounds, *a more fundamental
> rethinking of our Establishment Clause
> jurisprudence remains in order.*"[162]

Free Exercise of Religion

In general, modern "free exercise" law allows government to
intrude on legitimate religious practice only in the name of a
"compelling" governmental interest.[163]

The owner of residential rental property in Anchorage, Alaska,
consistently refused to rent to unmarried couples because of his sincere
religious belief that such cohabitation was a sin and that he would be
facilitating it by acting otherwise.[164] The Anchorage Equal Rights
Commission decided that the owner's policy violated various state laws
prohibiting discrimination based on marital status. The Alaska
Supreme Court agreed, ruling that the laws' application to the owner
did not violate his right to the free exercise of his religion.

The owner sought review in the Supreme Court of the United States, which was denied. Justice Thomas, however, wrote a "dissent," arguing that the Court should have granted certiorari:

> If, despite affirmative discrimination by Alaska on the basis of marital status [e.g., unmarried partner of deceased does not share in estate, absent last will and testament] and a complete absence of any national policy against such discrimination, the State's asserted interest in this case is allowed to qualify as a "compelling" interest—that is, a "paramount" interest, an interest "of the highest order"—then I am at a loss to know what asserted governmental interests are not compelling. The decision of the Alaska Supreme Court drains the word *compelling* of any meaning and seriously undermines the protection for exercise of religion . . . .[165]

In this unsuccessful attempt to convince three of his colleagues to grant certiorari and, by implication, hold the Alaska laws violative of the landlord's right to the free exercise of his anti-cohabitation religious beliefs, Thomas was suggesting that *a core First Amendment guarantee should be interpreted rationally, not by the fashionable criteria of political correctness.*

This approach is consistent with the methodology Thomas brings to statutory interpretation generally, and we will see it applied consistently to his opinions in other Bill of Rights cases.

Freedom of Speech

Although the First Amendment protects freedom of "speech," thus suggesting that there is but one type, the Supreme Court has sliced and diced that concept into various sub-categories. There is now "political speech," "commercial speech," "obscene speech," "defamatory speech," "symbolic speech," "anonymous speech," "hate speech," and more—several with their own "tests," and thus with their own degrees of protection, or the lack thereof.

While there is no official hierarchical ranking about which category of speech is more "important," most informed people would put "political speech" at the top of the list because of its relationship to the democratic process. As we shall see, the First Amendment has never had a stronger champion than Justice Thomas.

In the 1976 case of *Buckley v. Valeo*,[166] the Supreme Court recognized that government-imposed controls on political contributions and expenditures "operate in an area of the most fundamental First Amendment activities." Still, in *Buckley*, the Court *upheld* a federal statute's limits on political *contributions*, while at the same time *invalidating* the limits on political *expenditures*. This schizophrenic ruling rested on the Court's rationale that "[t]he expenditure limitations . . . represent substantial merely than theoretical restraints on the quantity and diversity of political speech," whereas "limitations upon the amount that any one person or group may contribute to a candidate or political committee entail only a marginal restriction upon the contributor's ability to engage in free communication."[167]

Twenty years later, the case of *Colorado Republican Federal Campaign Committee v. Federal Election Commission*[168] reached the Supreme Court. Before either political party had selected senatorial candidates, the Colorado Republican Party ran radio ads attacking the Democratic Party's likely candidate. The Federal Election Commission claimed the cost of the ads violated a dollar limit set by the Federal Election Campaign Act of 1971.

The Court ruled that "the First Amendment prohibits the application of [that] provision to the kind of expenditure at issue here— an expenditure that the political party has made independently, without coordination with any candidate."

Justice Thomas concurred in part and dissented in part. While he agreed with the Court's conclusion, he disagreed with how his colleagues reached it. Openly disagreeing with the *Buckley* ruling, Thomas believed that:

> contribution limits infringe as directly
> and as seriously upon freedom of
> political expression and association as do
> expenditure limits. *The protections of the*
> *First Amendment do not depend upon so*
> *fine a line as that between spending*
> *money to support a candidate or group*
> *and giving money to the candidate or*
> *group to spend for the same purpose.* In
> principle, people and groups give money
> to candidates and other groups for the
> same reason that they spend money in
> support of those candidates and groups:
> because they share social, economic, and
> political beliefs and seek to have those
> beliefs affect governmental policy. *I*
> *think that the Buckley framework for*
> *analyzing the constitutionality of*
> *campaign finance laws is deeply flawed.*
> Accordingly, I would not apply it.[169]

Instead, in analyzing the constitutionality of political campaign finance laws, justice Thomas would begin with "the premise that there is no constitutionally significant difference between campaign contributions and expenditures: Both forms of speech are central to the First Amendment. * * * I am convinced that under [the appropriate test of] traditional strict scrutiny, broad prophylactic caps on both spending and giving in the political process like [the challenged provision of the Federal Election Campaign Act of 1971] are unconstitutional."

Three years later, in *Nixon v. Shrink Missouri Government*,[170] provisions of Missouri's campaign finance law, limiting the amount of contributions to candidates in order to reduce the opportunity for political corruption, were before the Court. The limitations were upheld,[171] and, not surprisingly, Justice Thomas dissented. Again, he went after *Buckley*.

The introduction to Thomas's *Shrink Missouri* dissent began by his characterizing the Court's decision as "ratification" of "Missouri's sweeping repression of political speech," made possible by his colleagues' adopting the "analytic fallacies of our flawed decision in *Buckley*." Worse than merely applying *Buckley* to the Missouri statute, "[u]nfortunately, the Court is not content to merely adhere to erroneous precedent. Under the guise of applying *Buckley*, the Court proceeds to weaken the already enfeebled constitutional protection that *Buckley* afforded campaign contributions."

Next, adverting to his concurrence/dissent in the *Colorado Republican* case, Thomas stated flatly that the Court's *Buckley* decision was "in error" and, despite his respect for the principle of *stare decisis*, he "would overrule it." Then government restrictions on political campaign contributions would be subject to "strict scrutiny," and would survive only if they were "narrowly tailored" to serve a "compelling interest"—a burden that both the federal and state governments could rarely, if ever, carry.

In support of his position, Thomas began by stating a proposition that he regarded as "unassailable": "Political speech is the primary object of First Amendment protection."[172]

He then began where his analyses often begin: "The Founders sought to protect the rights of individuals to engage in political speech because a self-governing people depends upon the free exchange of political information. And that free exchange should receive the most protection when it matters the most—during campaigns for elective office."[173]

Recognizing that the Founders' principles were "solidly embedded in our precedents," Thomas stated flatly that "the Court today abandons them."

> For nearly half a century, this Court has extended First Amendment protection to a multitude of forms of "speech," such as making false defamatory statements, filing lawsuits, dancing nude, exhibiting drive-in movies with nudity, burning flags, and wearing military uniforms. Not surprisingly, the Courts of Appeals have followed our lead and concluded that the First Amendment protects, for example, begging, shouting obscenities, erecting tables on a sidewalk, and refusing to wear a necktie.

Yet, Thomas complained, these examples of protected speech "are less integral to the functioning of our Republic than campaign contributions."

Next, he went back into history and proceeded to dissect *Buckley* premise by premise, thoroughly discrediting the decision and thereby undermining the precedent upon which the Court rested its decision regarding the Missouri statute.

He followed this intellectual surgery by demonstrating that in *Shrink Missouri*, the Court did not apply the "strict scrutiny" test propounded but not applied in Buckley:

> Apart from its endorsement of *Buckley's*
> rejection of the intermediate standards of
> review used to evaluate expressive
> conduct . . . the Court makes no effort to
> justify its deviation from the tests we
> traditionally employ in free speech cases.

Applying strict scrutiny, and even conceding that the state of Missouri had a compelling interest in reducing political corruption sufficient to justify the state's limitation on political contributions, Thomas found that the statute was not narrowly tailored to achieve that end. A "blunderbuss approach" is what he called it, noting that other laws existed in Missouri to deal with corruption. "[W]hen it comes to significant infringement on our fundamental liberties," he wrote, "that some undesirable conduct may not be deterred is an insufficient justification to sweep in vast amounts of protected political speech."

Justice Thomas took on *Buckley* yet again in *Federal Election Commission v. Colorado Republican Federal Campaign Committee*.[174] The Supreme Court majority had ruled that under the Federal Election Campaign Act, expenditures by a political party that were coordinated with its *own* candidate for Congress could constitutionally be restricted. Thomas dissented "[b]ecause this provision sweeps too broadly, interferes with the party-candidate relationship, and has not been proved necessary to combat corruption." For good measure, he stated that he "continue[d] to believe that *Buckley* . . . should be overruled."

Quoting himself from earlier cases, Thomas wrote of the importance of political speech and how "it is the lifeblood of a self-governing people . . . ." Then, he expressed "baffle[ment] that [the] Court has extended the most generous First Amendment safeguards to filing lawsuits, wearing profane jackets, and exhibiting drive-in movies with nudity[175], but has offered only tepid protection to the core speech and associational rights that our Founders sought to defend."

In pointing out the majority's inconsistency in its First Amendment jurisprudence—let alone its warped hierarchy of free speech values—Thomas was, albeit collegially, underscoring the hypocrisy of Justices Stevens, O'Connor, Souter, Ginsburg, and Breyer, all of whom were proponents of free speech. Except when they weren't.[176]

As important to issues of political speech as the post-Buckley cases were, their significance was eclipsed by *McConnell v. Federal Election Commission*,[177] an extremely complicated case whose severely fragmented decision damaged the cause of free speech even more than did *Buckley*.

As the Harvard Law Review has explained,

> [W]ith the passage of the Bipartisan Campaign Reform Act of 2002 (BCRA)[178] , Congress declared that soft money was a blight on American politics best banned outright.[179] Last Term, in *McConnell v. FEC*[180], the Court largely approved that effort, upholding all but a few minor provisions of the Act. The majority's decision announced a far more sweeping definition of "corruption" than was articulated twenty-seven years earlier in Buckley v. Valeo[181], a definition justified with a voluminous record demonstrating the pervasive influence of soft money. As the dissenters in *McConnell* noted, however, the majority's expansive conception of corruption gives rise to the concern that a similar rationale might be employed to justify limitations on free speech in other contexts.[182]

Justice Thomas's opinion in *McConnell*—one of his finest on any subject— eloquently makes exactly that point. He opens with the obligatory quotation from the First Amendment ("Congress shall make no law . . ."), and follows with this categorical statement:

> Nevertheless, *the Court today upholds what can only be described as the most significant abridgment of the freedoms of speech and association since the Civil War.* With breathtaking scope, the Bipartisan Campaign Reform Act of 2002 (BCRA), directly targets and constricts core political speech, the primary object of First Amendment protection. * * * Because the First Amendment has its fullest and most urgent application to speech uttered during a campaign for political office * * * our duty is to approach these restrictions with the utmost skepticism and subject them to the strictest scrutiny."[183]

Thomas thus laid down his major premises: that core political speech is constitutionally protected, and that restrictions on it are subject to strict scrutiny. Those restrictions can survive constitutional challenge only by being narrowly tailored to serve a compelling governmental interest.

He then turned to the majority's rationale with an attack rooted in the Court's own precedents:

> Yet today the fundamental principle that "the best test of truth is the power of the thought to get itself accepted in the competition of the market" . . . is cast

> aside in the purported service of
> preventing "corruption," or the mere
> "appearance of corruption." * * *
> Apparently, the marketplace of ideas is to
> be fully open only to defamers, *New
> York Times Co. v. Sullivan* . . . ; nude
> dancers, *Barnes v. Glen Theatre, Inc.* . . .
> ; pornographers, *Ashcroft v. Free Speech
> Coalition* . . . ; flag burners, *United States
> v. Eichman* . . . ; and cross burners,
> *Virginia v. Black* . . . .

After addressing certain technical deficiencies of the statute and the majority's embrace of them, Thomas returned to the overarching principle involved in the law and in the Court's upholding of it.

> Today's holding continues a disturbing trend: the steady
> decrease in the level of scrutiny applied to restrictions
> on core political speech. * * * Although this trend is
> most obvious in the review of contribution limits, it has
> now reached what even this Court today would
> presumably recognize as a direct restriction on core
> political speech: limitations on independent
> expenditures.

In hammering away at *Buckley*'s unsupportable distinction between political "contributions" and "expenditures," and at the Court's suppression of even the latter by the device of applying a "softer" test than the requisite strict scrutiny, Thomas continued to argue that any restrictions on core political speech were unconstitutional.

A collateral issue to the *Buckley*-type "contribution/expenditure" cases is the activity of leafleting in connection with a public controversy.

For example, an Ohio statute prohibited the distribution of anonymous leaflets, and the leafleting opponent of a proposed school tax was convicted of violating the law. The Supreme Court held the ordinance unconstitutional in *McIntyre v. Ohio Elections Commission*,[184] and Justice Thomas was in the majority. However, rather than join the 7-2 majority opinion, he concurred. His concurring opinion can best be understood if it is contrasted not only with the majority ruling, but with a dissent by Justice Scalia (in which Chief Justice Rehnquist joined).

Scalia wrote:

> At a time when both political branches of Government and both political parties reflect a popular desire to leave more decision making authority to the States, today's decision moves in the opposite direction, adding to the legacy of the inflexible central mandate (irrevocable even by Congress) imposed by this Court's constitutional jurisprudence. In an opinion which reads like it is addressing some peculiar law like the Los Angeles municipal ordinance at issue in [an earlier Supreme Court case], the Court invalidates a species of protection for the election process that exists, in a variety of forms, in every State except California, and that has a pedigree dating back to the end of the 19th century. Preferring the views of the English utilitarian philosopher John Stuart Mill . . . to the considered judgment of the American people's elected representatives from coast to coast, the Court discovers a hitherto unknown

right-to-be-unknown while engaging in
electoral politics. I dissent from the
imposition of free-speech imperatives
that are demonstrably not those of the
American people today, and that there is
inadequate reason to believe were those
of the society that begat the First
Amendment or the Fourteenth.

Lest anyone think Scalia was completely turning his back on originalist interpretation of the Constitution, he openly admitted that the case was a close call for him: "In the present case, *absent other indications*, I would be inclined to agree with the concurrence [by Thomas] that a society which used anonymous political debate so regularly would not regard as constitutional even moderate restrictions made to improve the election process."[185]

The "other indications" that swung Scalia into dissent were that for many years virtually every state had prohibited anonymous leafleting, the ordinance did not prohibit any speech but required only non-anonymity, and, most important to Scalia (and Rehnquist), it was aimed at protecting the election process.

Justice Thomas's concurring opinion, though agreeing that the Ohio law was inconsistent with the First Amendment, parted company with the majority's rationale—i.e., anonymous speech should be protected because it has "value" and "an honorable tradition"—and instead identified the Court's sole task to be "determ[ining] whether the phrase 'freedom of speech, or of the press,' *as originally understood*, protected anonymous political leafleting."

To that end, Thomas made a convincing case that "the Framers engaged in anonymous political writing." That was enough to inform his interpretation of the phrase "freedom of speech, or of the press."

Justice Thomas, while "like Justice Scalia . . . loath to overturn a century of practice shared by almost all of the states," then parted company with his colleague, concluding that "*the historical evidence from the framing [of the Constitution] outweighs recent tradition.*" [186]

In sum, what separated Thomas from the majority was the justice's reliance on text and "original understanding," and what separated him from Scalia and Rehnquist was Thomas's unwillingness to sacrifice those interpretive tools on the altar of what amounted to virtually universal violation of the free speech of those who engaged in anonymous leafleting. [187]

If, as we have seen, core political speech can be abridged, what is to become of speech that is considered by some on the Court as "second-class" speech? The answer is found in an examination of the category referred to as "commercial speech."

In *Virginia Pharmacy Board v. Virginia Citizens Consumer Council, Inc.*, [188] the Supreme Court ruled that the commonwealth's blanket ban on prescription drug advertising violated the First Amendment. [189] If advertising was truthful and not misleading, it was protected speech, a principle that continued in Supreme Court jurisprudence for some two decades.

In the mid-nineties, the Supreme Court reviewed two Rhode Island statutes that regulated the advertising of alcoholic beverages. One, with a minor exception, prohibited "advertising in any manner whatsoever" the price of any alcoholic beverage offered for sale in the state. The other prohibited entirely all publication and broadcast of any advertisement that referred to "the price of any alcohol beverages."

In *44 Liquormart, Inc. v. Rhode Island* [190] —in reliance on several post – *Virginia Pharmacy Board* cases, especially *Central Hudson Gas & Electric Corp. v. Pub. Serv. Comm'n of N.Y.* [191] —the Supreme Court ruled each Rhode Island statute unconstitutional because they were more extensive than necessary to achieve the state's purported interest of fostering temperance.

Justice Thomas concurred, not because he disagreed with the result, but because he had serious reservations about speech being valued hierarchically—with, paraphrasing George Orwell, "some speech being more important than other speech."

Thomas noted that "[t]he Court has at times appeared to assume that 'commercial' speech could be censored in a variety of ways for any of a variety of reasons because, as was said without clear rationale in some post-Virginia Bd. of Pharmacy cases [especially Central Hudson], such speech was in a 'subordinate position in the scale of First Amendment values . . . .' * * * I do not see a philosophical or historical basis for asserting that 'commercial' speech is of 'lower value' than 'noncommercial' speech. Indeed, some historical materials suggest to the contrary."

A year later, the Court took another commercial speech case, *Glickman v. Wileman Brothers & Elliott, Inc.*[192]

At issue were certain regulations issued by the secretary of agriculture pursuant to a federal statute. According to the majority, "[t]he basic policy decision that underlies the entire statute rests on an assumption that in the volatile markets for agricultural commodities the public will be best served by *compelling cooperation* among producers in making economic decisions that would be made independently in a free market."[193]

As part of that coerced "cooperation" regarding the marketing of certain agricultural products, the government compelled growers, handlers, and processors of California fruit to pay for generic advertising. Some of the processors objected, complaining that they were being forced to underwrite speech with which they disagreed.

In a 5-4 decision—completely ignoring the *Central Hudson* precedent and its "test"[194] for acceptable government regulation of commercial speech—the Court ruled that the case did not even present a First Amendment issue. It viewed the compelled advertising payments as merely "economic regulation," well within the power of Congress under the Interstate Commerce Clause.

Justice Thomas dissented. Not because the majority failed to employ the *Central Hudson* test, with which he disagreed anyhow. Not even because Supreme Court precedents, with which he also disagreed, accorded commercial speech merely second-class status. His dissent, in two respects, was more fundamental.

One echoed the First Amendment principle he had expressed in *44 Liquormart*:

> I write separately to note my disagreement with the majority's conclusion that coerced funding of advertising by others does not involve "speech" at all and does not even raise a First Amendment "issue." * * * It is one thing to differ about whether a particular regulation involves an "abridgement" of the freedom of speech, but it is entirely another matter—and a complete repudiation of our precedent—for the majority to deny that "speech" is even at issue in this case. In numerous cases, this Court has recognized that paying money for the purposes of advertising involves speech. The Court also has recognized that compelling speech raises a First Amendment issue just as much as restricting speech. Given these two elemental principles of our First

> Amendment jurisprudence, it is incongruous [for the majority] to suggest that forcing fruit growers to contribute to a collective advertising campaign does not even *involve* speech, while at the same time effectively conceding [as the majority did] that *forbidding* a fruit grower to make those same contributions voluntarily would violate the First Amendment.[195]

The other aspect of Thomas's dissent, buried in a footnote, provides an insight into a fundamental value premise of his, albeit one not articulated expressly, that underlies much of his jurisprudence:

> The majority's excessive emphasis on the supposed *collectivization* of the fruit industry . . . fails to support its conclusion. Although . . . the government has a considerable range of authority in regulating the Nation's economic structure, part of the Constitution—the First Amendment— does enact a distinctly *individualistic* notion of "the freedom of speech," and Congress may not simply collectivize that aspect of our society, regardless of what it may do elsewhere.[196]

Prior to Justice Thomas's dissent in *Glickman*, only one other case in Supreme Court history had used the words "collectivize"/"collectivization" (but in an entirely different context). Thomas's use of them in *Glickman* demonstrates that *he is explicitly aware of the fundamental ethical/political distinction between individual rights* (e.g., freedom of speech) *and collectivism*[197] (e.g., the government's de facto takeover of the fruit-growing industry)—and that, at least regarding free speech, he is unwilling to allow the individual rights (e.g., those of the fruit growers) to be subordinated to the government's perceived need for "orderly" fruit markets.[198]

Glickman did not signal the end of commercial speech cases for the Supreme Court, nor of Justice Thomas's opposition to the second-class status to which the Court had relegated such speech. *Lorillard Tobacco Co. v. Reilly*[199] presented the Court with a Massachusetts regulation that imposed a sweeping ban on advertising (i.e., speech) about tobacco products. The Court ruled that the ban violated the First Amendment.

Justice Thomas concurred, taking the occasion to repeat that "when the government seeks to restrict truthful speech in order to suppress the ideas it conveys, strict scrutiny is appropriate, whether or not the speech in question may be characterized as 'commercial.'" Applying that test, all the Massachusetts tobacco advertising restrictions were unconstitutional.

Thomas then passed to a wider point, one which reveals his underlying belief in individual responsibility and constitutes a ringing endorsement of the "free market" of personal accountability:

> *No legislature has ever sought to restrict speech about an activity it regarded as harmless and inoffensive.* Calls for limits on expression always are made when the specter of some threatened harm is looming.[200]
>
> The identity of the harm may vary. People will be inspired by totalitarian dogmas and subvert the Republic. They will be inflamed by racial demagoguery and embrace hatred and bigotry. Or they will be enticed by cigarette

advertisements and choose to smoke,
risking disease. It is therefore no answer
for the State to say that the makers of
cigarettes are doing harm: perhaps they
are. But in that respect they are no
different from the purveyors of other
harmful products, or the advocates of
harmful ideas. When the State seeks to
silence them, they are all entitled to the
protection of the First Amendment.

What these political and commercial speech cases have in
common is the tension between the First Amendment's free speech
guarantee and government regulations imposed for the "greater good."
In cases where the speech value has been subordinated to government
power, Thomas has consistently come down on the side of speech—
depending on whether *speech*, or something else, was really involved.

The only case in Justice Thomas's tenure on the Court that has
sorely tested his judgment of "whether *speech*, or something else, was
really involved" was the 2003 case of *Virginia v. Black*.[201]

Three white men in Virginia burned a cross on a black
neighbor's lawn. They were convicted under a fifty-year-old Virginia
statute that prohibited cross-burning:

It shall be unlawful for any person or
persons, with the intent of intimidating
any person or group of persons, to burn,
or cause to be burned, a cross on the
property of another, a highway or any
other public place. Any person who shall
violate any provision of this section shall
be guilty of a Class 6 felony.

Any such burning of a cross shall be
prima facie evidence of an intent to
intimidate a person or group of persons.

There were two complementary parts to this Virginia statute: (1) it was illegal to burn a cross with a particular intent, and (2) the act of burning a cross showed an intent to intimidate (which shifted the burden to the defendant to *disprove* that he intended to intimidate).

The Virginia Supreme Court reversed the convictions, holding that the law unconstitutionally violated the First Amendment's guarantee of free speech.[202]   The Supreme Court of the United States agreed to review the case.

At the oral argument, Professor Rodney Smolla of the University of Richmond School of Law—one of America's foremost champions of free speech—characterized cross-burning as "horrible, evil and disgusting." Nonetheless, he attacked the Virginia anti-cross-burning statute as unconstitutional, arguing that the defendants' conduct was protected free speech akin to flag-burning and swastika displays which, though equally odious, had been held protected by the First Amendment.

The federal government's solicitor general's office argued in support of the Virginia statute, asserting that cross-burning was not "expression," but rather "akin to a threat to put somebody in fear of bodily harm." In other words, as the statute says, to "intimidate."

Justice Thomas, normally silent during oral arguments, was reported to have made these comments:

- "My fear is you are actually understating the symbolism of and effect of the burning cross."

- "I think what you're attempting to do is fit this into our jurisprudence rather than stating more clearly what the cross was intended to accomplish."

- "My fear is that there is no other purpose to the cross. There was no communication, no particular message. It was intended to cause fear and terrorize a population."

- "This was a reign of terror, and the cross was a symbol of that reign of terror. Isn't that significantly greater than intimidation or a threat?"

- "We had almost 100 years of lynching and activity in the South by the Knights of Camelia and the Ku Klux Klan."

This last comment reveals Justice Thomas's understandable reaction to cross-burning, one that sparked similar reactions from some of his fellow justices.

The Associated Press reported at the time that the subject of cross-burning "also evoked strong emotions from his colleagues, who joined in expressing concern about violence and racism . . . ." Justice Antonin Scalia, for example, noted that blacks would prefer to see a rifle-toting man in their front yard rather than a burning cross. Justice David Souter remarked that "[t]he cross has acquired a potency that is at least equal to that of a gun." One commentator contemporaneously wrote that "[a]ccording to accounts of those who were in the courtroom, it seemed as if Thomas brought the court around to the view that banning such expression is permissible under the First Amendment."

However, only a decade before, the Court had decided the case of *R.A.V. v. City of St. Paul, Minnesota*,[203] where teenagers had burned a cross in a black family's yard. A local ordinance provided that:

> Whoever places on public or private
> property a symbol, object, appellation,
> characterization or graffiti, including but
> not limited to, a burning cross or Nazi
> swastika, which one knows or has
> reasonable grounds to know arouses
> anger, alarm or resentment in others on
> the basis of race, color, creed, religion or
> gender commits disorderly conduct and
> shall be guilty of a misdemeanor.

The Court, prior to Thomas joining it, had held the St. Paul ordinance *unconstitutional* as a violation of free speech. Justice Scalia concluded his opinion for the Court in R.A.V. by forcefully observing: "Let there be no mistake about our belief that burning a cross in someone's front yard is reprehensible. But St. Paul has sufficient means at its disposal to prevent such behavior without adding the First Amendment to the fire."

In light of the similarity between the Virginia statute and the R.A.V. ordinance, it would have seemed that the Court could not easily escape being bound by the latter precedent. One would have thought that any attempt by the Court to distinguish the Virginia law from the St. Paul ordinance—on the ground that the former spoke of "with the intent of intimidating" (with which Justice Thomas appeared concerned) while the latter spoke of arousing "alarm"—would fail because the principles and intent of each statute would seem identical. Although the Virginia statute in *Black* contained no express reference to "race, color, creed, religion or gender," as did the St. Paul ordinance, it was clear (as Justice Thomas, among others on the Court, recognized) that Virginia's law had the same intent.

Besides R.A.V., other precedents would have seemed equally difficult to overcome. For example, in *Tinker v. Des Moines*

Independent Community School District[204] the Court had upheld the right of students to wear black armbands to protest the Vietnam War, because their conduct was "closely akin" to pure speech. Nor had the school district banned *all* political symbols: "A particular symbol—black armbands worn to exhibit opposition to this Nation's involvement in Vietnam—was singled out for prohibition."

So, too, in Virginia. Only burning *crosses*—not swastikas, as Professor Smolla argued, or photographs of bin Laden, or an effigy of Hillary Clinton—were prohibited. In *Virginia v. Black*—just as in *Tinker*—the unmistakable intent of the law was to censor a particular idea. In *Tinker* it was opposition to the Vietnam War. In *Black* it was opposition to a certain race. In both cases, the law sought to censor conduct "closely akin" to pure speech.

In *Texas v. Johnson*[205] the defendant had been prosecuted under a state law making it a crime to desecrate or otherwise mistreat the American flag in any manner "the actor knows will seriously offend one or more persons likely to observe or discover his actions." Johnson had doused a flag with kerosene and set it ablaze, while other protestors chanted "America, the red, white, and blue, we spit on you."

Johnson's conviction was reversed. He had engaged in expressive, albeit reprehensible, conduct.

Were the three defendants in *Black* similarly engaged in expressive, albeit reprehensible, conduct when they burned the cross? They certainly weren't trying to rid themselves of unwanted wood, to compensate for a broken street lamp, or to celebrate a holiday. They surely didn't burn the cross on a white person's property. They hadn't started the fire accidentally.

They were sending a message to that black family.

No matter how odious, bigoted, uncivilized, and un-American the message (and it was!), like the armband-wearing students in *Tinker* and the flag-burning defendant in *Johnson*, the cross-burners' message in *Black* would seem to have been protected by the First Amendment because it expressed an idea.

Justice O'Connor wrote the opinion for a very fragmented Court.[206] In essence, most of the justices believed that, in O'Connor's words, the Court had "conclude[d] that [1] while a State, consistent with the First Amendment, may ban cross burning carried out with the intent to intimidate, [2] the provision in the Virginia statute treating any cross burning as prima facie evidence of intent to intimidate renders the statute unconstitutional in its current form."

In other words, despite *Tinker, Johnson* and *R.A.V.* the Virginia cross-burning statute would ordinarily have been *constitutional*—but because it went a step further and, in effect, presumed the necessary criminal intent from the act of burning itself, the entire statute was *unconstitutional*.

Essentially, O'Connor and those for whom she wrote purported to "distinguish" R.A.V. The case did not apply to the Virginia statute, they ruled, because it did not apply to the Virginia statute. This tautology is all they offered. Neither *Tinker* nor *Johnson* was dealt with.[207]

Thomas dissented from the Court's conclusion, rejecting not its view that the anti-cross-burning statute would *ordinarily* be constitutional (a view with which he agreed), but rather with the Court's analysis that resulted in the laws being invalidated because of its "presumption of intent" provision.

To understand Thomas's dissent in *Virginia v. Black*, it is necessary first to consider a case from several years earlier, *Capitol Square Review and Advisory Board v. Pinette*.[208] The Court's ruling— that Ohio did not violate the Establishment Clause when it *allowed* the Ku Klux Klan to display an unattended cross on the state capitol grounds—is less important for our purposes than *why* Thomas *concurred* in *Pinette*:

> I join the Court's conclusion that
> petitioners' exclusion of the Ku Klux
> Klan's cross cannot be justified on
> Establishment Clause grounds. But the
> fact that the legal issue before us involves
> the Establishment Clause should not lead
> anyone to think that a cross erected by
> the Ku Klux Klan is a purely religious
> symbol. *The erection of such a cross is a
> political act, not a Christian one.*[209]

In *Black*, Justice Thomas began his dissenting opinion by observing that:

> In every culture, certain things acquire
> meaning well beyond what *outsiders* can
> comprehend. That goes for both the
> sacred . . . and the profane. I believe that
> cross burning is the paradigmatic
> example of the latter.[210]

Then, echoing his view in *Pinette*, Justice Thomas made a strong case that in the hands of the Klan a cross, let alone a burning cross, is a political/intimidation tool, not a religious symbol. It is because of this premise that Thomas parted company with the majority, which, in his judgment, "errs in imputing an expressive component" to the cross-burning that formed the basis of the prosecutions in *Black*.

> [T]his statute prohibits only conduct, not
> expression. And just as one cannot burn
> down someone's house to make a
> political point and then seek refuge in the
> First Amendment, those who hate cannot

terrorize and intimidate to make their
point. In light of my conclusion that the
statute here addresses only conduct, there
is no need to analyze it under any of our
First Amendment tests.[211]

Having made this point—that the *Black* prosecutions and the
Virginia statute upon which they were based involved not *expression*,
but *conduct*, and that thus the First Amendment should have not been
part of the Court's analysis—Justice Thomas could have let it go at
that. Instead, he went one step further, albeit in *dicta*, to emphasize a
contradiction, even hypocrisy, in the jurisprudence of certain of his
colleagues:

> That the First Amendment gives way to
> other interests is not a remarkable
> proposition.[[212]] What is remarkable is
> that, under the [Court's] analysis, the
> determination of whether an interest is
> sufficiently compelling [to trump free
> speech] depends not on the harm a
> regulation . . . seeks to prevent, but the
> *areas of society at which it aims.* For
> instance, in *Hill v. Colorado* . . . the
> Court upheld a restriction on protests
> near abortion clinics, explaining that the
> State had a legitimate interest, which was
> sufficiently narrowly tailored, in
> protecting those seeking services of such
> establishments from "unwanted advice"
> and "unwanted communication" . . . . In
> so concluding, the Court placed heavy
> reliance on the "vulnerable physical and
> emotional conditions" of patients. * * *
> Thus, when it came to the rights of *those
> seeking abortions,* the Court deemed

restrictions on "unwanted advice," which,
notably, can be given only from a
distance of at least eight feet from a
prospective patient, justified by the
countervailing interest in obtaining an
abortion. Yet, *here* [in the *Black* case],
the [Court] strikes down the statute
because one day an individual might wish
to burn a cross, but might do so without
an intent to intimidate anyone. That
cross burning subjects *its* targets, and,
sometimes, an unintended audience . . . to
extreme emotional distress, and is
virtually never viewed merely as
"unwanted communication," but rather,
as a physical threat, is of no concern to
the [Court]. Henceforth, under the
[Court's] view, physical safety will be
valued less than the right to be free from
unwanted communications.[213]

Right of Association

Although not expressly provided for in the First Amendment, in
1958 the Supreme Court found there a "right of association." It was
explained this way:

Effective advocacy of both public and
private points of view, particularly
controversial ones, is undeniably
enhanced by group association, as this
Court has more than once recognized by
remarking upon the close nexus between
the freedoms of speech and assembly . . .
. It is beyond debate that the freedom to
engage in association for the

> advancement of beliefs and ideas is an
> inseparable aspect of the "liberty"
> assured by the Due Process Clause of the
> Fourteenth Amendment, which embraces
> freedom of speech . . . . Of course, it is
> immaterial whether the beliefs sought to
> be advanced by association pertain to
> political, economic, religious or cultural
> matters, and *state action which may have
> the effect of curtailing the freedom to
> associate is subject to the closest
> scrutiny.*[214]

Otherwise, when state action imposes a lesser burden on associational rights, the governmental interest will be upheld if it is reasonable and non-discriminatory.

That individuals have an associational right to come together for political purposes may be a truism, but the *application* of that principle has not always been easy.

Oklahoma had a semi-closed primary system. Only a party's registered members could vote in its primary, unless the party allowed registered Independents to vote in it also. When the Libertarian Party attempted to open its primary to all registered voters, no matter how they were registered, it was prevented from doing so. Only registered Libertarians and Independents were allowed. Registered Libertarian, Democrat, and Republican voters then sued, alleging that the state's semi-closed primary law violated their political associational rights under the First Amendment.

Writing the majority opinion for a fragmented Court, Justice Thomas ruled the statute was *constitutional* because the justices were "persuaded that any burden Oklahoma's semi-closed primary imposes is minor and justified by legitimate state interests."

He began his opinion by recognizing that "[t]he Constitution grants States broad power to prescribe the 'Time, Places and Manner of holding Elections for Senators and Representatives' . . . which power is matched by state control over the election process for state offices."

Thomas then addressed whether Oklahoma's exercise of that "broad power" through its semi-closed primary law "burdened" associational rights.[215]

> But even if Oklahoma's semi-closed primary system burdens an associational right [which Thomas was apparently not conceding], the burden is less severe than others this Court has upheld as constitutional.
>
> For instance, in *Timmons*, we considered a Minnesota election law prohibiting multiparty, or "fusion," candidacies in which a candidate appears on the ballot as the nominee of more than one party. * * * Minnesota's law prevented the New Party, a minor party under state law, from putting forward the same candidate as a major party. The New Party challenged the law as unconstitutionally burdening its associational rights. * * * This Court concluded that the burdens imposed by Minnesota's law—though not trivial— were not severe.
>
> The burdens were not severe because the New Party and its members remained free to govern themselves internally and to communicate with the public as they wished. Minnesota had neither regulated

the New Party's internal decision making
process, nor compelled it to associate
with voters of any political persuasion . .
. . The New Party and its members
simply could not nominate as their
candidate any of "those few individuals
who both have already agreed to be
another party's candidate and also, if
forced to choose, themselves prefer that
other party."

Just as the burden in *Timmons* was minimal, so, too, was the
burden on the Oklahoma Libertarians. None of the party's internal
processes were regulated, they could exclude from membership
whomever they wanted (save for illegal or unconstitutional reasons),
and they were in no way restricted from communicating with the
public.

Since the burden was minimal, if at all, Oklahoma's important
regulatory interest would justify the state's semi-closed primary law, to
wit, "preserv[ing] [political] parties as viable and identifiable interest
groups . . . enhanc[ing] parties' electioneering and party-building
efforts . . . and guard[ing] against party raiding and 'sore loser'
candidacies by spurned primary contenders."

In closing his opinion for the Court, Justice Thomas adverted to
a favorite theme of his jurisprudence: Since the Constitution vests
power over state elections to the states, implementation of that power is
left to Oklahoma's democratic process. If the voters of that state want
semi-closed primaries, so be it. Absent a real burden on the First
Amendment right of association, the only function of a court, let alone
the Supreme Court of the United States, is to make sure that Oklahoma
has a legitimate reason. As he put the point:

Oklahoma remains free to allow the LPO
[Libertarian Party of Oklahoma] to invite

registered voters of other parties to vote
in its primary. But the Constitution leaves
that choice to the democratic process, not
to the courts.

Federalism and separation of powers, two of the three pillars of
American constitutionalism, were at work once again—with the third
pillar we have just examined, judicial review, making the process work.

ENDNOTES

[145] Amendment I, Constitution of the United States of America.

[146] Of the six guarantees of the First Amendment—establishment, free
exercise, speech, press, assembly, and petition—Justice Thomas has
written significantly only about the first three. Thus, the latter three
guarantees will not be discussed in this book.

[147] 536 U.S. 639, 122 S.Ct. 2460 (2002).

[148] 347 U.S. 483, 74 S.Ct. 686 (1954) (*Brown* (I)).

[149] In joining the majority, though in a concurring opinion, Justice
Thomas noted that "[t]o determine whether a federal program survives
scrutiny under the Establishment Clause, we have considered whether it
has a secular purpose and whether it has the primary effect of
advancing or inhibiting religion. * * * I agree with the Court that
Ohio's program easily passes muster under our stringent test . . . ."

[150] Footnote omitted.

[151] Emphasis added.

[152] Emphasis added. Footnote omitted.

[153] Emphasis added. Footnote omitted.

[154] Douglass Papers 623. Emphasis added.

Although *Zelman* was an establishment clause case, it was because of the inseparable racial aspects of the school voucher issue that in Thomas's concurring opinion he added some *dicta* about race, noting that "[w]hile the romanticized ideal of universal public education resonates with the cognoscenti who oppose vouchers, poor urban families just want the best education for their children, who will certainly need it to function in our high-tech and advanced society. As Thomas Sowell noted 30 years ago: 'Most black people have faced too many grim, concrete problems to be romantics. They want and need certain tangible results, which can be achieved only by developing certain specific abilities.' * * * The same is true today. * * * The failure to provide education to poor urban children perpetuates a vicious cycle of poverty, dependence, criminality, and alienation that continues for the remainder of their lives. If society cannot end racial discrimination, at least it can arm minorities with the education to defend themselves from some of discrimination's effects."

[155] 125 S.Ct. 2113 (2005).

[156] 42 United States Code, Section 2000cc-1(a)(1)-(2).

[157] Emphasis added.

[158] 125 S.Ct. 2854 (2005).

[159] Emphasis added.

[160] Emphasis added.

[161] Emphasis added.

[162] Emphasis added.

---

[163] See the Religious Freedom Restoration Act of 1993, 107 Stat. 1488, 42 United States Code, Section 2000bb *et seq.* (1988 ed., Supp. V).

[164] *Swanner* v. *Anchorage Equal Rights Commission*, 513 U.S. 979, 115 S.Ct. 460 (1994).

[165] Emphasis in original.

[166] 424 U.S. 1, 96 S.Ct. 612 (1976).

[167] The inherent historical and logical flaws in the *Buckley* decision have produced a substantial amount of adverse comment, scholarly and otherwise.

[168] 518 U.S. 604, 116 S.Ct. 2309 (1996).

[169] Emphasis added.

[170] 528 U.S. 377, 120 S.Ct. 897 (2000).

[171] It is interesting to note that the restrictions on political speech were upheld in an opinion by Justice Souter, joined by the chief justice and Justice O'Connor, with concurrences by Justices Stevens and Breyer, with whom Justice Ginsburg joined—four liberals, a half-liberal, and Rehnquist. Justices Kennedy and Scalia joined Justice Thomas in dissenting.

[172] In support of this proposition, Thomas cited Supreme Court decisions, constitutional treatises, law professors, and former law professor and judge Robert Bork.

[173] Immediately following this statement, Thomas quoted James Madison to the same effect.

[174] 533 U.S. 431, 121 S.Ct. 2351 (2001).

[175] Footnote omitted.

[176] In *Federal Election Commission* v. *Beaumont*, 539 U.S. 146, 123 S.Ct. 2200 (2003), the Court upheld certain provisions of the Federal Election Campaign Act and various regulations that created prohibitions on corporate contributions and other expenditures in connection with federal elections. Justice Thomas dissented, again arguing "that campaign finance laws are subject to strict scrutiny."

[177] 540 U.S. 93, 124 S.Ct. 619 (2003).

[178] Footnote omitted.

[179] Harvard's footnote to the text states that: "'Soft money' is funding not subject to disclosure requirement and amount and source limitations in the Federal Election Campaign Act (FECA). Though FECA bans the use of soft money to influence federal elections, the Federal Election Commission (FEC) gradually expanded the acceptable uses of soft money to include generic party advertising and 'legislative advocacy media advertisements' mentioning candidates for federal office."

[180] Citation omitted.

[181] Footnote omitted.

[182] 118 *Harvard Law Review* 364 (2004).

[183] Citations and interior quotation marks omitted. Emphasis added.

[184] 514 U.S. 334, 115 S.Ct. 1511 (1995).

[185] Emphasis in original.

[186] Emphasis added.

---

[187] Another election case of interest is *Buckley* v. *American Constitutional Law Foundation, Inc.*, 525 U.S. 182, 119 S.Ct. 636 (1999). Colorado law required that circulators of initiative petitions be registered voters, that they wear identification badges bearing their names, and that the initiative's proponents report the names and addresses of their paid circulators and how much they received. The Supreme Court majority ruled all three provisions unconstitutional as against the First Amendment.

Justice Thomas concurred, agreeing with the result but disagreeing with the watered-down test his colleagues used to reach it. He wrote:

> When a State's rule imposes severe burdens on speech or association, it must be narrowly tailored to serve a compelling interest; lesser burdens trigger less exacting review, and a State's important regulatory interests are typically enough to justify reasonable restrictions. * * * When a State's election law directly regulates core political speech, we have always subjected the challenged restriction to strict scrutiny . . . .

Applying his test of strict scrutiny, Thomas found the Colorado statutes to be unconstitutional.

[188] 425 U.S. 748, 96 S.Ct. 1817 (1976).

[189] Many observers, liberals and conservatives alike, though pleased with the case's ruling, were not happy with the Court's proffered rationale: "It is a matter of *public interest* that [economic] decisions . . . be intelligent and well informed. To this end, the free flow of commercial information is indispensable." (Emphasis added.)

In other words, "commercial" speech was entitled to First Amendment protection not because the speaker—in the Virginia case, the pharmacies—had a right to speak, but because consumers *needed* the information. Such a rationale was hardly a ringing endorsement of the principle of free speech.

[190] 517 U.S. 484, 116 S.Ct. 1495 (1996).

[191] 447 U.S. 557, 116 S.Ct. 1495 (1996).

[192] 521 U.S. 457, 117 S.Ct. 2130 (1997).

[193] Emphasis added.

[194] "In commercial speech cases . . . a four-part analysis has developed. At the outset, we must determine whether the expression is protected by the First Amendment. For commercial speech to come within that provision, it at least must concern lawful activity and not be misleading. Next, we ask whether the asserted governmental interest is substantial. If both inquiries yield positive answers, we must determine whether the regulation directly advances the governmental interest asserted, and whether it is not more extensive than is necessary to serve that interest." *Central Hudson Gas & Electric Corp.* v. *Public Service Commission of New York*, 447 U.S. 557, 100 S.Ct. 2343 (1980).

[195] Emphasis added. Footnotes omitted. It is interesting that the majority opinion, which was unable to find a First Amendment issue raised where the government compelled fruit growers to pay for advertising with which they disagreed, was authored by liberal Justice Stevens and joined by Justices O'Connor, Kennedy, Ginsburg, and Breyer. In addition to Justice Thomas, Justice Souter also wrote a strong dissent. Chief Justice Rehnquist and Justice Scalia also dissented.

[196] Emphasis added.

[197] As good a definition of "collectivism" that one can find is Ayn Rand's: "Collectivism means the subjugation of the individual to a group—whether to a race, class or state does not matter. Collectivism

holds that man must be chained to collective action and collective thought for the sake of what is called 'the common good.'" H. Binswanger, ed., The Ayn Rand Lexicon: Objectivism from A to Z (New York: NAL Books, 1986), 74.

[198] Two years later, in *Greater New Orleans Broadcasting Association, Inc.* v. *United States*, 527 U.S. 173, 119 S.Ct. 1923 (1999), Justice Thomas concurred in another "commercial speech" case in order to reiterate his adherence to his earlier expressed view that in cases where "the government's asserted interest is to keep legal users of a product or service ignorant in order to manipulate their choices in the marketplace, the *Central Hudson* test should not be applied because 'such an interest' is *per se* illegitimate and can no more justify regulation of 'commercial speech' than it can justify regulation of 'noncommercial' speech."

Two years after that, the Court had before it the case of *United States* v. *United Foods, Inc.*, 533 U.S. 405, 121 S.Ct. 2334 (2001), involving the improbably named Mushroom Promotion, Research, and Consumer Information Act (104 Stat. 3854, 7 U.S.C. Section 6101, *et seq.*). The majority distinguished *Glickman* v. *Wileman Brothers & Elliott, Inc.*, and held unconstitutional the act's requirement that mushroom handlers contribute assessments that were used to pay for advertising that promoted mushroom sales.

More important for our purposes is Justice Thomas's concurring opinion, where he reiterated his "views that 'paying money for the purposes of advertising involves speech,' and that 'compelling speech raises a First Amendment issue just as much as restricting speech.' * * * Any regulation that compels the funding of advertising must be subject to the most stringent First Amendment scrutiny."

[199] 533 U.S. 525, 121 S.Ct. 2404 (2001).

[200] Emphasis added. *Lorrilard* was followed the next year by *Thompson* v. *Western States Medical Center*, 535 U.S. 357, 122 S.Ct. 1497 (2002). The case involved provisions of the Food and Drug Administration Modernization Act prohibiting certain compounded drugs from being advertised and promoted. The Supreme Court majority held the provisions to be unconstitutional restrictions on commercial speech.

Justice Thomas concurred, again going his own way regarding this category of "second- class" speech: "I concur because I agree with the Court's *application* of [the *Central Hudson* test]." (Emphasis added.)

But, as we have seen, Thomas disagreed with the test *itself*. And he said so again: "I continue, however, to adhere to my view that cases such as this should not be analyzed under the *Central Hudson* test." He then repeated what he had written in *44 Liquormart*: "I do not believe that such a test should be applied to a restriction of 'commercial' speech, at least when, as here, the asserted interest is one that is to be achieved through keeping would-be recipients in the dark."

Eight months later, the Court denied certiorari in *Borgner* v. *Florida Board of Dentistry*, 537 U.S. 1080, 123 S.Ct. 688 (2002), and Justice Thomas dissented. Dr. Borgner's practice emphasized dental implants. However, under Florida law he was required in his advertising to make certain disclaimers. Applying the *Central Hudson* test, the federal court of appeals upheld the requirement of the disclaimers.

Thomas saw the case as presenting "an excellent opportunity to clarify some oft-recurring issues in the First Amendment treatment of commercial speech and to provide lower courts with guidance on the subject of state-mandated disclaimers." Only Justice Ginsburg joined Thomas's dissent from the Court's denial of certiorari.

[201] 538 U.S. 343, 123 S.Ct. 1536 (2003).

[202] The Court's ruling, limited to the cross-burning statute, did not address whether the defendants might be criminally responsible under other laws—e.g., conspiracy, trespass, arson, terror threats, malicious mischief, racially motivated assault—and civilly liable as well.

[203] 505 U.S. 377, 112 S.Ct. 2538 (1992).

[204] 393 U.S. 503, 89 S.Ct. 733 (1969).

[205] 491 U.S. 397, 109 S.Ct. 2533 (1989).

[206] "O'Connor, J., announced the judgment of the Court and delivered the opinion of the Court with respect to Parts I, II, and III, in which Rehnquist, C.J., and Stevens, Scalia, and Breyer, J.J., joined, and an opinion with respect to Parts IV and V, in which Rehnquist, C.J., and Stevens and Breyer, J.J., joined. Stevens, J., filed a concurring opinion . . . . Scalia, J., filed an opinion concurring in part, concurring in the judgment in part, and dissenting in part, in which Thomas, J., joined as to Parts I and II . . . . Souter, J., filed an opinion concurring in the judgment in part and dissenting in part, in which Kennedy and Ginsburg, J.J., joined . . . . Thomas, J., filed a dissenting opinion."

[207] Justices Souter, Kennedy, and Ginsburg concluded that the statute violated the First Amendment.

[208] 515 U.S. 753, 115 S.Ct. 2440 (1995).

[209] Emphasis added. Justice Thomas then explained the use of the cross in Klan activities, concluding that:

> [a]lthough the Klan might have sought to convey a message with some religious component, I think that the Klan had a primarily nonreligious purpose in erecting the cross. The Klan simply has appropriated one of the most sacred of religious symbols as a symbol of hate. In my mind, this suggests that this case may not have truly involved the Establishment Clause,

although I agree with the Court's disposition because of the manner in which the case has come before us. In the end, there may be much less here than meets the eye.

[210] Emphasis added.

[211] As to the reason the majority invalidated the statute, Justice Thomas added that "[e]ven assuming that the statute implicates the First Amendment, in my view, the fact that the statute permits the jury to draw an inference of intent to intimidate from the cross burning presents no constitutional problems. Therein lies my primary disagreement with the [Court]."

[212] One is reminded of Justice Holmes's observation about *falsely* shouting "fire" in a crowded theater.

[213] Emphasis added. Justice Thomas's *Black* dissent presented a strong argument that cross burning is *conduct*, wholly devoid of expressive content, and thus suppressible. In doing so, however, he occupies a gray zone of free speech jurisprudence inhabited by cases the Court has characterized as involving "symbolic speech," e.g., burning a draft card, while condemning conscription; displaying a red flag, to evidence opposition to organized government; "sitting in" at a southern lunch counter, to protest racial segregation; burning a flag, while condemning the Vietnam War; wearing black armbands in school, as part of political protest.

These have always been difficult cases, essentially because much "conduct" has "expressive" content, and it is often extremely difficult to draw a line where the former ends and the latter begins—no less than with cross-burning or, for that matter, neo-Nazis marching through a predominantly Jewish neighborhood shouting anti-semitic insults. Thus, it is worth remembering that "in the transition to statism, every infringement of human rights has begun with the suppression of a given right's least attractive practitioners. In this case [which involved pornography], the disgusting nature of the offenders makes it a good test of one's loyalty to a principle." (Ayn Rand, "Censorship: Local and Express," *The Ayn Rand Letter*, August 23, 1973.)

[214] *NAACP* v. *Alabama*, 357 U.S. 449, 78 S.Ct. 1163 (1958). Emphasis added.

[215] Justice Thomas, at some length, rejected the petitioners' argument that the Oklahoma statute required "strict scrutiny.

CHAPTER 7.

"Other enumerated rights"

FOURTH, FIFTH, SIXTH AND EIGHTH
AMENDMENTS

There are those, mostly historians and legal scholars, who believe that the First Amendment occupies a "preferred position" in the Bill of Rights. Apart from its clear negative language, "Congress shall make no law," the notion is that the guarantees of the First Amendment are, alone, indispensable for the operation and survival of democracy and the protection and furtherance of individual rights.[216]

However, the "preferred position" notion has never achieved any serious support from any justice of the Supreme Court, nor has it influenced the decision in any Supreme Court case. There are doubtless various reasons for this—among them, historical, textual, and logical— and one of them is that exalting the First Amendment would necessarily denigrate the other amendments, principally the Fourth, Fifth, Sixth, and Eighth.

While these amendments may be of less value to a worshiper, activist, or newspaper than they are to someone wrongly accused, they are of great value to an arrestee or criminal defendant—or someone whose home is coveted by the city to make way for a multiplex movie theater. It is hardly useful to attempt to weigh the value of petitioning the government "for a redress of grievances" against the value of preventing one's home being condemned for a public "use." Doubtless, for that reason, there are no "preferred position" discussions in Justice Thomas's opinions on the First Amendment, nor any concerning the Fourth, Fifth, Sixth, and Eighth Amendments.[217]

FOURTH AMENDMENT

> *The right of the people to be*
> *secure in their persons, houses,*
> *papers, and effects, against*
> *unreasonable searches and*
> *seizure, shall not be violated, and*
> *no Warrants shall issue, but*
> *upon probable cause, supported*
> *by Oath or affirmation, and*
> *particularly describing the*
> *place to be searched, and the*
> *persons or things to be seized.*[218]

The Supreme Court has long held that in evaluating the scope of the Fourth Amendment's guarantee of "security," it is necessary to look "to the traditional protections against unreasonable searches and seizures afforded by the common law at the time of the framing [of the Bill of Rights]."

An example of that inquiry, and of Justice Thomas's painstaking attention to historical detail and respect for those "traditional protections," is found in *Wilson v. Arkansas.*[219]

Drug sales to an informant resulted in a warrant being issued to search a private home, where a convicted felon and an armed individual resided. When the police arrived, the main door was open and "[w]hile opening an unlocked screen door and entering the residence, they identified themselves as police officers and stated they had a warrant."

The Supreme Court agreed to take the case "to resolve the conflict among the lower courts as to whether the common-law knock and announce principle forms a part of the Fourth Amendment reasonableness inquiry."

The Court ruled that it did and reversed the defendant's conviction—in a unanimous opinion written by Justice Thomas.

Guided by originalist principles, as to "reasonableness" Thomas wrote that "our effort to give content to this term may be guided by the meaning ascribed to it by the Framers of the [Fourth] Amendment. An examination of the common law of search and seizure leaves no doubt that the reasonableness of a search of a dwelling [which was involved in *Wilson]* may depend in part on whether law enforcement officers announced their presence and authority prior to entering."

Thomas then proceeded to examine the writings of "[s]everal prominent [English] founding-era commentators," English common-law statutes as old as 1275, and English cases from 1603, 1757, and 1774. He noted that "[t]he common-law knock and announce principle was woven quickly into the fabric of early American law," and that "[e]arly American courts similarly embraced the common-law knock and announce principle."

Not content to let his analysis go at that, Thomas examined the "knock and announce" principle's main exceptions—threat of physical violence, destruction of evidence, flight—by examination of English and American cases from 1603, 1822, 1833, and 1843.

In reversing the defendant's conviction, *Wilson v. Arkansas* is less remarkable for its ruling—the police should have "knocked and announced" when executing their warrant unless some exception applied[220] —than for *how* Thomas reached his conclusion.

He "defined" the Fourth Amendment's "reasonableness" requirement regarding "knock and announce" *by what it meant to those who wrote it into the Bill of Rights.* He refused to embrace, as his liberal colleagues had in other cases, some "Living Constitution" notion of "evolving standards of decency" (no doubt embraced by the United Nations). If the police had to "knock and announce," it was because that's what the "reasonableness" requirement of the Fourth Amendment had meant in its previous incarnations.[221]

The exclusion of illegally obtained evidence in a *criminal* trial is understandable given Supreme Court precedents. But what about exclusion in other contexts? Prior to Justice Thomas's joining the Supreme Court, the justices had ruled that "[t]he exclusionary rule is . . . a judicially created means of deterring illegal searches and seizures," that it does not "proscribe the introduction of illegally obtained evidence in all proceedings," and that it is to be employed "only where its remedial objectives are thought most efficaciously served."

Then came *Pennsylvania Bd. of Probation and Parole v. Scott,*[222] where the question for the Court was "whether the exclusionary rule, which generally prohibits the introduction at criminal trial of evidence obtained in violation of a defendant's Fourth Amendment rights, applies in parole revocation proceedings."

Because the Court had previously held that the exclusionary rule did not apply to grand jury proceedings, civil tax proceedings, and civil deportation proceedings,[223] in *Scott* Justice Thomas ruled for a 5-4 Court that the rule was also inapplicable to parole revocation proceedings. Again, while precedent and policy reasons dictated the result, the key to Thomas's opinion, strongly reflective of his Fourth Amendment jurisprudence, is found in three similar statements: "we have repeatedly declined to *extend* the exclusionary rule"; ". . . we refused to *extend* the exclusionary rule"; "we are asked to *extend* the exclusionary rule."[224]

It is anyone's guess whether, as an original question, had Thomas then been on the Court he would have voted to apply the exclusionary rule to the states at all. Clearly in *Scott*, he was unwilling to *extend* it to a proceeding he deemed civil and administrative in nature. This is consistent with his unwillingness on federalism and on separation of powers grounds to extend judicial rulings in other contexts, as well.[225]

FIFTH AMENDMENT

> *No person shall be held to answer*
> *for a capital, or otherwise*
> *infamous crime, unless on a*
> *presentment or indictment of a*
> *Grand Jury, except in cases*
> *arising in the land or naval*
> *forces, or in the Militia, when in*
> *actual service in time of War or*
> *public danger; nor shall any*
> *person be subject for the*
> *same offense to be twice put in*
> *jeopardy of life or limb, nor shall*
> *be compelled in any criminal case*
> *to be a witness against himself,*
> *nor be deprived of life, liberty,*
> *or property, without due process*
> *of law; nor shall private property*
> *be taken for public use without*
> *just compensation.*[226]

Self-incrimination[227]

During an altercation with police in which Oliverio Martinez grabbed an officer's weapon, Martinez was seriously wounded. In the hospital, a police supervisor questioned Martinez for roughly ten out of forty-five minutes about what had happened, and for the other thirty-five minutes medical personnel treated him. During the interview, Martinez admitted taking the officer's weapon and pointing it at him; he also admitted to regularly using heroin. At no time during the interview was Martinez given the "anything-you-say-may-be-used-against-you" "Miranda" warnings.[228]

Despite the altercation and Martinez's seizure of the officer's weapon, Martinez was never charged with any crime. Nor were his incriminating answers to the supervisor's questions ever used against him in any criminal prosecution.

Nonetheless, Martinez sued the supervisor, alleging that his Fifth Amendment right not to incriminate himself had been violated. In essence, Martinez claimed that even though no use was ever made of his un-Miranda-ized answers, the supervisor's interview was a *per se* violation of his constitutional right sufficient to sustain a civil action against the supervisor under the federal civil rights statute.

The Supreme Court, in *Chavez v. Martinez*,[229] disagreed, with Justice Thomas writing the majority opinion:

> We fail to see how, based on the text of the Fifth Amendment, Martinez can allege a violation of this right, since Martinez was never prosecuted for a crime, let alone compelled to be a witness against himself in a criminal case. * * * In our view, a "criminal case" at the very least requires the initiation of legal proceedings.

Even though this conclusion was sufficient by itself to dispose of the case, Thomas added that:

> We need not decide today the precise moment when a "criminal case" commences; it is enough to say that police questioning does not constitute a "case" any more than a private investigator's pre-complaint activities constitute a "civil case." * * * Although conduct by law enforcement officials prior to trial may ultimately impair that right [not to self-incriminate], *a*

> *constitutional violation occurs only at*
> *trial.*[230]

In sum, Justice Thomas once again resisted extending the reach of the Fifth Amendment's Self-Incrimination Clause by his ruling that "a violation of the constitutional right against self-incrimination occurs *only* if one has been compelled to be a witness against himself in a criminal case"—which, after all, is what the text of that amendment says.[231]

Due Process

Unlike the Fourteenth Amendment (which applies to the states), the Fifth Amendment (which applies to the federal government) contains no guarantee of equal protection of the laws. When in 1954 the Supreme Court needed a constitutional hook on which to hang its conclusion that racially segregated public schools in the District of Columbia were unequal, it simply endowed the Due Process Clause of the Fifth Amendment with equal protection content.

Building on that precedent, "federal equal protection" via the Fifth Amendment's Due Process Clause has often been invoked against federal statutes and administrative action.

An example from Justice Thomas's second term is the case of *Federal Communications Commission v. Beach Communications, Inc.*,[232] in which he wrote the majority opinion. Not surprisingly, Thomas's opinion transcended the narrow equal protection issue before the Court.

For the purposes of certain franchise requirements regarding operation of cable television systems, the Cable Communications Policy Act, a federal statute, made a distinction between, on the one hand, facilities that served separately owned and managed buildings and, on the other, facilities that served one or more buildings that were under common ownership and management. Claiming that this provision of the Act and the FCC's enforcement of it violated equal protection, a cable company sued.

Writing for a unanimous Court, Justice Thomas first acknowledged the constitutional (i.e., separation of powers) limits on equal protection jurisprudence:

> Whether embodied in the Fourteenth Amendment or inferred from the Fifth, equal protection is *not a license for courts to judge the wisdom, fairness, or logic of legislative choices.* In areas of social and economic policy, a statutory classification that neither proceeds along suspect [e.g., racial] lines nor infringes fundamental constitutional rights [e.g., voting] must be upheld against equal protection challenge if there is any reasonably conceivable state of facts that could provide a rational basis for the classification.[233]

Not content merely to state the obvious, Thomas then chose to explain the constitutional reason for the so-called "rational relation" test the Court uses to judge equal protection challenges (under either the due process umbrella of the Fifth Amendment, or the explicit equal protection guarantee of the Fourteenth):

> This standard of review is a paradigm of judicial restraint. "The Constitution presumes that, absent some reason to infer antipathy, even improvident decisions will eventually be rectified by the democratic process and judicial intervention is generally unwarranted no

matter how unwisely we make think a
political branch has acted."[234]

This is pure separation of powers jurisprudence. According to
Thomas, the courts generally and the Supreme Court in particular
should have no role to play in the democratic process of legislation—
except when constitutional rights are at stake, or statutory interpretation
is necessary. Regrettably, despite judicial restraint being the rule—at
least theoretically—too many justices ignore it.[235]

Many other Fifth Amendment due process cases do not involve
issues of separation of powers, but rather procedural regularity. A good
example is *United States v. James Daniel Good Real Property.*[236]
There, the majority ruled that civil forfeiture of a convicted drug
dealer's home was unconstitutional absent meaningful notice and an
opportunity to be heard (unless there were exigent circumstances).

In concurring and dissenting, Thomas agreed with the
majority's "focus on the protection of property rights—rights that are
central to our heritage." Although he was "disturbed by the breadth of
new civil forfeiture statutes," he disagreed that under the facts of the
case Good had been treated unconstitutionally.

Good *had* previously been convicted of a drug offense
involving the property later forfeited. The government *had* obtained a
warrant from a federal magistrate before seizing it, and no residents
were dispossessed.

This said, Thomas's main point was that:

> Given that current practice under [the
> forfeiture statute] appears to be far
> removed from the legal fiction upon
> which the civil forfeiture doctrine is
> based, it may be necessary—in an
> appropriate case—to reevaluate our

generally deferential approach to
legislative judgments in this area of civil
forfeiture. In my view, however, Good's
due process claim does not present that
"appropriate" case.

Thomas was suggesting that given the harsh effect on property
rights of civil forfeiture statutes, separation of powers doctrine could
eventually tilt the scales in favor of judicial power trumping the
legislation.

Unfortunately, as serious as civil forfeiture legislation is and as
dangerous as it can be, it is not the only, nor the most egregious, way
government can seize private property.

Eminent Domain

Indeed, among the most frightening non-criminal powers of the
federal government is its authority to seize privately owned real estate,
including people's homes. The only restraint on that power is the
Takings Clause of the Fifth Amendment—*and a Supreme Court willing
to enforce it.* Regrettably, among the last decisions of the Court's 2004
– 2005 term, in *Kelo v. City of New London*[237] a 5-4 majority applied
the *coup de grace* to whatever strength the Takings Clause may have
had left after the Court's many years of emasculating it.

The earlier case of *Tahoe-Sierra Preservation Council, Inc. v.
Tahoe Regional Planning Agency*[238] was a way station on the way to
Kelo. In Tahoe-Sierra, the agency had ordered that no development
take place in the Lake Tahoe basin for thirty-two months. When the
case reached the Supreme Court, the four liberals (Stevens, Souter,
Ginsburg, and Breyer), joined by fellow-traveling liberals O'Connor
and Kennedy, in an opinion by Stevens, ruled that the nearly three-year
suspension of use was not a "taking" under the Fifth Amendment.

Justice Thomas dissented, scoffing at the majority's assurance that "a temporary prohibition on economic use" could not be a "taking" because, according to the Court, "the property will recover value as soon as the prohibition is lifted." Thomas observed that "the 'logical' assurance that a 'temporary restriction . . . merely causes a diminution in value' . . . is cold comfort to the property owners in this case or any other. After all," Thomas wrote, "'[i]n *the long run we are all dead'.*"[239]

Three years later came the Kelo case. Essentially, the City of New London condemned private residences in order to turn the homeowners' property over to private developers. Why? In the approving words of Justice Stevens's relatively short opinion, "to capitalize on the arrival of the Pfizer [pharmaceutical] facility and the new commerce it was expected to attract. In addition to creating jobs, generating tax revenue, and helping to build momentum for the revitalization of downtown New London . . . the plan was also designed to make the City more attractive and to create leisure and recreational opportunities on the waterfront and in the park."

This time, the Court's imprimatur on the City of New London's condemnation of Kelo's and the others' homes was too much even for O'Connor. The vote was 5-4—the predictable liberal bloc of Stevens, Souter, Ginsburg, and Breyer, plus Kennedy, the fellow-traveling liberal, who concurred.

Justice Thomas dissented. His opinion, longer than Stevens's majority, is among the finest Thomas produced during his fourteen terms on the Court.

Invoking English common-law treatises and the Framers of our Constitution, Thomas, as usual, began at the beginning, with the words of the Fifth Amendment: The taking must be for "public use."

> Defying this understanding, the Court
> replaces the Public Use Clause with

"Public Purpose Clause" . . . (or perhaps
the "Diverse and Always Evolving Needs
of Society" Clause . . .), a restriction that
is satisfied, the Court instructs, so long as
the purpose is "legitimate" and the means
"not "irrational" . . . . This deferential
shift in phraseology enables the Court to
hold, against all common sense, that a
costly urban-renewal project whose
stated purpose is a vague promise of new
jobs and increased tax revenues, but
which is also suspiciously agreeable to
the Pfizer Corporation, is for a "public
use." I cannot agree. *If such "economic
development" takings are for a "public
use," any taking is, and the Court has
erased the Public Use Clause from our
Constitution . . . .*[240]

Thomas went on to note that he agreed fully with O'Connor's separate dissent, adding that he did not believe that "this Court can eliminate liberties expressly enumerated in the Constitution."

But Thomas did not stop there. He wrote that *Kelo* was only the latest in a line of cases virtually reading the Takings Clause out of the Constitution "without the slightest nod to its *original meaning*. In my view," he continued, "the Public Use Clause, originally understood is a meaningful limit on the government's eminent domain power. *Our cases have strayed from the Clause's original meaning, and I would reconsider them.*"[241]

There follows in Thomas's dissenting opinion a thorough analysis of the Public Use clause—definitionally, historically, and logically—that demonstrates convincingly why the Court's *Kelo* ruling was unsupportable, as were the precedents it relied on in reaching its conclusion.

After dissecting those cases, this was Thomas's unavoidable conclusion:

> When faced with a clash of constitutional
> principle and a line of unreasoned cases
> wholly divorced from the text, history,
> and structure of our founding document,
> *we should not hesitate to resolve the*
> *tension in favor of the Constitution's*
> *original meaning.*"[242]

This was a restatement of Justice Thomas's unambiguous and consistent originalist jurisprudence, pertaining not only to the Fifth Amendment's Eminent Domain Clause but to all of constitutional law.

Although it was *dicta* (a statement not necessary for the decision of the case), Justice Thomas offered a dire prediction of where the *Kelo* decision would lead, and who would be its worst, most innocent victims:

> The consequences of today's decision are
> not difficult to predict, and promise to be
> harmful. So-called "urban renewal"
> programs provide some compensation for
> the properties they take, but no
> compensation is possible for the
> subjective value of these lands to the
> individuals displaced and the indignity
> inflicted by uprooting them from their
> homes. Allowing the government to take
> property solely for public purposes is bad
> enough, but extending the concept of
> public purpose to encompass any
> economically beneficial goal guarantees
> that these losses will fall
> disproportionately on poor communities.

Those communities are not only systematically less likely to put their lands to the highest and best social use, but are also the least politically powerful. If ever there were justification for intrusive judicial review of constitutional provisions that protect "discrete and insular minorities" . . . surely that principle would apply with great force to the powerless groups and individuals the Public Use Clause protects.

The deferential standard [of review] this Court has adopted for the Public Use Clause is therefore deeply perverse. It encourages "those citizens with disproportionate influence and power in the political process, including large corporations and development firms" to victimize the weak.

Those incentives have made the legacy of this Court's "public purpose" test an unhappy one. In the 1950's, no doubt emboldened in part by the expansive understanding of "public use" this Court adopted in [the] *Berman* [case], cities "rushed to draw plans" for downtown development. B. Frieden & L. Sagalayn, Downtown, Inc. How America Rebuilds Cities 17 (1989). "Of all the families displaced by urban renewal from 1949 through 1963, 63 percent of those whose race was known were nonwhite, and of these families, 56 percent of nonwhites and 38 percent of whites had incomes low enough to qualify for public housing, which, however, was seldom available to them." * * * Public works projects in the 1950's and 1960's destroyed predominantly minority communities in St. Paul, Minnesota, and Baltimore, Maryland. * * * In 1981, urban planners in Detroit, Michigan, uprooted the largely "lower-income and elderly" Poletown neighborhood for the benefit of the General Motors Corporation. J. Wylie, Poletown: Community Betrayed 58 (1989). Urban renewal projects have long been associated with the displacement of blacks; "in cities across the country, urban renewal came to be known as 'Negro removal.'" Pritchett, The "Public Menace" of Blight: Urban Renewal and the Private Uses of Eminent Domain, 21 *Yale L. & Pol'y Rev. 1*, 47 (2003). Over 97 percent of the individuals forcibly removed from their homes by the "slum-clearance" project upheld by this Court in *Berman* were black. * * *

Regrettably, the predictable consequence of the Court's decision will be to exacerbate these effects.

SIXTH AMENDMENT

> *In all criminal prosecutions, the accused shall enjoy the right to a speedy and public trial, by an impartial jury of the State and*

*district wherein the trial shall
have been committed; which
district shall have been previously
ascertained by law, and to be
informed of the nature and cause
of the accusation; to be
confronted with the witnesses
against him; to have compulsory
process for obtaining witnesses in
his favor, and to have the
assistance of counsel for his
defence.*[243]

Speedy Trial[244]

Doggett v. United States[245] was a drug conspiracy case where eight and a half years had elapsed between Doggett's *indictment and trial*—not between the crime and arrest or indictment, and not between arrest and indictment. The reason for the long delay between Doggett's indictment and trial was that he had left the jurisdiction, and the authorities were not looking for him.

The Supreme Court majority ruled that one element of "speedy" is prejudice to the defendant's ability to defend himself because of the passage of time. Ostensibly, not an irrational position.

However, Thomas dissented. Examining precedent, he identified "two conflicting lines of authority, the one declaring that 'limit[ing] the possibility that the defense will be impaired' is an independent and fundamental objective of the Speedy Trial Clause . . . and the other declaring that it is not."

The majority in *Doggett* had ruled that the former lines of authority were controlling. Thomas relied on the latter: "[a] lengthy pretrial delay, of course, may prejudice an accused's ability to defend himself. But . . . prejudice to the defense is not the sort of impairment of *liberty*[246] against which the Clause is directed."

The following quotation makes Thomas's point:

> Prejudice to the defense stems from the interval between *crime* and trial, which is quite distinct from the interval between *accusation* [formal charge] and trial. If the Clause were indeed aimed at safeguarding against prejudice to the defense, then it would presumably limit *all* prosecutions that occur long after the criminal events at issue. A defendant prosecuted 10 years after a crime is just as hampered in his ability to defend himself whether he was indicted the week after the crime or the week before the trial—but no one would suggest that the Clause protects him in the latter situation, where the delay did not substantially impair his liberty, either through oppressive incarceration or the anxiety of known criminal charges.[247]

Accordingly, Thomas saw "no basis for the Court's conclusion that Doggett was entitled to relief under the Speedy Trial Clause *simply* because the Government was [concededly] negligent in prosecuting him and because the resulting delay may have prejudiced his defense."[248] If that defense had been prejudiced—something Thomas denied from the facts of the case—it is not that Doggett would have been without recourse. He could have argued, like defendants in other criminal cases, that the prejudice to his defense violated his rights under the Due Process Clause of the Fourteenth Amendment.

This is a subtle but important difference: procedural and substantive "due process" is a "Jack-of-all-remedies," with its touchstone being the deprivation of a "liberty" interest. While the delay in Doggett's case *may* have been a deprivation of a Fourteenth Amendment due process liberty interest, it was *not* a violation of the federal Constitution's Sixth Amendment right to a speedy trial.

Confrontation

In *Randall v. Illinois*,[249] Justice Thomas's second opinion during his first term, the Court ruled unanimously that because of an exception to a federal evidentiary rule, a four-year-old sexual assault victim's out-of-court statements were admissible at trial even though she did not testify in court.

Justice Thomas concurred in the ruling, agreeing with the result because of Supreme Court precedents, but writing separately in order to identify and correct what he perceived to be a fundamental flaw in the Court's Confrontation Clause/rules of evidence jurisprudence.

Essentially, Thomas sought a narrower reading of the clause than that given it by seven other members of the Court. He "suggest[ed] that our Confrontation Clause jurisprudence has evolved in a manner that is perhaps inconsistent with the text and history of the Clause itself."

Thus, in this early Thomas opinion, we see two elements of his jurisprudence that developed more fully in later terms and on other constitutional subjects: *his beliefs that text and history are fundamental, and that cases erroneously decided need to be at least revisited, and perhaps overruled.*

EIGHTH AMENDMENT

> *Excessive bail shall not be required, nor*
> *excessive fines imposed, nor cruel and*
> *unusual punishments inflicted.*[250]

Excessive Fines[251]

Not until 1998 did the Supreme Court strike down a fine as unconstitutional under the Excessive Fines Clause of the Eighth Amendment. It did so in *United States v. Bajakajian.*[252]

If any case demonstrates the absurdity of charges that JusticeThomas decides cases in lockstep with other conservatives on the Court, it is this one. In *Bajakajian*, Thomas wrote the majority opinion for himself and Justices Stevens, Souter, Ginsburg, and Breyer—against the dissents of Rehnquist, O'Connor, Kennedy, and Scalia.

Federal law required individuals physically departing the United States with more than $10,000 in currency to report it to the authorities. Willful violation results in forfeiture to the government of "any property . . . involved in such offense."

Mr. Bajakajian was caught at Los Angeles International Airport (by currency-smelling dogs!) with $230,000 in his checked luggage. A search of all the departing family's other bags turned up $357,144 in cash.

Bajakajian pleaded guilty to the reporting violation. The trial judge found that the entire $357,144 had been "involved in" the offense, but that despite the words of the statute, a forfeiture of the entire amount would violate the Excessive Fines Clause of the Eighth Amendment. Accordingly, the trial judge ordered forfeiture of only $15,000 and sentenced

Bajakajian to three years probation and a $5,000 fine, the maximum under the sentencing guidelines.[253]

In the Supreme Court, where the government sought forfeiture of the entire $357,144, Thomas's majority opinion traced the history of forfeiture laws, concluding that "[b]ecause the forfeiture of [Bajakajian's] currency constitutes punishment and is thus a 'fine' within the meaning of the Excessive Fines Clause," the next question was "whether it is 'excessive.'"

Under earlier Supreme Court decisions, "[t]he touchstone of the constitutional inquiry under the Excessive Fines Clause is the principle of proportionality: The amount of the forfeiture must bear some relationship to the gravity of the offense that it is designed to punish." However, because neither the text nor the history of the clause provided any formula by which to *quantify* excessiveness, and because in the Court's Cruel and Unusual Punishments Clause jurisprudence it had ruled "that judgments about the appropriate punishment for an offense belong in the first instance to the legislature," Thomas used the latter clause's test for analyzing the former: "gross disproportionality"— measuring the "amount of the forfeiture to the gravity of the defendant's offense. If the amount of the forfeiture is grossly disproportionate to the gravity of the defendant's offense, it is unconstitutional."

Identifying that "the essence of [Bajakajian's] crime [was] a *willful failure to report*[254] his removal from the United States" of currency that he had every right to transport, Thomas noted that the federal sentencing guidelines provided only minimum penalties for the crime itself.[255] Also, he observed that the defendant was not within the category of persons sought to be deterred by the forfeiture law (money launderers, drug dealers, tax evaders), and that Bajakajian's failure to report caused minimal harm (loss of information to the government that $357,144 was leaving the country).

178

Given these factors, Thomas ruled that forfeiture of the entire $357,144 was grossly disproportionate to the nature of the crime.

When one reads closely Thomas's majority opinion and then the strong dissent by Kennedy, it is easy to understand how Thomas could easily have joined the dissent rather than the majority. The most plausible explanation of why he did not is found in his apparent belief that Bajakajian was "clean," and in Thomas's number crunching for his "harm caused" analysis:

> It is impossible to conclude . . . that the harm [Bajakajian] caused is anywhere near 30 times greater than that caused by a hypothetical drug dealer who willfully fails to report taking $12,000 out of the country in order to purchase drugs.

In other words, Bajakajian's $360,000 (in round numbers) would be forfeited just as would the drug dealer's $12,000—a thirty-fold difference. Thomas was making the point that in no way would the former have caused thirty times the harm caused by the latter.

The punishment simply did not fit the crime.

Cruel and Unusual Punishments

The Eighth Amendment's Cruel and Unusual Punishments Clause has been bedeviling the Supreme Court in recent years and appears to be an area of special interest to Justice Thomas.

Although the amendment became effective in 1791, not until 1910 in *Weems v. United States*[256] did the Supreme Court look closely at the amendment's English history, the rationale for its inclusion in the Bill of Rights, the Court's earlier construction of the provision, and how state courts had interpreted similar proscriptions.

And not until 1976, sixty-six years after *Weems*, did the Supreme Court measure a *prisoner's* alleged injuries against the yardstick of the Eighth Amendment.

The case was *Estelle v. Gamble*.[257] A Texas prisoner, J. W. Gamble, hurt his back during a work assignment. Dissatisfied with the medical treatment he received, Gamble sued the warden and other prison officials under 42 United States Code, Section 1983,[258] for alleged violation of his civil rights, to wit: his Eighth Amendment right to be free of "cruel and unusual punishments."

Noting that the amendment "proscribes more than physically barbarous punishments," that the government has an "obligation to provide medical care for those whom it is punishing by incarceration," and that this requirement is mandated by "contemporary" and "*evolving standards of decency,*"[259] the Court's majority formulated a test to evaluate prisoner allegations that their Eighth Amendment rights were violated: Have prison officials shown "deliberate indifference to serious medical needs"?[260]

Fifteen years later, the Court had occasion to elaborate the *Estelle v. Gamble* test, refining it into two parts: a *subjective* element, "deliberate indifference" (a culpable state of mind), and an *objective* element, the "serious" medical need (brain surgery, not removal of a hangnail).

Against this background, and during Justice Thomas's first term, the Court decided *Hudson v. McMillian*.[261] As the result of a beating by guards, "Hudson suffered minor bruises and swelling of his face, mouth, and lip. Blows also loosened Hudson's teeth and cracked his partial dental plate, rendering it unusable for several months." Predictably, he sued for violation of his Eighth Amendment – guaranteed civil right to be free of "cruel and unusual punishments."

In her opening paragraph for the Court's 7-2 majority, Justice O'Connor wrote:

> This case requires us to decide whether
> *the use of excessive physical force*
> *against a prisoner* may constitute cruel
> and unusual punishment when the inmate
> does not suffer serious injury. *We*
> *answer that question in the affirmative.*[262]

Justice Thomas, in dissent, saw the matter differently:

> In my view, a use of force that causes
> only insignificant harm to a prisoner may
> be immoral, it may be tortious [an
> actionable civil wrong], it may be
> criminal, and it may even be remediable
> under other provisions of the Federal
> Constitution, but it is not cruel and
> unusual punishment.

(So much for the liberals who, when the *Hudson* case came down, lambasted Thomas wrongly—and viciously—for being a justice indifferent to physical abuse of a prisoner.)

Thomas then explained his principal reasons for reaching this conclusion.

First, "[f]or generations, judges and commentators regarded the Eighth Amendment as applying only to torturous punishments meted out by statutes or sentencing judges, and not generally to any hardship that might befall a prisoner." Indeed, Thomas reminded the majority, not until the *Estelle* case in 1976 had the Supreme Court ever applied the Eighth Amendment "to a prisoner's complaint for a deprivation suffered in prison."

Next, Thomas explained that when the Court "cut the Eighth Amendment loose from its historical moorings and applied it to a broad range of prison deprivations," the *quid pro quo* was creation of the new test: official culpability (subjective) *and* serious injury (objective) had to be present.

He went on to expose the *Hudson* majority's abandonment of the "objective" prong of the test:

> The Court announces that "[t]he objective component of an Eighth Amendment claim is . . . contextual and responsive to contemporary standards of decency." * * * In the context of claims alleging the excessive use of physical force, the Court then asserts, the serious deprivation requirement is satisfied by *no serious deprivation at all.*[263]   [According to the Court,] "[w]hen prison officials maliciously and sadistically use force to cause harm, contemporary standards of decency always are violated." * * * [According to the Court,] [a]scertaining prison officials' state of mind, in other words, is the *only* relevant inquiry in deciding whether such cases involve cruel and unusual punishment.

Thomas disagreed, seeing "this approach [as] an unwarranted and unfortunate break with our Eighth Amendment jurisprudence."

Justice Thomas's *Hudson* dissent tells us at least three things about his legal philosophy in general and his Eighth Amendment jurisprudence in particular.

In general, rightly decided precedents and historical commentaries are the bedrock upon which subsequent decisions should be built.

More particularly, explicit criteria, both subjective and objective, for assessing Eighth Amendment deprivation claims are important and should not be lightly discarded, let alone less than two decades after they were first formulated.

Finally, abandonment of the objective component—"serious injury"—of the Eighth Amendment's "conditions of confinement" test in prisoner cases, substituting instead the empty liberal bromide "contemporary standards of decency," opens prison doors wide to baseless inmate complaints. Inevitably, decision-by-bromide can only embolden the incarcerated population, cause prison wardens and guards to endanger themselves by altering their handling of prisoners, and clutter the courts with endless claims of "civil rights"/"cruel and unusual" violations.

Something more can be found in Thomas's *Hudson* conclusion (once again, an important point central to his federalism jurisprudence):

> *Today's expansion of the Cruel and Unusual Punishments Clause beyond all bounds of history and precedent is, I suspect, yet another manifestation of the pervasive view that the Federal Constitution must address all ills in our society.* Abusive behavior by prison guards is deplorable conduct that properly evokes outrage and contempt. But that does not mean that it is invariably unconstitutional. The Eighth Amendment is not, and should not be turned into, a National Code of Prison Regulation. To reject the notion [as Thomas does] that the infliction of concededly "minor" injuries can be considered either "cruel" or "unusual" punishment (much less cruel *and* unusual punishment) is not to say that it amounts to acceptable conduct. Rather, it is to recognize [as Thomas does] that *primary responsibility for preventing and punishing such conduct rests not with the*

> *Federal Constitution but with the laws*
> *and regulations of the various States.*[264]

Thomas's prophesy about where *Hudson* would lead was borne out in the Court's next term, in a case entitled *Helling v. McKinney.*[265]

A Nevada state prisoner, McKinney, sued his warden and other prison officials for violating his federal civil rights. According to Justice White, author of the Court's majority opinion, McKinney's complaint

> alleged that [he] was assigned to a cell
> with another inmate who smoked five
> packs of cigarettes a day. * * * The
> complaint also stated that cigarettes were
> sold to inmates without properly
> informing of the health hazards a
> nonsmoking inmate would encounter by
> sharing a room with an inmate who
> smoked . . . and that certain cigarettes
> burned continuously, releasing some type
> of chemical . . . . [Helling] complained
> of certain health problems allegedly
> caused by exposure to cigarette smoke.

Which of the inmate's federal constitutional rights were violated? Naturally, his right to be free from "cruel and unusual punishments," as guaranteed by the Eighth Amendment. And not just free from *immediate* harm, but, as the Supreme Court read his complaint, free from harm to the prisoner's *future* health.[266]

In light of Justice Thomas's dissent in *Hudson*, it would not have been difficult to predict on which side he would be in *McKinney*.

He began by observing that in *Hudson* the Court had expanded the Eighth Amendment by ruling that it is violated by a use of force causing only a *minor* injury. Now, in *McKinney*, the Court was expanding the Cruel and Unusual Punishments prohibition to embrace only *risk* of injury. Henceforth, under the Cruel and Unusual Punishments Clause, it would suffice for a prisoner to state a litigable claim simply by alleging that conduct by prison authorities caused a *mere risk of minor injury.*

Consistent with Thomas's approach to statutory interpretation, he began with the words of the Eighth Amendment itself. In doing so, he cut to the heart of the Supreme Court's Eighth Amendment jurisprudence: The majority's "decision, like every other 'conditions of confinement' case since *Estelle v. Gamble* . . . rests on the premise that deprivations suffered by a prisoner constitute 'punishment' for Eighth Amendment purposes, even when the deprivations have not been inflicted as part of a *criminal* sentence."

In other words, if the Cruel and Unusual Punishments Clause barred only cruel and unusual *punishments*, because McKinney had not complained about *those punishments* he had no case.

Thomas then demonstrated that "[a]t the time the Eighth Amendment was ratified, the word 'punishment' referred to the penalty imposed for the commission of a crime. * * * That is also the primary definition of the word today. As a legal term of art, 'punishment' has always meant a 'fine, penalty, or confinement inflicted upon a person by the authority of the law and the judgment and sentence of a court, for some crime or offense committed by him'." He found no historical evidence to the contrary.

Indeed, the "cruell and unusuall Punishments"[267] provision of the English Declaration of Rights of 1689, the "antecedent to our constitutional text," was a response to *sentencing* abuses.

Nor, in the considerable discourse concerning the formation of the Constitution and creation of the Bill of Rights, was there anywhere a suggestion that the concern over cruel and usual punishments included harsh prison conditions.

As a matter of fact, Thomas noted, the Founders had an example they could have emulated if they were concerned with harsh prison conditions. The 1792 Delaware (state) constitution expressly provided that "Excessive bail shall not be required, nor excessive fines imposed, nor cruel or[268] unusual punishments inflicted." However, the Delaware constitution continued, *as the Eighth Amendment does not*: *"and in the construction of jails a proper regard shall be had to the health of prisoners."*269 (From the perspective of constitutional interpretation, this historical fact is devastatingly convincing.)

In making these points, and by a surgical analysis of *Estelle* and its antecedent cases, Thomas was challenging the premise upon which the Supreme Court's entire Eighth Amendment "conditions of confinement" jurisprudence had been built since Estelle was decided in 1976.

> Although the evidence is not overwhelming, I believe that the text and history of the Eighth Amendment, together with the decisions interpreting it, support the view that judges or juries— not jailers—impose "punishment." At a minimum, I believe that the original meaning of "punishment," the silence in the historical record, and the 185 years of uniform precedent shift the burden of persuasion to those who would apply the Eighth Amendment to prison conditions.

That burden, he argued, had not been carried by the majority.

In closing his dissent, Thomas lamented where the Court's Eighth Amendment jurisprudence was heading. More important, he articulated a conflict that would affect his own role on the Court for years to come: *adherence to the principle* of stare decisis *in the face of wrongly decided cases that create "constitutional rights" out of the "Living Constitution's" thin air*:

> In *Hudson*, the Court extended *Estelle* to cases in which the prisoner had suffered only minor injuries; here, it extends *Estelle* to cases in which there has been no injury at all.[270] Because I seriously doubt that *Estelle* was correctly decided, I decline to join the Court's holding. *Stare decisis* may call for hesitation in overruling a dubious precedent, but it does not demand that such a precedent be *expanded* to its outer limits.[271]

This is an important insight into Thomas's jurisprudence. Even though he believed the *Estelle* precedent to be wrong, he also believed that the principle of *stare decisis* is an important limitation on judicial activism that cautions hesitancy in overruling prior cases. However, as his dissent makes clear, he draws the line at *extending* a wrongly decided precedent.[272]

The Supreme Court was at it again in *Farmer v. Brennan*.[273] A preoperative male transsexual who projected feminine characteristics made a "deliberate indifference" claim based on having been housed in the prison's general population, and there assaulted and raped.

For the first time, the Court defined "deliberate indifference": "a prison official cannot be found liable under the Eighth Amendment for denying an inmate humane conditions of confinement unless the official knows of and disregards an excessive risk to inmate health or safety; the official must both be aware of facts from which the inference could be drawn that a substantial risk of serious harm exists, and he must also draw the inference." Because the Court believed the record from the trial court may not have adequately developed the facts, the case was remanded.

Justice Thomas concurred. His opinion reflects the concerns he expressed earlier in *Hudson and Helling*. The Court was again "refin[ing] the 'National Code of Prison Regulation,' otherwise known as the Cruel and Unusual Punishments Clause," which is inappropriately applied to anything other than *judicial* punishment. What happened to Farmer—*and it was certainly wrong*—was not "punishment," and thus the inmate, who may have had recourse under other laws, should have had *no* recourse under the Eighth Amendment.

Thomas did acknowledge that "in approaching this case . . . we do not write on a clean slate. * * * Beginning with *Estelle v. Gamble . . .* the Court's prison condition jurisprudence has been guided, not by the text of the Constitution, but rather by 'evolving standards of decency that mark the progress of a maturing society.'" Although he "doubt[ed] that mode of constitutional decision making," in the name of *stare decisis* he concurred in the Court's judgment. But "[i]n doing so, however, [he] remain[ed] hopeful that the Court will reconsider *Estelle* in light of the constitutional text and history."

Thomas had remained steadfast in his Eighth Amendment jurisprudence: the Cruel and Unusual Punishments Clause applied only to punishments imposed in a criminal sentence, *Estelle v. Gamble* was wrongly decided, it should be "reconsidered," and in the meantime its reach should not be expanded—let alone should its applicability be measured by whether the prison authorities' conduct comported with "evolving standards of decency that mark the progress of a maturing society."[274]

The Cruel and Unusual Punishments Clause is most notoriously implicated in cases involving the death penalty.

In 1975 Charles Kenneth Foster was sentenced to death for a brutal murder. Twenty-seven years later—having utilized every procedural device available to him—he had finally shot every arrow in his "prisoner's rights" quiver and was close to execution. He then sought certiorari from the Supreme Court,[275] contending that his execution after all those years would constitute "cruel and unusual punishment."

Foster garnered only one vote of the four necessary to grant certiorari, that of Justice Breyer.

In his dissent from the Court's denial of certiorari, Breyer argued that "the combination of uncertainty of execution and long delay is arguably 'cruel.' * * * Courts of other nations have found that delays of 15 years or less can render capital punishment degrading, shocking, or cruel [citing a case from Jamaica in the United Kingdom's Privy Council, another from the European Court of Human Rights, and a third from the Supreme Court of Canada]."

Not surprisingly, Justice Thomas concurred in the Court's denial of certiorari. He answered Breyer by making two points, the first rooted in separation of powers:

> Justice Breyer has only added another foreign court to his list while still failing to ground support for [his] theory in any decision by an American court. * * * While Congress, as a *legislature*, may wish to consider the actions of other nations on any issue it likes, this Court's Eighth Amendment jurisprudence should not impose foreign moods, fads, or fashions on Americans.[276]

Thomas's second point was a refreshingly commonsensical one:

> Murderers such as [Foster] who are not apprehended and tried suffer from the

fear and anxiety that they will be one day
caught and punished for their crimes—
perhaps even sentenced to death. Will
Justice Breyer next have us consider the
constitutionality of capital murder trials
that occur long after the commission of
the crime simply because the criminal
defendants, who have evaded capture,
have been so long suffering?

Foster could long ago have ended his
"anxieties and uncertainties" . . . by
submitting to what the people of Florida
have deemed him to deserve: execution.
Moreover, this judgment would not have
been made had [Foster] not slit Julian
Lanier's throat, dragged him into bushes,
and then, when [Foster] realized that he
could hear Lanier breathing, cut his
spine.[277]

ENDNOTES

[216] See *United States* v. *Rumley*, 345 U.S. 41, 73 S.Ct. 543 (1953); *Beauharnais* v. *Illinois*, 343 U.S. 250, 72 S.Ct. 725 (1952); *Breard* v. *City of Alexandria*, 341 U.S. 622, 71 S.Ct. 920 (1951).

[217] As will appear from the sections below, in fourteen terms on the Supreme Court, Justice Thomas has written considerably more on the Fifth and Eighth Amendments than on the Fourth and Sixth Amendments.

[218] Amendment IV, Constitution of the United States of America.

[219] 514 U.S. 927, 115 S.Ct. 1914 (1995).

[220] Whether an exception applied was something to be decided in the trial court on remand.

[221] Justice Thomas wrote another "reasonableness" majority opinion for the Court in *Board of Education of Independent School District No. 92 of Pottawatomie County* v. *Earls*, 536 U.S. 822, 122 S.Ct. 2559 (2002). An Oklahoma school district initiated a drug testing policy affecting students involved in competitive extracurricular activities. In a 6-3 decision, the Court upheld the policy because the testing "effectively serves the School District's interest in protecting the safety and health of its students."

[222] 524 U.S. 357, 118 S.Ct. 2014 (1998).

[223] The rationale for non-application included policy reasons relating to the nature of those proceedings and a weighing of the costs versus benefits of exclusion.

[224] Emphasis added.

[225] Predictably, the dissenters in *Scott* were Justices Stevens, Souter, Ginsburg, and Breyer.

[226] Amendment V, Constitution of the United States of America.

[227] In his fourteen terms on the Court, Justice Thomas has not written significantly on the "Presentment/Indictment" or "Double Jeopardy" Clauses of the Fifth Amendment.

[228] *Miranda* v. *Arizona*, 384 U.S. 436, 86 S.Ct.1602 (1966).

[229] 538 U.S. 760, 123 S.Ct. 1994 (2003).

[230] Emphasis in original.

[231] Emphasis added.

In *United States* v. *Patane*, 542 U.S. 630, 124 S.Ct. 2620 (2004), Justice Thomas wrote for a divided Court that the failure of a police officer to finish giving an arrestee the Miranda warnings—because the arrestee interrupted the officer after his first sentence, claiming to know what his rights were—did not require suppression at trial of a pistol found by the officer as a result of the arrestee's voluntary statement.

[232] 508 U.S. 307, 113 S.Ct. 2096 (1993).

[233] Emphasis added.

[234] Quotation marks in original; citation omitted.

[235] On the merits, Justice Thomas found that at least two rationales supported the distinction made in the statute. "The assumptions," he wrote, "underlying those rationales may be erroneous, but the very fact that they are 'arguable' is sufficient on rational-basis review to 'immuniz[e]' the congressional choice from constitutional challenge."

[236] 510 U.S. 43, 114 S.Ct. 492 (1993).

[237] _U.S._, 125 S.Ct. 2655 (2005).

[238] 535 U.S. 302, 122 S.Ct. 1465 (2002).

[239] Emphasis in original. As a source for this quotation, Thomas cited "J. Keynes, Monetary Reform 88 (1924)." The sentence appears also, almost verbatim, in the mouth of Cuffy Meigs, one of the villains in Ayn Rand's *Atlas Shrugged*: "In the long run, we'll all be dead." (ninth Random House edition, 843).

[240] Emphasis added.

[241] Emphasis added.

[242] Emphasis added.

---

[243] Amendment VI, Constitution of the United States of America.

[244] In his fourteen terms on the Court, Justice Thomas has not written significantly on the "Impartial Jury," "Accusation," "Compulsory Process," or "Assistance of Counsel" Clauses of the Sixth Amendment.

[245] 505 U.S. 647, 112 S.Ct. 2686 (1992).

[246] Emphasis added.

[247] Emphasis added.

[248] Emphasis added.

[249] 502 U.S. 346, 112 S.Ct. 736 (1992).

[250] Amendment VIII, Constitution of the United States of America.

[251] In his fourteen terms on the Court, Justice Thomas has not written significantly on the Excessive Bail Clause of the Eighth Amendment.

[252] 524 U.S. 321, 118 S.Ct. 2028 (1998).

[253] On appeal from the district court, the court of appeals ruled that, in its view of precedent, the property forfeited must be an "instrumentality" of the crime committed and the currency was not that (as, for example, a house might be the "instrumentality" of a drug-manufacturing operation), because the crime was failure to report the money, not its possession.

[254] Emphasis added.

[255] The maximum imprisonment was six months, and the maximum fine $15,000.

[256] 217 U.S. 349, 30 S.Ct. 544 (1910).

[257] 429 U.S. 97, 97 S.Ct. 285 (1976).

[258] "Every person who, under color of any statute, ordinance, regulation, custom, or usage, of any State or Territory, subjects, or causes to be subjected, any citizen of the United States or other person within the jurisdiction thereof to the deprivation of any rights, privileges, or immunities secured by the Constitution and laws, shall be liable to the party injured in an action at law, suit in equity, or other proper proceeding for redress."

[259] Emphasis added.

[260] As to Gamble himself, after examining the facts, the Court in an 8-1 decision (Justice Stevens dissented) ruled against the prisoner.

[261] 503 U.S. 1, 112 S.Ct. 995 (1992).

[262] Emphasis added.

[263] Emphasis added.

[264] Emphasis added.

[265] 509 U.S. 25, 113 S.Ct. 2475 (1993).

[266] The Supreme Court sent the case back to the federal district court, "to provide an opportunity for McKinney to prove his allegations, which will require him to prove both the subjective ['deliberate indifference'] and objective [actual injury] elements necessary to prove an Eighth Amendment violation." In addition, on remand "the prisoner must show that the risk of which he complains is not one that today's society chooses to tolerate."

[267] Thomas quoted the historically correct spelling.

[268] The Eighth Amendment language is "cruel *and* unusual" punishments.

[269] Emphasis added.

[270] Footnote omitted.

[271] Emphasis added.

[272] In the 1993 term, Thomas dissented in *Fogerty* v. *Fantasy, Inc.*, 510 U.S. 517, 114 S.Ct. 1023 (1994), a case involving attorney fees under a federal statute. Citing *Helling,* he noted that "while *stare decisis* may call for hesitation in overruling a dubious precedent, it does not demand that such a precedent be expanded to its outer limits."

[273] 511 U.S. 825, 114 S.Ct. 1970 (1994).

[274] In *Overton* v. *Bazzetta*, 539 U.S. 126, 123 S.Ct. 2162 (2003), for the reasons he gave in *Hudson*, Justice Thomas reiterated that the Eighth Amendment's Cruel and Unusual Punishments Clause was limited to a criminal case's *sentence*: "[R]egulations pertaining to visitations are not punishment within the meaning of the Eighth Amendment."

A corollary of Justice Thomas's Cruel and Unusual Punishments jurisprudence is his position on government financing of prisoners' "rights." In *Lewis* v. *Casey*, 518 U.S. 343, 116 S.Ct. 2174 (1996), where Arizona prison inmates unsuccessfully sued to obtain an extensive "in-house" law library and other legal resources, Thomas concurred. To express his views, he quoted with approval former chief justice Burger in an earlier case: "The Court leaves us unenlightened as to the source of the 'right of access to the courts' which it perceives, or of the requirement that States 'foot the bill' for assuring such access for prisoners who want to act as legal researchers and brief writers."

Seven years later, in his *Christopher* v. *Harbury*, 536 U.S. 403, 122 S.Ct. 2179 (2000), concurrence, Thomas adverted to his *Lewis* concurrence: "In *Lewis* . . . after a review of the constitutional text, this Court's precedent, and tradition, I could find no basis 'for the conclusion that the constitutional right of access [to the courts] imposes affirmative obligations on the States to finance and support prisoner litigation.' * * * Likewise, I find no basis in the Constitution for a 'right of access to courts' that effectively imposes an affirmative duty on Government officials either to disclose matters concerning national security or to provide information in response to informal requests."

[275] *Foster* v. Florida, 537 U.S. 990, 123 S.Ct. 470 (2002).

[276] Emphasis in original.

[277] Implicit in death sentences is the principle of "proportionality." In *Harmelin* v. *Michigan*, 501 U.S. 957, 111 S.Ct. 2680 (1991), decided before Clarence Thomas joined the Court, Justice Scalia acknowledged "that the Eighth Amendment contains a narrow proportionality principle . . . ." Proportionality being "the notion that the punishment should fit the crime . . . ."

In *Ewing* v. *California*, 537 U.S. 11, 123 S.Ct. 1179 (2003), the Court upheld the conviction, under California's "three-strikes law," of a man sentenced to 25 years to life for his last crime of stealing three golf clubs. Thomas concurred, not only because he believed that the proportionality test "is incapable of judicial application," but because even if it were "perfectly clear . . . I would not feel compelled by *stare decisis* to apply it. In my view, the Cruel and Unusual Punishments Clause of the Eighth Amendment contains no proportionality principle."

CHAPTER 8.

"No State shall"

FOURTEENTH AMENDMENT

No State shall make or enforce any law
which shall abridge the privileges or
immunities of citizens of the United States;
nor shall any State deprive any person of
life liberty, or property, without due process
of law, nor deny to any person within its
jurisdiction the equal protection of the
laws.[278]

Privileges or Immunities

In the *Slaughter-House Cases* of 1873,[279] the Supreme Court ruled that the Privileges or Immunities Clause of the Fourteenth Amendment did *not* "incorporate" any provision of the Bill of Rights, that it did *not* protect every right of individual citizens, and that it did *not* protect rights derived from state (e.g., New York) citizenship. On the contrary, if anything was protected, it was, as the amendment states, "the privileges or immunities of citizens of the United States"—meaning, *rights derived uniquely from being a citizen of the federal government.*

Under that interpretation, then, what would those rights be? According to the 1873 Court, voting in federal elections, traveling and engaging in interstate commerce, petitioning Congress, and entering federal lands.

Accordingly, the states could not terminate these federal rights, and only once since the founding of the Republic had the Court ruled that a state did violate the Privileges or Immunities Clause.[280] Until 1999.

A California statute limited "Temporary Assistance to Needy Families" benefits during the first year of residence in the Golden State to the amount the needy would have received in the state of their prior residence.

The Supreme Court in *Saenz v. Roe*[281] held the statute unconstitutional, as a violation of the Privileges or Immunities Clause of the Fourteenth Amendment.

Justice Thomas dissented, revealing a methodology of constitutional/historical analysis that epitomizes originalism. He noted that "[u]nlike the Equal Protection and Due Process Clauses, which have assumed near-talismanic status in modern constitutional law, the [Supreme] Court all but read the Privileges or Immunities Clause out of the Constitution in [the *Slaughter-House Cases*]."

For Thomas, there were two contemporary questions: What does the clause mean, and how does it apply to the California statute?

Typically, and "[u]nlike the majority," Thomas wrote, "I would look to history to ascertain the original meaning of the Clause."[282] He began with the 1606 Charter of Virginia and other colonial charters, extensively documenting his view that:

> [t]he colonists repeated assertions that
> they maintained the rights, privileges,
> and immunities of persons 'born within
> the realm of England' and 'natural born'
> persons suggests that, at the time of the
> founding, the terms 'privileges' and
> 'immunities' (and their counterparts)
> were understood to refer to those
> fundamental rights and liberties

specifically enjoyed by English citizens
and, more broadly, by all persons.

He followed with a presumption, albeit an entirely reasonable
one: The members of the Second Continental Congress *had* to have
understood this historical meaning when they employed the terms in
the Articles of Confederation. So, too, did the Framers of the
Constitution when they provided, in Article IV, Section 2, Clause 1,
that "[t]he Citizens of each State shall be entitled to all Privileges and
Immunities of Citizens in the several States" (some eighty-one years
before the Fourteenth Amendment).

From the colonial experience, to the Articles of Confederation,
to the Constitution, this unbroken line of understanding led to early
Supreme Court decisions. Thomas cited *Corfield v. Coryell*,[283] where
New Jersey prohibited anyone not an "actual inhabitant and resident"
from harvesting oysters from New Jersey waters. Rejecting a
constitutional challenge based on Article IV's Privileges and
Immunities Clause, Justice Bushrod Washington ruled that "citizens of
the several states are [not] permitted to participate in all the rights
which belong exclusively to the citizen of any other particular state,
merely upon the ground that they are enjoyed by those citizens."

What, then, did the Article IV Privileges and Immunities Clause
mean? According to Justice Washington, it protected those "which are,
in their nature, *fundamental.*"[284]

Thomas pointed out that among the specific fundamental rights
Justice Washington listed were:

> Protection by the government; the
> enjoyment of life and liberty, with the
> right to acquire and possess property of
> every kind, and to pursue and obtain
> happiness and safety . . . . The right of a
> citizen of one state to pass through, or to

reside in any other state, for purposes of
trade, agriculture, professional pursuits,
or otherwise. To claim the benefit of the
writ of habeas corpus; to institute and
maintain actions of any kind in the courts
of the state; . . . and an exemption from
higher taxes or impositions than are paid
by the other citizens of the state; . . . the
elective franchise . . . . These, and many
others which might be mentioned, are,
strictly speaking, privileges and
immunities.[285]

From Justice Washington's ruling in 1825, Thomas jumped to
the post – Civil War amendments: "When Congress gathered to debate
the Fourteenth Amendment, Members frequently, if not as a matter of
course, appealed to *Corfield*, arguing that the Amendment was
necessary to guarantee the fundamental rights that Justice Washington
identified in his opinion."[286]

Despite this historical evidence, Thomas—hardly the
doctrinaire conservative his critics falsely accuse him of being—saw
only an "inference that at the time the Fourteenth Amendment
[containing the Privileges or Immunities Clause that was being asserted
against the California statute] was adopted, people understood that
'privileges and immunities of citizens' were fundamental rights, rather
than every public benefit established by positive law."

But the inference was enough to put him at odds with the *Saenz*
majority because, given originalist interpretation of the Privileges or
Immunities Clause, California's needy benefits were no different from
New Jersey's oysters.

Thomas concluded by expressing a fear that because of the
Saenz decision, "the Privileges or Immunities Clause will become yet
another convenient tool for inventing new rights, limited solely by the

'predilections of those who happen at the time to be Members of this Court.'"

Given the Court's modern history, and its decisions since Justice Thomas wrote his 1999 *Saenz* dissent, his fear was well grounded.

Due Process

The Fifth[287] and Fourteenth Amendments provide that no one shall be deprived of life, liberty, or property without "due process" of law—neither procedurally nor substantively, neither civilly nor criminally. "Fundamental fairness" is the touchstone.

That the Due Process Clause of the Fourteenth Amendment "incorporates" most if not all of the Bill of Rights, making the latter's provisions applicable to the states,[288] is a now-settled controversy. Still, because the concept of "fundamental fairness" is so ephemeral, this clause has engendered considerable disagreement among the justices of the Supreme Court.

It is hardly surprising that over the years the Court has expressed the "fundamental fairness" principle in different ways. For example: "those fundamental principles of liberty and justice which lie at the base of all our civil and political institutions"[289] ; "those settled usages and modes of proceeding existing in the common and statute law of England"[290]; "privileges long recognized at common law as essential to the orderly pursuit of happiness by free men"[291]; and so on.

A succinct statement of what the contemporary Due Process Clause means to most of the justices can be found in Chief Justice Rehnquist's majority opinion in *Washington v. Glucksberg,*[292] which Justice Thomas joined.

> The Due Process Clause guarantees more
> than fair process, and the "liberty" it

protects includes more than the absence
of physical restraint.

Our established method of substantive-
due-process analysis has two primary
features. First, we have regularly
observed that the Due Process Clause
specially protects those fundamental
rights and liberties which are,
objectively, deeply rooted in this
Nation's history and tradition . . . .
Second, we have required in substantive-
due-process cases a careful description of
the asserted fundamental liberty interest.
* * * Our Nation's history, legal
traditions, and practices thus provide the
crucial guideposts for responsible
decision making . . . that direct and
restrain our exposition of the Due Process
Clause. As we stated recently . . . the
Fourteenth Amendment forbids the
government to infringe . . . fundamental
liberty interests *at all,* no matter what
process is provided, unless the
infringement is narrowly tailored to serve
a compelling state interest.[293]

As Chief Justice Rehnquist observed, the concept of "due
process" has both a procedural aspect (e.g., adequate notice and an
opportunity to be heard) and a substantive aspect (e.g., sending one's
children to a private, rather than a public, school). Such claims of due
process violations arise in both criminal and civil cases. Examples
follow.

Procedural due process

Justice Thomas's third dissent during his first term on the Court was in a criminal- law procedural due process case entitled *Dawson v. Delaware.*[294]

Dawson was convicted of capital murder and other crimes. To determine his punishment, at the penalty phase the judge allowed the jury to hear a stipulation that had been entered into by the prosecution and, apparently unwillingly, by the defense. The stipulation provided that "[t]he Aryan brotherhood refers to a white racist prison gang that began in the 1960s in California in response to other gangs of racial minorities. Separate gangs calling themselves the Aryan Brotherhood now exist in many state prisons including Delaware." In addition, the prosecution introduced evidence that Dawson's nickname was that of one of Satan's disciples, that the defendant wore an "Aryan Brotherhood" tattoo, and that he had a lengthy criminal record. Dawson was sentenced to death.

When the case reached the Supreme Court, according to the majority "[t]he question . . . [was] whether the First [right of association] and Fourteenth [due process] Amendments prohibit the introduction in a capital sentencing proceeding of the fact that the defendant was a member of an organization called the Aryan Brotherhood, where the evidence has no relevance to the issues being decided in the [penalty] proceeding."

The Court, in an 8-1 vote, ruled that the evidence was inadmissible. Justice Thomas, again not in lockstep with the Court's conservatives, was the lone dissenter, going against all of his eight colleagues, including Chief Justice Rehnquist (who wrote the majority opinion) and his frequent ally, Justice Scalia.

Thomas began his dissent by noting that at the sentencing hearing, Dawson had introduced mitigating "character" evidence: acting kindly toward his family, good time credit earned while in prison, and "membership and participation in various respectable organizations." To rebut that evidence the prosecution had shown that Dawson belonged to the Aryan Brotherhood prison gang. Each side had been allowed to introduce their evidence pursuant to a Delaware statute.

Thomas then parted company with his colleagues' conclusion that the prosecution's evidence was irrelevant because, said the majority, the "State failed to prove the Aryan Brotherhood's [criminal] activities." Thomas wrote:

> [A] jury reasonably could conclude from Dawson's membership in a prison gang that he had engaged in some sort of forbidden activities while in prison. The evidence also tended to establish future dangerousness and to rebut Dawson's attempt to show that he was kind to others.

Once the majority had ruled the Aryan Brotherhood evidence irrelevant— because Dawson's Aryan Brotherhood membership was an "associational" interest protected by the First Amendment—the Court ruled further that admission against him of evidence of that membership violated his constitutional rights.

In rejoinder, Thomas noted that "[o]nce the Court concludes that the gang membership evidence 'has no relevance to the issues being decided in the sentencing proceeding,'" that should eliminate the First Amendment (association) issue, turning the inquiry into a routine question of improper admission of evidence that is normally tested by the Due Process Clause.

Due process—a "fundamentally fair trial"—is, however, not irrelevant. Thus, rather than minimizing the procedural due process rights of criminal defendants, as many of Thomas's critics have wrongly accused him of doing, his *Dawson* dissent reveals a Supreme Court justice not afraid to stand alone against all eight colleagues and to employ appropriate due process criteria to judge the fairness of criminal trials.[295]

Thomas took the same approach in another procedural due process dissent two months later.

Terry Foucha barged into a private residence waving a .357 Magnum revolver, chased the married residents out, and then shot at the police as he fled. No one disputed these facts, including Foucha. He was charged under Louisiana law with aggravated burglary and illegal use of a weapon. Foucha's defense was to claim that a mental illness prevented him from knowing right from wrong.

After a hearing, the trial judge ruled that Foucha was "unable to appreciate the usual, natural and probable consequences of his acts; that he is unable to distinguish right from wrong; that he is a menace to himself and others; and that he was insane at the time of the commission of [his] crimes and that he is presently insane."

Foucha thus became what is called an "insanity acquittee"—a criminal defendant who committed the act with which he was charged, but who avoids punishment because at that time he suffered from a mental illness rendering him incapable of knowing right from wrong.

Foucha was committed to an appropriate facility. Four years later, the facility's superintendent recommended that Foucha be released. As Louisiana law required, a panel of physicians examined him and concluded that there was no longer any evidence of mental illness—*but did not address the question of whether Foucha was still dangerous*. The panel recommended that Foucha be conditionally released.

The trial judge held a hearing at which Foucha had the burden of proving that he could be released without danger to himself or

others. Two experts testified that though Foucha was in remission—
that is, he no longer suffered from a mental illness—they could not
certify that he would not be a danger to himself or others if released.[296]

After the hearing, the trial judge—absent any disagreement
from the state that Foucha was in remission and accepting the experts'
testimony that he was—found that Foucha remained dangerous to
himself and others, and, *on that basis alone*, refused to release him.

When the case reached the Supreme Court,[297] a 5-4 majority
turned Foucha loose, ruling that an insanity acquittee is entitled to go
free *even if he remained dangerous.* Continued confinement would,
according to the Court, violate the Due Process Clause of the
Fourteenth Amendment. In essence, it would be "fundamentally
unfair."

Justice Thomas dissented.

He noted that the appropriate analytical framework for due
process claims such as Foucha's was this: state legislation affecting
"fundamental rights" (e.g., voting, worshiping, speaking) is subject to
judicial "strict scrutiny," and will be invalidated unless the state proves
a "compelling interest"—and proves further that only through the
challenged legislation can the state accomplish its goal, which must be
legitimate. Otherwise, "the substance of state legislation under the Due
Process Clause of the Fourteenth Amendment is not exacting."

In other words, if the legislation bears a "reasonable
relationship" to a legitimate state goal, it will be sustained against
constitutional challenge.

Thus, according to Thomas, "[t]he critical question here . . . is
whether *insanity acquittees* [[298]] have a fundamental right to 'freedom
from bodily restraint' [[299]] that triggers strict scrutiny of their
confinement." His answer was "no," based not only on Supreme Court
precedent but on the unacceptable implications of the majority opinion.

> If the Court indeed means to suggest that *all[*[300]] restrictions on "freedom from bodily restraint" are subject to strict scrutiny, it has (at a minimum) wrought a revolution in the treatment of the mentally ill. Civil commitment as we know it would almost certainly be unconstitutional; only in the rarest of circumstances will a State be able to show a "compelling interest," and one that can be served in no other way, in involuntarily institutionalizing a person.

As strong as this reasoning was, however, there was another basis for Justice Thomas's dissent, one which speaks volumes about his view of federalism and his humility when it comes to asserting federal judicial power:

> Removing insanity acquittees from mental institutions may make eminent sense as a *policy* matter, but *the Due Process Clause does not require the States to conform to the policy preferences of federal judges.* "The Court is most vulnerable and comes nearest to illegitimacy when it deals with judge-made constitutional law having little or no cognizable roots in the language or design of the Constitution."[301]

For Thomas, then, if the people of the state of Louisiana, through their two-house legislature and governor, decided that "sane" but dangerous persons who had committed criminal acts were to be confined until they were no longer a threat to themselves and others, the federal courts in general, *and the Supreme Court of the United*

States in particular, had no right to interfere with the state's political judgment. If the citizens of Louisiana don't like the law, they possess adequate *political* (i.e., legislative) recourse—a recourse, Thomas was saying, entirely lacking against the rulings of five unelected, life-tenured justices of the Supreme Court.[302] If the citizens of Louisiana chose not to change their law, their refusal to do so in no way deprives the Fouchas of the world of due process.

Nor, for that matter, was due process deprived in a case discussed in the previous chapter, *Chavez v. Martinez.* There, Justice Thomas ruled for the Court that Martinez's in-hospital interview by a police supervisor did not violate the perpetrator's Fifth Amendment right not to incriminate himself, because his answers were never used against him in any criminal proceeding.

Nor did it violate his right to procedural due process, despite what Martinez claimed. As Justice Thomas explained:

> The Fourteenth Amendment provides that no person shall be deprived "of life, liberty, or property, without due process of law." Convictions based on evidence obtained by methods that are "so brutal and so offensive to human dignity" that they "shock the conscience" violate the Due Process Clause. *Rochin v. California*, 342 U.S. 165, 172, 174, 72 S. Ct. 205 (1952) (overturning conviction based on evidence obtained by involuntary stomach pumping). See also *Breithaupt v. Abram*, 352 U.S. 432, 435, 77 S. Ct. 408 (1957) (reiterating that evidence obtained through conduct that "shocks the conscience" may not be used to support a criminal conviction). Although *Rochin* did not establish a civil

remedy for abusive police behavior, we
recognized in *County of Sacramento* v.
Lewis, 523 U.S. 833, 846, 118 S. Ct.
1708 (1998), that deprivations of liberty
caused by "the most egregious official
conduct" . . . may violate the Due
Process Clause. While we rejected, in
Lewis, a Section 1983 plaintiff's
contention that a police officer's
deliberate indifference during a high-
speed chase that caused the death of a
motorcyclist violated due process, we left
open the possibility that unauthorized
police behavior in other contexts might
"shock the conscience" and give rise to
[civil rights violation] liability.

However, "conscience shocking" cases like *Rochin* and
Breithaupt are a far cry from the in-hospital, non-coercive interview of
Martinez, where no force of any kind was applied. Using *Rochin* and
Breithaupt as a litmus test, Justice Thomas explained:

We are satisfied that Chavez's
questioning did not violate Martinez's
due process rights. Even assuming [for
the sake of argument] that the persistent
questioning of Martinez somehow
deprived him of a liberty interest, we
cannot agree with Martinez's
characterization of Chavez's behavior as
"egregious" or "conscience shocking."

As we noted in Lewis, the official
conduct "most likely to rise to the
conscience-shocking level," is the
"conduct intended to injure in some way

unjustifiable by any government
interest." * * * Here, there is no
evidence that Chavez acted with a
purpose to harm Martinez by
intentionally interfering with his medical
treatment. Medical personnel were able
to treat Martinez throughout the
interview . . . and Chavez ceased his
questioning to allow tests and other
procedures to be performed. * * * Nor
is there evidence that Chavez's conduct
exacerbated Martinez's injuries or
prolonged his stay in the hospital.

Moreover, the need to investigate
whether there had been police
misconduct constituted a justifiable
government interest given the risk that
key evidence would have been lost if
Martinez had died without the authorities
ever hearing his side of the story.

Substantive due process

Chavez v. Martinez is a good example also of the principle of
"substantive," as compared to "procedural," due process.

As Justice Thomas explained the former:

The Court has held that the Due Process
Clause also protects certain "fundamental
liberty interests" from deprivation by the
government, *regardless of the procedures
provided,* unless the infringement is
narrowly tailored to serve a compelling
state interest. *Washington v. Glucksberg,*

210

521 U.S. 702, 721, 117 S.Ct. 2258, 117
S. Ct.2302 (1997). Only fundamental
rights and liberties which are "deeply
rooted in this Nation's history and
tradition" and "implicit in the concept of
ordered liberty" qualify for such
protection. * * * Many times, however,
we have expressed our reluctance to
expand the doctrine of substantive due
process . . . in large part "because
guideposts for responsible decision
making in this unchartered area are
scarce and open-ended."[303]

Glucksberg requires a "careful
description" of the asserted fundamental
liberty interest for the purposes of
substantive due process analysis; vague
generalities, such as "the right not to be
talked to," will not suffice. * * *

We therefore must take into account the
fact that Martinez was hospitalized and in
severe pain during the interview, but also
that Martinez was a critical non-police
witness to an altercation resulting in a
shooting by a police officer, and that the
situation was urgent given the perceived
risk that Martinez might die and crucial
evidence might be lost. In these
circumstances, we can find no basis in
our prior jurisprudence, see, *e.g.,*
Miranda . . . ("It is an act of responsible
citizenship for individuals to give
whatever information they may have to
aid in law enforcement"), or in our

Nation's history and traditions to suppose
that freedom from unwanted police
questioning is a right so fundamental that
it cannot be abridged absent a
"compelling state interest." * * * We
have never required such a justification
for a police interrogation, and we decline
to do so here. The lack of any
"guideposts for responsible decision
making" in this area, and our oft-stated
reluctance to expand the doctrine of
substantive due process, further counsel
against recognizing a new "fundamental
liberty interest" in this case.

Deck v. Missouri [304] is another textbook example of how
Justice Thomas analyzes substantive due process claims in the context
of criminal law:

Deck was convicted of the murders and
robbery [of a helpless elderly couple] . . .
and sentenced to death. The death
sentence was overturned on appeal. Deck
then had another sentencing hearing, at
which he appeared in leg irons, a belly
chain, and handcuffs. At the hearing, the
jury heard evidence of Deck's numerous
burglary and theft convictions and his
assistance in a jailbreak by two prisoners.
On re-sentencing, the jury unanimously
found six aggravating factors. * * * The
jury recommended, and the trial court
imposed, two death sentences.

Post-conviction, Deck claimed that his shackling deprived him
of due process of law. The Court agreed. Justice Thomas dissented.

Understanding his role as a judge, especially that of a Supreme Court justice interpreting the Constitution, Thomas clearly saw that his "legal obligation is not to determine the wisdom or the desirability of shackling defendants, but to decide a purely legal question: *Does the Due Process Clause of the Fourteenth Amendment preclude the visible shackling of a defendant.* Therefore, I examine whether there is a deeply rooted legal principle that bars that practice."[305]

Thomas's examination included English common law and a survey of scores of state cases. In the end, he had no trouble concluding that no such legal principle existed and thus that Deck's due process rights were not violated when, as a convicted criminal with an horrendous record, he was shackled during sentencing (as compared to trial, when he was still presumed innocent).

However, Thomas went further, explaining—presciently, in light of recent courtroom shooting episodes around the country—that people like Deck are dangerous in the extreme and that judges, jurors, court personnel, and the trial-attending public have a right to be free of the threats posed by criminals like him.

> Jurors no doubt also understand that it makes sense for a capital defendant to be restrained at sentencing. By sentencing, a defendant's situation is at its most dire. He no longer may prove himself innocent, and he faces either life without liberty or death. Confronted with this reality, a defendant no longer has much to lose should he attempt escape and fail, it is still lengthy imprisonment or death that awaits him. For any person in these circumstances, the reasons to attempt escape are at their apex. A defendant's best opportunity to do so is in the

courtroom, for he is otherwise in jail or restraints. * * *

In addition, having been convicted, a defendant may be angry. He could turn that ire on his own counsel, who has failed in defending his innocence. See, e.g., *State v. Forrest* (defendant brutally attacked his counsel at sentencing). Or, for that matter, he could turn on a witness testifying at his hearing or the court reporter. See, e.g., *People v. Byrnes* (defendant lunged at witness during trial); *State v. Harkness* (defendant attacked court reporter at arraignment). Such thoughts could well enter the mind of any defendant in these circumstances, from the most dangerous to the most docile. That a defendant now convicted of his crimes appears before the jury in shackles thus would be unremarkable to the jury. To presume that such a defendant suffers prejudice by appearing in handcuffs at sentencing does not comport with reality.

The Court's decision risks the lives of courtroom personnel, with little corresponding benefit to defendants. This is a risk that due process does not require.

Apparently, that risk did not bother Chief Justice Rehnquist and Justices Stevens, O'Connor, Souter, Kennedy, Ginsburg, and Breyer, who voted to reverse Deck's conviction.

Thomas's restrictive analysis of substantive due process cases makes it obvious, particularly if one considers cases like *Griswold v. Connecticut*, that in the hands of others the doctrine has been a tool-for-all-seasons. When enough non-originalist justices dislike the *content* of a particular law, they raise the banner of substantive due process and strike the statute down—even if they have to invent some constitutional peg on which to hang their hats, some hitherto unknown "fundamental right" (doubtless lurking in Justice Douglas's "penumbras" and "emanations").

For example, the paternal grandparents of children born out of wedlock sued for visitation under a Washington state statute that provided "[a]ny person may petition the court for visitation rights at any time" if "visitation may serve the best interests of the child." The Washington Supreme Court held the statute unconstitutional because it infringed on the fundamental right of parents to rear their children.

The Supreme Court of the United States agreed.[306]

Justice O'Connor's opinion for the majority made essentially two points. First, that "[w]e have long recognized that the [Fourteenth] Amendment's Due Process Clause, like its Fifth Amendment counterpart, 'guarantees more than fair process.' * * * The Clause also includes a substantive component that 'provides heightened protection against government interference with certain fundamental rights and liberty interests.'" Second, she stressed that "[t]he liberty interest at issue in this case—the interest of parents in the care, custody, and control of their children—is perhaps the oldest of the fundamental liberty interests recognized by this Court." With those two premises in place, it was easy for the Court to hold the "any person may petition" statute unconstitutional.

Justice Thomas concurred in the *result*, but he was apparently unable to resist, yet again, expressing skepticism about the "substantive due process" precedents upon which the majority's ruling was based.

He noted, perhaps wistfully, that "neither party has argued that our substantive due process cases were wrongly decided and that the original understanding of the Due Process Clause precludes judicial enforcement of unenumerated rights [like parents rearing children] under *that*[307] constitutional provision." Accordingly, he expressed no view on the merits of the case, agreeing only that the Washington statute was unconstitutional, and left "the resolution of that issue for another day."

Griswold v. Connecticut, discussed in the Introduction, and its first progeny, *Roe v. Wade*,[308] were "substantive due process" decisions. In the former, Douglas invented a "right of privacy" regarding the use of contraceptives that trumped a Connecticut statute. In the latter, Blackmun leveraged Douglas's "right of privacy" into a "right of abortion." In both cases, the Supreme Court majority concluded that the state laws at issue "substantively" (i.e., because of the alleged "fundamental" rights they prohibited) were unconstitutional.

Following *Roe,* an ebb and flow of cases relating to state regulation of abortion were decided by the Supreme Court.

Then came *Planned Parenthood of Southeastern Pennsylvania v. Casey*.[309] The case decided that state regulations of abortion furthering legitimate state interests, but not designed to strike at the core of the abortion "right" itself, were constitutional—*but only as long as they did not impose an "undue burden" on a woman's presumably "fundamental" right to obtain an abortion.* Translation: henceforth, only state regulations that placed a substantial obstacle in the woman's path to abort her fetus would be unconstitutional.

Then came *Stenberg v. Carhart*,[310] the infamous, euphemistically characterized "partial-birth" abortion case.

Nebraska law banned the partial-birth abortion procedure. Basing their decision on the statute's failure to incorporate any exemption for the health of the mother, and on the statute's prohibition of an abortion method one step short of partial-birth abortion, Justices Breyer (the author), Stevens, Souter, Ginsburg, and the so-called "moderate," O'Connor, held the statute unconstitutional because of its "undue burden" on the abortion choice.

Predictably, Justice Thomas dissented. The opinion is among his best.

He began by tracing the history of Supreme Court abortion jurisprudence and brought it up to date with *Casey*—whose opinion, he stated bluntly,

> was constructed by its authors out of whole cloth. *The standard set forth in the Casey . . .* [decision] *has no historical or doctrinal pedigree. The standard is a product of its authors' own philosophical views about abortion, and it should go without saying that it has no origins in or relationship to the Constitution* and is, consequently, as illegitimate as the standard it purported to replace. * * * Today, the Court inexplicably holds that the States cannot constitutionally prohibit a method of abortion that millions find hard to distinguish from infanticide and that the Court hesitates even to describe.[311]

But Thomas did not hesitate to describe it.

In the next section of his dissent he noted that:

> In the almost 30 years since *Roe,* this Court has never described the various

methods of aborting a second- or third-trimester fetus. From reading the majority's sanitized description, one would think that this case involves state regulation of a widely accepted routine medical procedure. Nothing could be further from the truth. The most widely used method of abortion during this state of pregnancy is so gruesome that its use can be traumatic even for the physician and medical staff who perform it. * * * And the particular procedure at issue in this case, "partial birth abortion," so closely borders on infanticide that 30 States have attempted to ban it.

There follows, on pages 984 to 989 of the official reports of the Supreme Court of the United States, Thomas's descriptions of "medical" procedures so ghastly that thesaurus synonyms—terrible, frightening, appalling, horrible, grisly, horrifying—are woefully inadequate.

The partial-birth abortion procedure, whose details have always been avoided by Court majorities upholding the practice, read as though they are to be found only in the depths of the depths of Dante's Inferno, not in a supposedly enlightened twentieth- century American culture.[312] Justice Thomas deserves the utmost gratitude and respect for his courage in pulling back the curtain that—until his dissent—obscured for far too long what had been a dirty secret sanitized in judicial euphemisms.[313]

With the facts in place, Thomas turned next to the law—specifically, to the appropriate interpretation of the Nebraska statute. After a lengthy analysis, he concluded that:

The majority and Justice O'Connor reject the plain language of the statutory definition, refuse to read that definition in light of the statutory reference to "partial birth abortion," and ignore the doctrine of constitutional avoidance. [[314]] In doing so, they offer scant statutory analysis of their own. * * * In their brief analyses, the majority and Justice O'Connor disregard all of the statutory language except for the final definitional sentence, thereby violating the fundamental canon of construction that statutes are to be read as a whole.

After demolishing what the Court's opinion rested on, Justice Thomas concluded by returning to the earlier case, *Casey:*

We were reassured repeatedly in Casey that not all regulations of abortion are unwarranted and that the States may express profound respect for fetal life. Under *Casey,* the regulation before us today should easily pass constitutional muster. *But the Court's abortion jurisprudence is a particularly virulent strain of constitutional exegesis* [interpretation]. *And so today we are told that 30 States are prohibited from banning one rarely used form of abortion that they believe to border on infanticide.* It is clear that the Constitution does not compel this result.[315]

The abortion and abortion-related cases were not the only progeny of the Court's discovery of "penumbras" and "emanations" in *Griswold*. *Lawrence v. Texas*[316] was another.

To understand Justice Thomas's dissent in that case, it is necessary to establish the context for it. A Texas statute criminalized certain intimate sexual contact between two same-gender individuals. This was a *state* statute, enacted by Texas under the Constitution's Tenth Amendment, guaranteeing to the states all powers—especially those relating to the public health, safety, welfare, and morals—(1) not expressly delegated to the federal government in the Constitution, or (2) not expressly denied to the states in the Constitution.

In other words, Texas had every right to pass the law, and it was constitutional unless some provision of the *federal* Constitution invalidated it.[317]

Two adult men were convicted in Texas for engaging in consensual homosexual conduct in a private home. The case eventually reached the Supreme Court of the United States. There, Justices Kennedy (the opinion's author), Stevens, O'Connor, Souter, Ginsburg, and Breyer ruled the statute unconstitutional on "substantive due process" grounds because they found in the Constitution's Due Process Clause a "liberty interest" the men possessed entitling them to engage in that conduct.

Justice Thomas's dissent articulated why he parted company with the majority, underscoring the obvious difference between a legislature and a court:

> If I were a member of the Texas
> Legislature, I would vote to repeal [the
> statute].
>
> Notwithstanding this, I recognize that as
> a Member of this Court, I am not

empowered to help petitioners and others
similarly situated. My duty, rather, is to
decide cases agreeably to the
Constitution and laws of the United
States. * * * And, like Justice Stewart
[dissenting in *Griswold*], I can find
neither in the Bill of Rights nor in any
other part of the Constitution a general
right of privacy . . . or as the Court terms
it today, the "liberty of the person both
in its spatial and more transcendent
dimensions . . . ."[318]

Here was a statute that, in Thomas's words, quoting Justice
Stewart in *Griswold*, was "uncommonly silly." However, Texas had a
constitutional right to enact it. And although Thomas would have
voted against it as a legislator, as a Supreme Court justice he could find
no *federal constitutional* right—let alone a "liberty" or "privacy"
right—that the law violated, any more than there was such a right in
Griswold or *Roe*.

Thomas's dissent shows the jurisprudential connection between
his view of federalism, and ersatz rights created by liberal justices in
the name of "evolving social norms": *the exercise of state power should
fall only if it violates a provision of the federal Constitution, fairly
interpreted according to its text and originalist principles.*

Fundamental rights should not be cooked up in a social science
laboratory.

Also very revealing of Justice Thomas's "fundamental rights"
jurisprudence is his dissent in the relatively obscure case of *City of
Chicago v. Morales.*[319]

The city enacted an anti-gang loitering ordinance, but it did not
make loitering per se illegal. When a policeman observed a group of

people in a public place without an apparent purpose, and in the company of a gang member known to the police, the officers were authorized to order the loiterers to disperse. It was failure to obey that order that was illegal.

In the Supreme Court, the core liberals (Stevens, Souter, Ginsburg, and Breyer) and O'Connor and Kennedy, the two fellow traveling liberals (or, as Senate majority leader Harry Reid calls them when it suits him, "moderates"), found hidden in the Constitution (perhaps in "penumbras" and "emanations") a "Fundamental Freedom to Loiter"[320]—a Due Process Clause "liberty" interest supposedly benefiting vicious gang members.

In his dissent, Justice Thomas stated categorically that "there is no fundamental right to loiter." On the merits, that was that.

But in his concluding paragraph we see an insight, albeit *dicta*, of a core value of Justice Thomas's:

> Today, the Court focuses extensively on the "rights" of gang members and their companions. It can safely do so—the people who will have to live with today's opinion do not live in our neighborhoods. Rather, the people who will suffer from our lofty pronouncements are people like Ms. Susan Mary Jackson; people who have seen their neighborhoods literally destroyed by gangs and violence and drugs. They are good, decent people who must struggle to overcome their desperate situation, against all odds, in order to raise their families, earn a living, and remain good citizens. As one resident described: "There is only about maybe one or two percent of the people in the

city causing these problems maybe, but
it's keeping 98 percent of us in our
houses and off the streets and afraid to
shop." * * *

By focusing exclusively on the imagined
"rights" of the two percent, the Court
today has denied our most vulnerable
citizens the very thing that Justice
Stevens [author of the Court's opinion] . .
. elevates above all else—the "freedom of
movement." And that is a shame.

Equal Protection

The most famous equal protection case of modern times is the
1954 public school desegregation case of *Brown v. Board of
Education*,[321] whose reverberations have been felt for generations.

In 1992, the Supreme Court faced yet another case of *Brown*'s
progeny, *United States v. Fordice*.[322] There, the Court ruled that a
state "does not satisfy its [constitutional] obligation to dismantle a dual
system of *higher* education merely by adopting race-neutral policies for
the future administration of that system." According to the Court, "[i]f
policies traceable to the . . . system are still in force and have
discriminatory effects, those policies too must be reformed to the extent
practicable and consistent with sound educational practices."

Although Justice Thomas agreed with that ruling, he wrote a
separate concurring opinion emphasizing that he did not read the
majority opinion to "compel the elimination of all observed racial
imbalance [and thus] it portends neither the destruction of historically
black colleges nor the severing of those institutions from their
distinctive histories and traditions."

Thomas's concern for, and his apparent valuing of, black colleges has been a little-noticed corner of his jurisprudence and, accordingly, his reasons have gone largely unnoticed—though his *Fordice* concurring opinion, in a reproach to those who have accused him of racism, makes his position very clear.

He concurred because he wanted to be sure that the majority opinion was not thought to "foreclose the possibility that there exists 'sound educational justification' for maintaining historically black colleges *as such.* " [323] He emphasized that "I do not understand our opinion to hold that a state is *forbidden* to do so. It would be ironic, to say the least, if the institutions that sustained blacks during segregation were themselves destroyed in an effort to combat its vestiges."[324]

Pursuant to the equal protection decision in *Brown* (I), a host of cases have been decided over the years concerning the appropriate remedy for the official racial segregation in schools there ruled unconstitutional.

One such case—*Missouri v. Jenkins*[325] —lasted some eighteen years.

In 1985, the federal district court in Missouri issued a remedial order, the intention of which was to eliminate all vestiges of state-imposed public school segregation in Kansas City. Hundreds of millions were spent, and by the time *Jenkins* was back in the Supreme Court in 1995, the "remedial" cost was $2 million *annually.*

Before the Court were two orders by the federal district judge. One imposed salary increases for all but three of the district's approximately 5,000 employees, teachers and staff alike. The other created a "magnet school," designed to attract non-minority students into largely minority schools.

The common question was whether, in issuing those orders, the federal district judge exceeded his constitutional power. "In short," wrote Chief Justice Rehnquist for the 5-4 majority, "the State has challenged the scope of the District Court's remedial authority."

Justice Thomas voted with the majority, but wrote a separate concurrence. He began by getting something bothersome off his chest:

> It never ceases to amaze me that the
> courts are so willing to assume that
> anything that is predominantly black
> must be inferior. Instead of focusing on
> remedying the harm done to those black
> schoolchildren by segregation, the
> District Court here sought to convert the
> Kansas City, Missouri, School District
> (KCMSD) into a "magnet district" that
> would reverse the "white flight" caused
> by *desegregation*.[326]

What came next in Thomas's concurring opinion was astonishing by any standard.

The second black Supreme Court justice in history, and the only one among the nine justices at that time, in words revelatory of his moral stature, took aim at the sacrosanct 1954 desegregation decision— albeit not its result, but its methodology.

What Thomas wrote about the Constitution, race, and racial segregation in *Jenkins* is more apt (let alone more eloquent) than the unanimous Court opinion authored by then – Chief Justice Earl Warren in *Brown* (I).

> Two threads in our jurisprudence have
> produced this unfortunate situation, in
> which a District Court has taken it upon
> itself to experiment with the education of
> the KCMSD's black youth. First, the

[district] court has read our cases to support the theory that black students suffer an unspecified psychological harm from segregation that retards their mental and educational development.[327] This approach not only relies upon questionable social science research rather than constitutional principle, but *it also rests on an assumption of black inferiority.* Second, we have permitted the federal courts to exercise virtually unlimited equitable powers to remedy this alleged constitutional violation.

The exercise of this authority has trampled upon principles of federalism and the separation of powers and has freed courts to pursue other agendas unrelated to the narrow purpose of precisely remedying a constitutional harm.[328]

Thomas then cut to the core of the case: "The District Court inferred a continuing constitutional violation from two primary facts: the existence of *de jure* [legal] segregation in the KCMSD prior to 1954, and the existence of *de facto* [actual] segregation *today* [in 1995]."[329]

The problem with that approach, however, was the lack of causality—of a link—between the former and the latter. Thomas addressed it:

It should by now be clear that the existence of one-race schools is not by itself an indication that the State is practicing segregation. * * * That certain

schools are overwhelmingly black in a
district that is now more than two-thirds
black is hardly a sure sign of intentional
state action. * * * District Courts must
not confuse the consequences of [pre-
1954] *de jure* segregation with the results
of larger social forces or private
decisions. * * * When a district court
holds the State liable for discrimination
almost 30 years after the last official state
action, it must do more than show that
there are schools with high black
populations or low test scores. * * * But
*I question the District Court's conclusion
that because the State had enforced
segregation until 1954, its actions, or
lack thereof, proximately caused the
"racial isolation" of the predominately
black schools in 1984.*[330]

Returning to *Brown* (I), Justice Thomas took it head on.

It is clear that the District Court
misunderstood the meaning of *Brown* I.
Brown I did not say that "racially
isolated" schools were inherently
inferior; the harm that it identified was
tied purely to de jure ["by law"]
segregation. Indeed, *Brown I itself did
not need to rely upon any psychological
or social-science research in order to
announce the simple, yet fundamental,
truth that the government cannot
discriminate among its citizens on the
basis of race.*[331]

Brown (I), Thomas was saying, should not have rested on pseudo-scientific Swedish social science, but rather on a straightforward application of the Equal Protection Clause of the Fourteenth Amendment: "Psychological injury or benefit is irrelevant to the question whether state actors have engaged in intentional discrimination—the critical inquiry for ascertaining violations of the Equal Protection Clause."

There was no evidence that the KCMSD had, so that was that.

Thomas was by no means finished. He wrote: "The time has come for us to put the genie back in the bottle." He was talking about the virtual blank check the Supreme Court had given the *federal* district courts to craft "remedies" for the consequences of official racial discrimination—while, at the same time, "not permit[ing] constitutional principles such as federalism or the separation of powers to stand in the way of our drive to reform the schools."

The "massive expenditures" ordered by the district court in this case were an example. Thomas blamed earlier Court decisions for the "judicial overreaching we see before us today," acknowledging that it was perhaps "the price we now pay for our approval of such extraordinary remedies in the past." And not just in the realm of public education, because "[j]udges have directed or managed the reconstruction of entire institutions and bureaucracies, with little regard for the inherent limitations on their authority."

Because the Framers intended no such extravagant remedial powers, and because such powers cut against the core principles of federalism (*federal* judges running *state* institutions) and separation of powers (*courts* running *executive branch* departments, like schools and prisons), Thomas rejected them *in principle.* He knew what those remedial powers were really used for: "The federal courts . . . also should avoid using racial equality as a pretext for solving social problems that do not violate the Constitution."

In the end, Thomas observed:

> The desire to reform a school district, or
> any other institution, cannot so captivate
> the judiciary that it forgets its
> constitutionally mandated role.
> Usurpation of the traditionally local
> control over education not only takes the
> judiciary beyond its proper sphere, it also
> deprives the States and their elected
> officials of their constitutional powers.
> *At some point, we must recognize that the*
> *judiciary is not omniscient, and that all*
> *problems do not require a remedy of*
> *constitutional proportions.*"[332]

A non-omniscient judiciary. Now *there's* an idea.[333]

The paternalism to which Justice Thomas alluded in *Missouri v. Jenkins* reared its head in a case decided the same day, *Adarand Constructors, Inc. v. Pena.*[334]

There, the low bidder on a highway contract lost out because, under federal law, it was not controlled by "socially and economically disadvantaged individuals," who were "presume[d]" to "include Black Americans, Hispanic Americans, Native Americans, Asian Pacific Americans, and other minorities, or any other individual found to be disadvantaged by the [Small Business] Administration."

The Supreme Court ruled that all racial classifications, employed by any level of government, must be evaluated by the "strict scrutiny" test, and sent the case back to the trial court to determine whether the federal scheme was narrowly tailored to achieve a compelling interest. The majority consisted of Justice O'Connor, who authored the opinion, Chief Justice Rehnquist, and Justices Kennedy,

Scalia, and Thomas. Justices Stevens, Souter, Ginsburg, and Breyer dissented.

Thomas wrote a revealing concurring opinion. "I agree with the majority's conclusion that strict scrutiny applies to *all[335*] government classifications based on race. I write separately, however, to express my disagreement with the premise underlying Justice Stevens' and Justice Ginsburg's dissents: *that there is a racial paternalism exception to the principle of equal protection.*[336]

Thomas was saying the dissenters were admitting that, yes, the Equal Protection Clause does require equal treatment for all races, that government action not treating them equally must be scrutinized strictly, and that unequal treatment based on race cannot survive unless narrowly tailored to achieve a compelling interest—except, according to the dissent echoing George Orwell, sometimes some races are more equal than others.

Thomas explained it this way:

> I believe that there is a "moral [and]
> constitutional equivalence" . . . between
> laws designed to *subjugate* a race and
> those that distribute benefits on the basis
> of race in order to foster some current
> notion of equality. *Government cannot
> make us equal; it can only recognize,
> respect, and protect us as equal before
> the law.*[337]

Because Thomas's concurring opinion in *Adarand* is of such great importance in revealing not only his jurisprudence on issues of race, but also his uncompromising constitutional values, it is necessary to quote his opinion at length.

That these programs may have been motivated, in part, by good intentions cannot provide refuge from the principle that under our Constitution, *the government may not make distinctions on the basis of race.*

As far as the Constitution is concerned, it is irrelevant whether a government's racial classifications are drawn by those who wish to oppress a race or by those who have a sincere desire to help those thought to be disadvantaged. There can be no doubt that *the paternalism that appears to lie at the heart of this [federal contract] program is at war with the principle of inherent equality that underlies and infuses our Constitution. See Declaration of Independence* ("We hold these truths to be self-evident, that all men are created equal, that they are endowed by their Creator with certain unalienable Rights, that among these are Life, Liberty, and the pursuit of Happiness").

These programs not only raise grave constitutional questions, they also undermine the moral basis of the equal protection principle. Purchased at the price of immeasurable human suffering, the equal protection principle reflects our Nation's understanding that such classifications ultimately have a destructive impact on the individual and our society.

Unquestionably, [per Justice Stevens] "[i]nvidious [racial] discrimination is an engine of oppression" . . . . It is also true that "[r]emedial" racial preferences may reflect "a desire to foster equality in society" . . . . But there can be no doubt that *racial paternalism and its unintended consequences can be as poisonous and pernicious as any other form of discrimination.*

So-called "benign" discrimination teaches many that because of chronic and apparently immutable handicaps, minorities cannot compete with them without their patronizing indulgence. Inevitably, such programs engender attitudes of superiority or, alternatively, provoke resentment among those who believe that they have been wronged by the government's use of race. *These programs stamp minorities with a badge of inferiority and may cause them to develop dependencies or to adopt an attitude that they are "entitled" to preferences.* * * *

In my mind, government-sponsored racial discrimination based on benign prejudice is just as noxious as discrimination inspired by malicious prejudice.[338] In each instance, it is racial discrimination, plain and simple.[339]

"Stamp[ing] minorities with a badge of inferiority" is hardly limited to construction contracts. Perhaps the worst example is in the context of affirmative action.

There are many cases that underscore the profound differences in jurisprudence between Justice Thomas and the recently retired Sandra Day O'Connor, whose beatification by the Left for some of her swing votes is, for them, not without good reason.

One of those cases is *Grutter v. Bollinger*,[340] an affirmative action case that showed O'Connor at her worst and Thomas at his best.

In essence, the question for the Court, in O'Connor's words, was "whether the use of race as a factor in student admissions by the University of Michigan Law School . . . is unlawful."

Ruling for herself and the (other) four liberals, Stevens, Souter, Ginsburg, and Breyer, O'Connor decided that the school had a "compelling" interest in the creation and maintenance of a "diverse" student body, and that because that interest was "narrowly tailored," the use of race as an admissions criterion was constitutional.

Thomas began his dissent, as he had done at least once in the past, by quoting the eloquent ex-slave Frederick Douglass from a speech made almost a century and a half earlier—making a point "lost on today's majority":

> [I]n regard to the colored people, there is
> always more that is benevolent, I
> perceive, than just, manifested toward us.
> What I ask for the negro is not
> benevolence, not pity, not sympathy, but
> simply *justice*. The American people
> have always been anxious to know what
> they shall do with us . . . . I have had but
> one answer from the beginning. Do

nothing with us! Your doing with us has
already played the mischief with us. Do
nothing with us! If the apples will not
remain on the tree of their own strength,
if they are worm-eaten at the core, if they
are early ripe and disposed to fall, let
them fall! And if the negro cannot stand
on his own legs, let him fall also. All I
ask is, give him a chance to stand on his
own legs! Let him alone! . . . [Your]
interference is doing him positive
injury.[341]

Thomas, like Douglass, eschews paternalism in all its forms. In
Grutter he argued the law school had no "compelling" interest in the
racial discrimination that even the majority admitted pervaded the
school's admissions policy.

But more important than Thomas's devastating rebuttal to the
Court's "compelling interest" premise (which sufficed to destroy the
majority's entire argument), is that he exposed what actually animated
its ruling—one with both dangerous implications and pernicious
consequences:

The absence of any articulated legal
principle supporting the majority's
principal holding suggests another
rationale. I believe what lies beneath the
Court's decision today are the benighted
notions that one can tell when racial
discrimination benefits (rather than hurts)
minority groups . . . and that racial
discrimination is necessary to remedy
general societal ills. This Court's
precedents supposedly settled both
issues, but clearly the majority still

cannot commit to the principle that racial classifications are per se harmful and that almost no amount of benefit in the eye of the beholder can justify such classifications.

Then, Justice Clarence Thomas spoke the unspeakable, saying what few other notables of his race[342] have said publicly:

The Law School tantalizes unprepared students with the promise of a University of Michigan degree and all of the opportunities that it offers. *These overmatched students take the bait, only to find that they cannot succeed in the cauldron of competition.* And this mismatch is not restricted to elite institutions. * * * Indeed, to cover the tracks of the aestheticists, this cruel farce of racial discrimination must continue— in selection for the Michigan Law Review . . . and in hiring at law firms and for judicial clerkships—until the "beneficiaries" are no longer tolerated. While these students may graduate with law degrees, there is no evidence that they have received a qualitatively better legal education (or become better lawyers) than if they had gone to a less "elite" law school for which they were better prepared. And the aestheticists will never address the real problems facing "underrepresented" minorities, instead continuing their social experiments on other people's children.[343]

Thus did Thomas in *Grutter* lay bare the legal and moral bankruptcy of the Court liberals' jerrybuilt majority opinion, their own patronizing racial discrimination, and the attendant consequences for their minority "wards." In doing so, once again Thomas proved that he understands not only the meaning of the Equal Protection Clause and the case law the Court has developed in its adjudications of it, but also that *decisions have consequences.*

Thomas concluded:

> The majority has placed its *imprimatur* on a practice that can only weaken the principle of equality *embodied in the Declaration of Independence* and the Equal Protection Clause. "Our Constitution is color-blind, and neither knows or tolerates classes among citizens." * * *

> It has been nearly 140 years since Frederick Douglass asked the intellectual ancestors of the Law School to "[d]o nothing with us!" and the Nation adopted the Fourteenth Amendment. Now we must wait another 25 years to see this principle of equality vindicated.[344]

Equal protection issues based on racial classifications also arise in the context of prison administration.

These are the pertinent facts from Justice Thomas's dissenting opinion in *Johnson v. California.*[345] The legal conclusions Thomas drew from them dramatically demonstrate the practical awareness that separates him from those of his wooly colleagues who have spent little time in the real world:

When an inmate like Johnson is admitted
into the California prison system or
transferred between . . . institutions, he is
housed initially for a brief period—
usually no more than 60 days—in one of
California's prison reception centers for
men.

[S]ome prisoners, like Johnson, neither
require confinement in a single cell nor
may be safely housed in a dormitory.
The CDC houses these prisoners in
double cells during the 60-day period. In
pairing cellmates, race is indisputably the
predominant factor. * * * California's
reason is simple: Its prisons are
dominated by violent gangs. * * * And
as the largest gangs' names indicate—the
Aryan Brotherhood, the Black Guerrilla
Family, the Mexican Mafia, the Nazi
Low Riders, and La Nuestra Familia—
they are organized along racial lines.

[W]hen Johnson was admitted in 1987,
he was a member of the Crips, a black
street gang. * * * He was therefore
ineligible to be housed with nonblack
inmates.

Johnson complained that he was being racially discriminated
against in violation of the Equal Protection Clause of the Fourteenth
Amendment.

According to Justice Thomas:

The questions presented in this case
require us to resolve two conflicting lines
of precedent. On the one hand, as the
Court stresses, this Court has said that *all*
racial classifications reviewable under the
Equal Protection Clause must be strictly
scrutinized. [Citing *Gratz* and
Adarand.][346] On the other, this Court
has no less categorically said that "the
[relaxed] standard of review we adopted
in *Turner*. . . applies to *all* circumstances
in which the needs of prison
administration implicate constitutional
rights."[347]

Despite Thomas's devastating analysis, the four liberals on the
Court and fellow-travelers O'Connor and Kennedy turned a blind eye
toward their analytical and precedential shortcomings. Choosing strict
scrutiny, they remanded the case so the lower court could ascertain if
the prison policy was narrowly tailored to achieve a compelling state
interest.

If the policy could not survive strict scrutiny, Thomas noted,
then "Johnson may well have won a Pyrrhic victory."[348]

ENDNOTES

[278] Amendment XIV, Constitution of the United States of America.

[279] *Slaughter-House Cases*, 83 U.S. (16 Wall.) 36 (1873).

[280] Five years later, that decision was overruled.

[281] 526 U.S. 489, 119 S.Ct. 1518 (1999).

[282] Here, Justice Thomas inserted the following footnote: "Legal scholars agree on little beyond the conclusion that the Clause does not mean what the Court said it meant in 1873."

[283] 6 Fed. Cas. 546 (No. 3,230) (CCED Pa. 1825).

[284] Emphasis added.

[285] Justice Thomas added a footnote stating that "[d]uring the first half of the 19th century, a number of legal scholars and state courts endorsed Justice Washington's conclusion that the Clause protected only fundamental rights."

[286] In text and footnotes, Thomas provided several examples.

[287] The Fifth Amendment provides that: "No person shall be . . . deprived of life, libertyor property, without due process of law."

[288] The "Incorporation Doctrine" is discussed in Chapter 2.

[289] *Hurtado* v. *California*, 110 U.S. 516, 45 S.Ct. 111 (1884).

[290] *Adamson* v. *California*, 332 U.S. 46, 67 S.Ct. 1672 (1947).

[291] *Meyer* v. *Nebraska*, 262 U.S. 390, 43 S.Ct. 625 (1923).

[292] 521 U.S. 702, 117 S.Ct. 2258 (1997).

[293] Inner quotation marks omitted. Among the "fundamental" rights the Court has identified are the rights to marry, to have children, to direct their upbringing and education, to marital "privacy," to use contraception, to bodily integrity, and to abortion. Perhaps also "the traditional right to refuse unwanted lifesaving medical treatment."

[294] 503 U.S. 159, 112 S.Ct. 1093 (1992).

Justice Thomas certainly accepts and applies the *principle* of due process "fundamental fairness." But it can be argued that occasionally he has come down on the wrong side of its *application*.

One such case is *Bennis* v. *Michigan*, 516 U.S. 442, 116 S.Ct. 994 (1996). A man engaged in sexual activity with another person in an automobile he owned jointly with his wife. When the husband was convicted of "gross indecency," even though the wife had no advance knowledge of her husband's conduct, the state then sued husband and wife under a Michigan statute to forfeit their car as a "nuisance."

Chief Justice Rehnquist and Justices O'Connor, Scalia, and Ginsburg upheld the forfeiture—with Thomas providing a fifth vote in a concurring opinion. Even though all nine justices agreed that the wife was wholly innocent of any connection with her husband's crime—except through joint ownership of the family car—the majority ruled that the forfeiture did not violate her right to due process.

Though Thomas's vote was essential to the majority's forfeiture, one can sense from his opinion that he was uneasy:

> This case is ultimately a reminder that the Federal Constitution [especially the Fourteenth Amendment's Due Process Clause] does not prohibit everything that is intensely undesirable. * * * The limits on *what* property can be forfeited as a result of what wrongdoing . . . are not clear to me. * * * Improperly used, forfeiture could become more like a roulette wheel employed to raise revenue from innocent but hapless owners whose property is unforeseeably misused, or a tool wielded to punish those who associate with criminals, than a component of a system of justice.

Still, Thomas helped form the majority. He explained why:

> Forfeiture of property without proof of the owner's wrongdoing, merely because it was "used" in or was an "instrumentality" of crime *has been permitted in England and this country, both before and after the adoption of the Fifth and Fourteenth Amendments.* (Emphasis added).

For Thomas, history and precedent trumped what can only be characterized as a due process violation of the innocent wife's substantive rights to an interest in her jointly owned car.

There was another reason Thomas approved the forfeiture—this one entirely consistent with his constitutional jurisprudence:

> When the property sought to be forfeited has been entrusted by its owner to one who uses it for crime, however, the Constitution apparently assigns to the States and to the political branches of the Federal Government the primary responsibility for avoiding that result.

Translation: Michigan has the power under the Tenth Amendment to enact a draconian forfeiture law—such laws having been repeatedly upheld by the Supreme Court as a matter of constitutional law—subject to state constitutional scrutiny and, conceivably, congressional action (if an Article I power can be found to justify the legislation). Federalism, again.

[296] At the time of the hearing, the state did not contend that Foucha suffered from a mental illness.

[297] *Foucha* v. *Louisiana*, 504 U.S. 71, 112 S.Ct. 1780 (1992).

[298] Emphasis in original.

[299] This phrase appeared in the majority opinion.

[300] Emphasis in original.

[301] Emphasis added. Quotation marks in original.

[302] In *Kelly* v. *South Carolina*, 534 U.S. 246, 122 S.Ct. 726 (2002), consistent with his position in *Foucha*, Justice Thomas observed that the majority decision "allows the Court to meddle further in a State's sentencing proceedings under the guise that the Constitution requires us to do so. I continue to believe, without qualification, that 'it is not this Court's role to micromanage state sentencing proceedings.' * * * As a matter of *policy*, it may be preferable for a trial court to give such an instruction [concerning parole ineligibility], but these are 'matters that the Constitution leaves to the states.'" (Emphasis added.)

[303] Emphasis added.

[304] 125 S.Ct. 2007 (2005).

[305] Emphasis added.

[306] *Troxel* v. *Granville*, 530 U.S. 57, 120 S.Ct. 2054 (2000).

[307] Emphasis added.

[308] 410 U.S. 113, 93 S.Ct. 705 (1973).

[309] 505 U.S. 833, 112 S.Ct 2791 (1992).

[310] 530 U.S. 914, 120 S.Ct. 2597 (2000).

[311] Emphasis added.

[312] **WARNING**: The squeamish, and those for whom infant life is sacred, *may be better off not reading the following testimony of a nurse who observed a partial-birth abortion.* It appears on page 1007 of volume 530 of the United States [Supreme Court] Reports.

The baby's little fingers were clasping and unclasping, and his little feet were kicking. Then the doctor stuck the scissors in the back of his head, and the baby's arms jerked out, like a startle reaction, like a flinch, like a baby does when he thinks he is going to fall. The doctor opened up the scissors, stuck a high-powered suction tube into the opening, and sucked the baby's brains out. Now the baby went completely limp.

[313] It is worth noting that contributing to the invalidation of the Nebraska statute that attempted to outlaw the barbarism of partial-birth abortion were two women, O'Connor and Ginsburg. One would think that female judges would be especially sensitive to near full-term infants being savagely dismembered.

[314] The doctrine of constitutional avoidance holds that if the Court can construe a statute so as to avoid ruling it unconstitutional, it should do so. The doctrine has been applied in many Supreme Court and lower court cases.

[315] Emphasis added.

Justice Scalia also dissented, and although this book is about Justice Thomas's jurisprudence it would be unfair not to acknowledge Scalia's powerful contribution to exposing the poverty of the *Stenberg* majority opinion.

He began by putting *Stenberg* v. *Carhart* in "its rightful place in the history of this Court's jurisprudence beside *Korematsu* [the World War II Japanese "relocation" case] and *Dred Scott* [the pre – Civil War decision that "legitimized" African slavery].

Some of Justice Scalia's comments follow:

> The method of killing a human child—one cannot even accurately say an entirely unborn human child—proscribed by

this statute is so horrible that the most clinical description of it evokes a shudder of revulsion. * * * The notion that the Constitution of the United States, designed, among other things, "to establish Justice, insure domestic Tranquility, . . . and secure the Blessings of Liberty to ourselves and our Posterity," prohibits the States from simply banning this visibly brutal means of eliminating our half-born posterity is quite simply absurd. * * * I have joined Justice Thomas's dissent because I agree that today's decision is an "unprecedented expansion" of our prior cases . . . "is not mandated" by *Casey's* "undue burden" test . . . and can even be called . . . "obviously irreconcilable" with *Casey's* explication of what its undue-burden standard requires . . . . * * *

There is no cause for anyone who believes in *Casey* to feel betrayed by this outcome. It has been arrived at by precisely the process *Casey* promised—*a democratic vote by nine lawyers, not on the question whether the text of the Constitution has anything to say about this subject* (it obviously does not); *nor even on the question* (also appropriate for lawyers) *whether the legal traditions of the American people would have sustained such a limitation upon abortion* (they obviously would); *but upon the pure policy question whether this limitation upon abortion is "undue"—i.e., goes too far.* [Emphasis added.] * * * And those who believe that a 5-to-4 vote on a policy matter by unelected lawyers should not overcome the judgment of 30 state legislatures have a problem, not with the *application* of *Casey*, but with its *existence*. *Casey* must be overruled. * * *

I cannot understand why those who *acknowledge* that, in the opening words of Justice O'Connor's concurrence, "[t]he issue of abortion is one of the most contentious and controversial in contemporary American society" . . . persist in the belief that this Court, armed with neither constitutional text nor accepted tradition, can resolve that contention and controversy rather than be consumed by it. If only for the sake of its own preservation, the Court should return this matter to the people—where the Constitution, by its silence on the subject, left it—and let *them* decide, State by State, whether this practice should be allowed. *Casey* must be overruled. [All other emphasis in original.]

[316] 539 U.S. 558, 123 S.Ct. 2472 (2003).

[317] A Texas court had the power to declare the statute unconstitutional under the state constitution, but that was not an issue in the case.

[318] Inner quotation marks omitted.

[319] 527 U.S. 41, 119 S.Ct. 1849 (1999).

[320] The capitalization of this "Freedom" appears in Justice Scalia's dissent.

[321] 347 U.S. 483, 74 S.Ct. 686 (1954) (*Brown* I).

[322] 505 U.S. 717, 112 S.Ct. 2727 (1992).

[323] Emphasis in original.

[324] Emphasis added.

[325] 515 U.S. 70, 115 S.Ct. 2038 (1995).

[326] Emphasis in original.

[327] Thomas was alluding to the junk sociology that served as much of *Brown* (I)'s foundation.

[328] Emphasis added.

---

[329] Emphasis added.

[330] Emphasis added.

[331] Emphasis added.

[332] Emphasis added.

[333] A classic example of district court remedial powers run amok is *Lewis* v. *Casey*, 518 U.S. 343, 116 S.Ct. 2174 (1996). Justice Thomas's concurring opinion lays bare the excesses of the trial court, at the intersection of federalism and separation of powers.

> The Constitution charges federal judges with deciding cases and controversies, not with running state prisons. Yet, too frequently, federal district courts in the name of the Constitution effect wholesale takeovers of state correctional facilities and run them by judicial decree. This case is a textbook example. Dissatisfied with the quality of the law libraries and the legal assistance at Arizona's correctional institutions, the District Court imposed a statewide decree on the Arizona Department of Corrections (ADOC), dictating in excruciating minute detail a program to assist inmates in the filing of lawsuits—right down to permissible noise levels in library reading rooms.

> Such gross overreaching by a *federal* district *court* simply cannot be tolerated in our federal system. Principles of *federalism* and *separation of powers* dictate that exclusive responsibility for administering state prisons resides with the State and its officials. * * * Even when compared to the *federal judicial overreaching* to which we now have become accustomed, this is truly a remarkable case. The District Court's order vividly demonstrates the danger of continuing to afford *federal judges* the virtually unbridled power that we have for too long sanctioned.

We have here yet another example of a *federal judge* attempting
to direc[t] or manag[e] the reconstruction of entire institutions
and bureaucracies, with little regard for the inherent limitations
on [his] authority." [Citing *Missouri* v. *Jenkins*; emphasis
added.]

[334] 515 U.S. 200, 115 S.Ct. 2097 (1995).

[335] Emphasis in original.

[336] Emphasis added.

[337] Emphasis added.

[338] Footnote omitted.

[339] Emphasis added.

[340] 539 U.S. 306, 123 S.Ct. 2325 (2003).

[341] Emphasis in original.

[342] Others who have spoken the unspeakable include, but are not
limited to, Thomas Sowell, Walter Williams, and Larry Elder.

[343] Emphasis added.

To those who would deny the validity of the argument made by Justice
Thomas, I offer evidence from personal experience. For twenty-one
years, I was a professor at Brooklyn Law School (and, for a while, an
associate dean). During that time I saw example after example of what
Justice Thomas describes. I witnessed the devastating consequences—
psychological, professional, social, and economic—to the
"beneficiaries" of my law school's liberal-driven, misguided efforts to
make two and two equal five. Though I had not then been aware of
Frederick Douglass's statement, some of us faculty and administrators

attempted to implement the principles he articulated. We were met with defamatory insults. *We* were the "racists," rather than the liberal do-gooders who preened, gloating that they had helped the "unfortunate," when, in reality, they were severely injuring them.

[344] Emphasis added.

On the same day the Court handed down its decision in *Grutter*, it decided *Gratz* v. *Bollinger*, 539 U.S. 244, 123 S.Ct. 2411 (2003), ruling that the use of racial preferences for admission to *an undergraduate college* at the University of Michigan was *unconstitutional*. Justice Thomas concurred because of the result, but wrote separately to emphasize that "a State's use of racial discrimination in higher education admissions is categorically prohibited by the Equal Protection Clause."

[345] 125 S.Ct. 1141 (2005).

[346] Emphasis in original.

[347] Emphasis in original.

[348] While *Brown* and its progeny have spawned considerable equal protection jurisprudence related to racial issues, other cases arising under that clause of the Fourteenth Amendment exist on a spectrum much wider than race, and embrace gender discrimination, jury selection, state taxation, and more.

Typically, equal protection analysis is not easy. As with due process analysis, a determination must be made of what "test" to apply, and then the facts, often in dispute, have to be measured by the test.

A good example is the case of *Nordlinger* v. *Hahn*, 505 U.S. 1, 112 S.Ct. 2326 (1992). California's Proposition 13 capped property taxes, reassessing them based on new construction cost or change in ownership, thus creating a tax disparity between newer and older owners. The state constitutional amendment was attacked on equal protection grounds.

The first question for the Court was what test to apply. For the majority, Justice Blackmun wrote that:

> As a general rule, "legislatures are presumed to have acted within their constitutional power despite the fact that, in practice, their laws result in some inequality." * * * Accordingly, this Court's cases are clear that, unless a classification warrants some form of heightened review because it jeopardizes exercise of a fundamental right [e.g., voting] or categorizes on the basis of an inherently suspect characteristic [e.g., race], the Equal Protection Clause requires only that the classification rationally further a legitimate state interest.

Blackmun applied the "rational relation" test, found that California had sufficiently valid reasons for the tax disparity, and upheld Proposition 13's constitutionality.

Justice Thomas concurred in the result but was troubled because it seemed to him in conflict with an earlier decision of the Court. In that case, according to Thomas, the Court "struck down an assessment method . . . that operated precisely the same way as the California scheme" challenged in *Nordlinger*. Important here is not whether Thomas was correct in his reading of the two cases (he was), but rather his willingness to question the earlier decision and imply that rather than the majority distinguishing it the Court should have overruled it.

> I understand that the Court prefers to distinguish [the earlier case], but in doing so, I think, the Court has left our equal protection jurisprudence in disarray. The analysis appropriate to this case is straightforward. Unless a classification [here, newer owners versus older owners] involves suspect classes or fundamental rights, judicial scrutiny under the Equal Protection

Clause demands only a conceivable rational basis for the challenged state distinction. * * * Proposition 13, I believe, satisfies this standard—but so, for the same reasons, did the scheme employed in [the earlier case].

CONCLUSION

Tens of thousands of words ago in the Introduction to this book, I wrote that "[a]ttacks on Justice Thomas have been unconscionable distortions of an unambiguous and distinguished record. Simple justice requires they be rebutted, because his opinions, often eloquent, reveal him as a thoughtful conservative who understands the role of a Supreme Court justice, the methodology of proper constitutional and statutory adjudication, and the appropriate resolution of the many issues that have come to the Court during his tenure."

To prove my case, I culled and analyzed some 327 opinions of Justice Thomas, many dealing with the most fundamental questions confronting our republic: separation of powers, federalism, judicial review, the 1791 Bill of Rights, and the Fourteenth Amendment.

From those majority, concurring, and dissenting opinions, I selected scores that best reflect Justice Thomas's constitutional jurisprudence.

Finally, I chose to quote from Thomas's opinions at considerable length so that his words would, without need for anyone's "interpretation," speak for themselves.

And that they surely do, often eloquently. They demonstrate a constitutional originalism, rooted in a deep, near-worshipful respect for the founding documents of this nation, and for those who gave them life.

That originalism has been demonstrated time and again in Justice Thomas's interpretation of the Constitution and federal statutes:

> Thus, history provides an answer for the
> constitutional question posed by this
> case. . . . The dissent identifies no

evidence that the Framers intended to
disable religious entities from
participating on neutral terms in
evenhanded government programs.
(*Rosenberger v. Rector and Visitors of
University of Virginia.*)

Justice Thomas understands that originalist interpretation is of
crucial importance in cases involving the *scope* of federal power—be it
exercised pursuant to the Commerce Clause or *restrained* by the Tenth
Amendment:

The Court has encouraged the Federal
Government to persist in its view that the
Commerce Clause has virtually no limits.
Until this Court replaces its Commerce
Clause jurisprudence with a standard
more consistent with the original
understanding, we will continue to see
Congress appropriating state . . . powers
under the guise of regulating commerce.
(*United States v. Lopez.*)

In each State, the remainder of the
people's powers—"[t]he powers not
delegated to the United States by the
Constitution, nor prohibited by it to the
States," Amdt. 10—are either delegated
to the state government or retained by the
people. The Federal Constitution does
not specify which of these two
possibilities obtains; it is up to the
various state constitutions to declare
which powers the people of each state
have delegated to their state government.
(*U.S. Term Limits v. Thornton.*)

Justice Thomas's commitment to the principle of separation of powers pervades many of his opinions on other subjects. This is especially true of *federalism* and the nature and scope of *judicial review*—all of which are implicated when the *federal* Supreme *Court* is asked to invalidate the work of a *state legislature*. Thomas is acutely aware that at stake are federal-state relations, judicial-legislative relations, and the reach of judicial review:

> *This Court* has no power to decide questions concerning the admissibility of evidence under *Nevada law.* * * * Except in cases involving a violation of a specific *constitutional* provision such as the Confrontation Clause . . . *this Court* may not reverse a *state* trial judge's action in the *admission of evidence* unless the evidentiary ruling "so infuse[s] the trial with unfairness as to deny due process of law." (*Riggins v. Nevada*; emphasis added.)

Probably nothing has expanded the power of the federal courts, from top to bottom, like the Incorporation Doctrine. Unlike most justices throughout history, and certainly those who have served in modern times, Justice Thomas consistently challenges the notion of "incorporation"—that wellspring of twentieth century judicially created ersatz "rights":

> [A]s a matter of first principles, I question whether this [Supreme Court Establishment Clause] test should be applied to the States. * * * But that protection is as a matter of due process of law, not because the Establishment Clause itself operates against the states. (*Zelman v. Simmons-Harris*.)

In First Amendment law, Justice Thomas's view of the Establishment Clause, even accepting its "incorporation," is iconoclastic, to say the least:

> On its face . . . [the statute] is not a law "respecting an establishment of religion." This provision does not prohibit or interfere with state establishments, since no State has established (or constitutionally could establish . . .) a religion. Nor does the provision require a State to establish a religion: It does not force a State to coerce religious observance or payment of taxes supporting clergy, or require a State to prefer one religious sect over another. *It is a law respecting religion, but not one respecting an establishment of religion.* (*Cutter v. Wilkinson*; emphasis added.)

As to the First Amendment's guarantee of free speech, Justice Thomas is virtually, if not actually, alone in reproaching the Court for having cherry-picked among various kinds of speech, anointing some varieties as more worthy of protection than others:

> I do not see a philosophical or historical basis for asserting that "commercial" speech is of "lower value" than "noncommercial" speech. Indeed, some historical materials suggest to the contrary. (*44 Liquormart* v. *Rhode Island.*)

Justice Thomas's jurisprudence concerning criminal procedure is informed by multiple core principles—separation of powers, federalism, the appropriate scope of judicial review—and by originalist interpretive tools. Nowhere is this more apparent than in his Eighth Amendment opinions, especially regarding the Court's Cruel and Unusual Punishments Clause:

> I believe that the text and history of the Eighth Amendment, together with the decisions interpreting it, support the view that judges or juries—not jailers—impose "punishment." At a minimum, I believe that the original meaning of "punishment," the silence in the historical record, and the 185 years of uniform precedent shift the burden of persuasion to those who would apply the Eighth Amendment to prison conditions. (*Helling v. McKinney*).

> Today's expansion of the Cruel and Unusual Punishments Clause beyond all bounds of history and precedent is, I suspect, yet another manifestation of the pervasive view that the Federal Constitution must address all ills in our society. Abusive behavior by prison guards is deplorable conduct that properly evokes outrage and contempt. But that does not mean that it is invariably unconstitutional. The Eighth Amendment is not, and should not be turned into, a National Code of Prison Regulation (*Hudson v. McMillian.*)

Justice Thomas's fidelity to the Founders' protection of property rights was powerfully expressed in the 2004 – 2005 term's Eminent Domain Clause case:

> [T]he Court replaces the Public Use
> Clause with "Public Purpose Clause" . . .
> (or perhaps the "Diverse and Always
> Evolving Needs of Society" Clause . . .),
> a restriction that is satisfied, the Court
> instructs, so long as the purpose is
> "legitimate" and the means "not
> "irrational" . . . . This deferential shift in
> phraseology enables the Court to hold,
> against all common sense, that a costly
> urban-renewal project whose stated
> purpose is a vague promise of new jobs
> and increased tax revenues, but which is
> also suspiciously agreeable to the Pfizer
> Corporation, is for a "public use." I
> cannot agree. If such "economic
> development" takings are for a "public
> use," any taking is, and the Court has
> erased the Public Use Clause from our
> Constitution . . . . (*Kelo v. City of New
> London.*)

Then there is Justice Thomas's jurisprudence under the Due Process and Equal Protection Clauses of the Fourteenth Amendment.

In his procedural due process opinions, Thomas has painstakingly assessed what "process" the defendants received, and measured it against the "fundamental fairness" standard.

In substantive due process cases, Justice Thomas digs deep to ascertain whether a fundamental right is actually at stake. He wrote of the Texas sodomy statute:

> I recognize that as a Member of this
> Court, I am not empowered to help
> petitioners and others similarly situated.

> My duty, rather, is to decide cases
> agreeably to the Constitution and laws of
> the United States. * * * And, like Justice
> Stewart [dissenting in *Griswold*], I can
> find neither in the Bill of Rights nor in
> any other part of the Constitution a
> general right of privacy . . . . (*Lawrence
> v. Kansas.*)

Finally, it is in Justice Thomas's Fourteenth Amendment equal protection jurisprudence dealing with race that we see the expression of constitutional values not seen in any other justice.

In *United States v. Fordice*, Thomas challenged, not the ruling of the sacrosanct *Brown* (I), but the Swedish social science *methodology* of the Court's unanimous decision.

In *Adarand Constructors, Inc. v. Pena*, Thomas strongly disagreed "with the premise underlying Justice Stevens' and Justice Ginsburg's dissents: that there is a *racial paternalism exception* to the principle of equal protection."

In *Grutter v. Bollinger*, Thomas spoke the unspeakable: that the elites' presumptuous *paternalism* harms minorities even more than the racial discrimination it purportedly seeks to eliminate.

To say that the kind of jurisprudence one sees flowing consistently from Justice Thomas's pen is unique is an understatement.

Having taught constitutional law for some two decades, I have read countless Supreme Court opinions—from those antedating even the legendary *Marbury v. Madison* in the early 1800s to the abominable *Kelo v. City of New London* at the end of the recent 2004 – 2005 term. Those opinions were authored by scores of justices, from *Marbury's* John Marshall to *Kelo's* John Paul Stevens. Yet in no opinions I have read, especially in modern times, has there been the *consistent* originalism and dedication to founding principles and documents that one sees in the Supreme Court jurisprudence of Justice Thomas.

Why not?

Given what we have seen in Justice Thomas's opinions, the answer is not hard to come by.

In matters of statutory interpretation, Justice Thomas, unlike his colleagues, begins with the plain text, and, if he must go further, he relies on definition, syntax, history, context, and reason.

In matters of constitutional interpretation, he relies on historical sources, founding documents, contemporaneous evidence such as the *Federalist*, and timeless principles of natural law.

In a book review by Professor John C. Eastman of Ken Foskett's *Judging Thomas: The Life and Times of Clarence Thomas,* Eastman writes:

> Thomas himself sought out Claremont
> Institute political scientists Ken Masugi
> and John Marini to help him with his
> inquiry into the natural-law principles of
> the American founding.

Further, as chairman of the Equal Employment Opportunity Commission, Thomas "put political theorists on his staff to conduct seminars with him about the principles of the American Founding."

Eastman adds:

> Chairman Thomas hired Masugi and
> Marini "to serve as his intellectual
> mentors . . . ." He [Foskett] describes
> how the self-selected course of study led
> Thomas to a profound appreciation for

the natural-law principles articulated in
the Declaration of Independence and in
Martin Luther King, Jr.'s, "Letter from a
Birmingham Jail," as well as the color-
blind jurisprudence espoused most
forcefully by the late 19th-century
Supreme Court Justice John Harlan in his
famous dissent in *Plessy v. Ferguson*.

If, as Professor Eastman says, "it is becoming clear that
Thomas's own jurisprudential philosophy is more in line with the
principles of our nation's founders, and hence with the Constitution
they framed, than any other sitting Justice's is," the reason can be
found in his acceptance, and application, of the natural-rights
philosophy in which the United States is rooted.

That philosophy is manifest in the Virginia Declaration of
Rights, the Declaration of Independence, the Constitution, the
Federalist, the Bill of Rights, and the post – Civil War amendments. It
is seen in what occurred on July 4, 1776, when the Declaration of
Independence was born; on September 17, 1787, when the Constitution
was promulgated; and on December 15, 1791, when the Bill of Rights
was ratified. It is reflected in the works, and words, of Founders
Alexander Hamilton, Tom Paine, Patrick Henry, Samuel Adams,
Thomas Jefferson, James Otis, and many others—including, especially,
James Madison, considered by many to be the most important of the
Founders.

It is because of Associate Justice of the Supreme Court of the
United States Clarence Thomas's uncompromising fealty to those
founding documents, to those who mid-wifed their birth, and to the
political explosions to which they gave life, that he deserves to be
recognized as The Keeper of the Flame.

259

APPENDIX "A"

OPINIONS OF JUSTICE THOMAS

44 Liquormart, Inc. v. Rhode Island, 517 U.S. 484, 116 S.Ct. 1495 (1996).[349]

Aetna Health Inc. v. Davila, 542 U.S. 200, 124 S.Ct. 2488 (2004).[350]

Alaska v. Native Village of Venetie Tribal Government, 522 U.S. 520, 118 S.Ct. 948 (1998).[351]

Albertsons, Inc. v. Kirkingburg, 527 U.S. 555, 119 S.Ct. 2162 (1999).[352]

Allied-Bruce Terminix Companies, Inc. v. Dobson, 513 U.S. 265, 115 S.Ct 834 (1995).[353]

American Trucking Associations, Inc. v. Michigan Public Service Commission, _U.S._, 125 S.Ct. (2005).[354]

Anderson v. Edwards, 514 U.S. 143, 115 S.Ct. 1291 (1995).[355]

Apprendi v. New Jersey, 530 U.S. 466, 120 S.Ct. 2348 (2000).[356]

Archer v. Warner, 538 U.S. 314, 123 S.Ct. 1462 (2003).[357]

Arizona Department of Revenue v. Blaze Construction Company, Inc., 526 U.S. 32, 119 S.Ct. 957 (1999).[358]

Ashcroft v. American Civil Liberties Union, 535 U.S. 564, 122 S.Ct. 1700 (2002).[359]

Ashcroft v. Free Speech Coalition, 535 U.S. 234, 122 S.Ct. 1389 (2002).[360]

Associated Industries of Missouri v. Lohman, 511 U.S. 641, 114 S.Ct. 1815 (1994).[361]

AT&T Corporation v. Iowa Utilities Board, 525 U.S. 366, 119 S.Ct. 721 (1999).[362]

Banks v. Dretke, 540 U.S. 668, 124 S.Ct. 1256 (2004).[363]

Baral v. United States, 528 U.S. 431, 120 S.Ct. 1006 (2000).[364]

Barnhart v. Peabody Coal Co., 537 U.S. 149, 123 S.Ct. 748 (2003).[365]

Barnhart v. Sigmon Coal Company, Inc., 534 U.S. 438, 122 S.Ct. 941 (2002).[366]

Bates v. Dow Agrosciences LLC, _U.S._, 125 S.Ct. 1788 (2005).[367]

Beard v. Banks, 542 U.S. 406, 124 S.Ct. 2504 (2004).[368]

Beck v. Prupis, 529 U.S. 494, 120 S.Ct. 1609 (2000).[369]

Bedroc Limited, LLC v. United States, 541 U.S. 176, 124 S.Ct. 1587 (2004).[370]

Bell v. Quintero, _U.S._, 125 S. Ct. 2240 (2005).[371]

Bennis v. Michigan, 516 U.S. 442, 116 S.Ct. 994 (1996).[372]

Board of Education of Independent School District No. 92 of Pottawatomie County v. Earls, 536 U.S. 822, 122 S.Ct. 2559 (2002).[373]

Boeing Company v. United States, 537 U.S. 437, 123 S.Ct.1099 (2003).[374]

Bogan v. Scott-Harris, 523 U.S. 44, 118 S.Ct. 966 (1998).[375]

Borgner v. Florida Board of Dentistry, 537 U.S. 1080, 123 S.Ct. 688 (2002).[376]

Brentwood Academy v. Tennessee Secondary School Athletic Association, 531 U.S. 288, 121 S.Ct. 924 (2001).[377]

Buckley v. American Constitutional Law Foundation, Inc., 525 U.S. 182, 119 S.Ct. 636 (1999).[378]

Burlington Industries, Inc. v. Ellerth, 524 U.S. 742, 118 S.Ct. 2257 (1998).[379]

Bush v. Vera, 517 U.S. 952, 116 S.Ct. 1941 (1996).[380]

California Department of Corrections v. Morales, 514 U.S. 499, 115 S.Ct 1597 (1997).[381]

California Division of Labor Standards Enforcement v. Dillingham Construction, N.A., Inc., 519 U.S. 316, 117 S.Ct. 832 (1997).[382]

Campbell v. Louisiana, 523 U.S. 392, 118 S.Ct. 1418 (1998).[383]

Camps Newfound/Owatonna, Inc. v. Town of Harrison, Maine, 520 U.S. 564, 117 S.Ct. 1590 (1997).[384]

Capitol Square Review and Advisory Board v. Pinette, 515 U.S. 753, 115 S.Ct. 2440 (1995).[385]

Cargill, Incorporated v. United States, 516 U.S. 955, 116 S.Ct. 407 (1995).[386]

Caron v. United States, 524 U.S. 308, 118 S.Ct. 2007 (1998).[387]

Carter v. United States, 530 U.S. 255, 120 S.Ct. 2159 (2000).[388]

Cass County, Minnesota v. Leech Lake Band of Chippewa Indians, 524 U.S. 103, 188 S.Ct. 1904 (1998).[389]

Cedar Rapids Community School District v. Garret F., 526 U.S. 66, 119 S.Ct. 992 (1999).[390]

Chavez v. Martinez, 538 U.S. 760, 123 S.Ct. 1994 (2003).[391]

Chen v. City of Houston, 532 U.S. 1046, 121 S.Ct. 2020 (2001).[392]

Cheney v. United States, 542 U.S. 367; 124 S.Ct. 2576 (2004).[393]

Christensen v. Harris County, 529 U.S. 576, 120 S.Ct. 1655 (2000).[394]

Christopher v. Harbury, 536 U.S. 403, 122 S.Ct. 2179 (2000).[395]

City of Edmonds v. Oxford House, Inc., 514 U.S. 725, 115 S.Ct. 1776 (1995).[396]

City of Chicago v. Morales, 527 U.S. 41, 119 S.Ct. 1849 (1999).[397]

City of Indianapolis v. Edmond, 531 U.S. 32, 121 S.Ct. 447 (2000).[398]

City of West Covina v. Perkins, 525 U.S. 234, 119 S.Ct. 678 (1999).[399]

Clark v. Martinez, _U.S._, 125 S.Ct. 716 (2005).[400]

Clingman v. Beaver, _U.S._, 125 S.Ct. 2029 (2005).[401]

Colorado Republican Federal Campaign Committee v. Federal Election Commission, 518 U.S. 604, 116 S.Ct. 2309 (1996).[402]

Columbia Union College v. Clarke, 527 U.S. 1013, 119 S.Ct. 2357 (1999).[403]

Commissioner of Internal Revenue v. Lundy, 516 U.S. 235, 116 S.Ct. 647 (1996).[404]

Commissioner of Internal Revenue v. Soliman, 506 U.S. 168, 113 S.Ct. 701 (1993).[405]

Concrete Pipe and Products of California, Inc. v. Construction Laborers Pension Trust for Southern California, 508 U.S. 602, 113 S.Ct. 2264 (1993).[406]

Connecticut National Bank v. Germain, 503 U.S. 249, 112 S.Ct. 1146 (1992).[407]

Consolidated Rail Corporation v. Gottshall, 512 U.S. 532, 114 S.Ct. 2396 (1994).[408]

Cook v. Gralike, 531 U.S. 510, 121 S.Ct. 1029 (2001).[409]

Cooper Industries, Inc. v. Aviall Services, Inc., _U.S._, 125 S. Ct. 577 (2004).[410]

Cooper Industries, Inc. v. Leatherman Tool Group, Inc., 532 U.S. 424, 121 S.Ct. 1678 (2001).[411]

CSX Transportation, Inc. v. Easterwood, 507 U.S. 658, 113 S.Ct. 1732 (1993).[412]

Cunningham v. Hamilton County, Ohio, 527 U.S. 198, 119 S.Ct. 1915 (1999).[413]

Cutter v. Wilkinson, _U.S._, 125 S.Ct. 2113 (2005).[414]

Dawson v. Delaware, 503 U.S. 159, 112 S.Ct. 1093 (1992).[415]

Deck v. Missouri, _U.S._, 125 S. Ct. 2007 (2005).[416]

Delaware v. New York, 507 U.S. 490, 113 S.Ct. 1550 (1993).[417]

Denver Area Educational Telecommunications Consortium, Inc. v. Federal Communications Commission, 518 U.S. 727, 116 S.Ct. 2374 (1996).[418]

Department of Transportation v. Public Citizen, 541 U.S. 752, 124 S. Ct. 2204 (2004).[419]

Desert Palace, Inc. dba Caesars Palace Hotel & Casino v. Costa, 539 U.S. 90, 123 S. Ct. 2148 (2003).[420]

Director of Revenue of Missouri v. Cobank ACB, 531 U.S. 316, 121 S.Ct. 941 (2001).[421]

District of Columbia v. Greater Washington Board of Trade, 506 U.S. 125, 113 St.Ct. 580 (1992).[422]

Doctor's Associates, Inc. v. Casarotto, 517 U.S. 681, 116 S.Ct. 1652 (1996).[423]

Doggett v. United States, 505 U.S. 647, 112 S.Ct. 2686 (1992).[424]

Dooley v. Korean Air Lines Co., Ltd., 524 U.S. 116, 118 S.Ct. 1890 (1998).[425]

Department of Transportation v. Public Citizen, 541 U.S. 752, 124 S.Ct. 2204 (2004).[426]

Easley v. Cromartie, 532 U.S. 234, 121 S.Ct. 1452 (2001).[427]

Eastern Enterprises v. Apfel, 524 U.S. 498, 118 S.Ct. 2131 (1998).[428]

Edelman v. Lynchburg College, 535 U.S. 106, 122 S.Ct. 1145 (2002).[429]

Egelhoff v. Egelhoff, 532 U.S. 141, 121 S.Ct. 1322 (2001).[430]

Elk Grove Unified School District v. Newdow, 542 U.S. 1, 124 S.Ct. 2301 (2004).[431]

Entergy Louisiana, Inc. v. Louisiana Public Service Commission, 539 U.S. 39, 123 S.Ct. 2050 (2003).[432]

Equal Employment Opportunity Commission v. Waffle House, Inc., 534 U.S. 279, 122 S.Ct. 754 (2002).[433]

Evans v. United States, 504 U.S. 255, 112 S.Ct. 1881 (1992).[434]

Ewing v. California, 538 U.S. 11, 123 S.Ct. 1179 (2003).[435]

Exxon Company, U.S.A. v. Sofec, Inc., 517 U.S. 830, 116 S.Ct. 1813 (1996).[436]

Faragher v. City of Boca Raton, 524 U.S. 775, 118 S.Ct. 2275 (1998).[437]

Farmer v. Brennan, 511 U.S. 825, 114 S.Ct. 1970 (1994).[438]

Farrar v. Hobby, 506 U.S. 103, 113 S.Ct. 566 (1992).[439]

Federal Communications Commission v. Beach Communications, Inc., 508 U.S. 307, 113 S.Ct 2096 (1993).[440]

Federal Deposit Insurance Corporation v. Meyer, 510 U.S. 471, 114 S.Ct. 996 (1994).[441]

Federal Election Commission v. Beaumont, 539 U.S. 146, 123 S.Ct. 2200 (2003).[442]

Federal Election Commission v. Colorado Republican Federal Campaign Committee, 533 U.S. 431, 121 S.Ct 2351 (2001).[443]

Federal Maritime Commission v. South Carolina State Ports Authority, 535 U.S. 743, 122 S.Ct. 1864 (2002).[444]

Feltner v. Columbia Pictures Television, Inc., 523 U.S. 340, 118 S.Ct. 1279 (1998).[445]

Fischer v. United States, 529 U.S. 667, 120 S.Ct. 1780 (2000).[446]

Florida v. White, 526 U.S. 559, 119 S.Ct. 1555 (1999).[447]

Freightliner Corporation v. Myrick, 514 U.S. 280, 115 S.Ct. 1483 (1995).[448]

Fogerty v. Fantasy, Inc., 510 U.S. 517, 114 S.Ct. 1023 (1994).[449]

Foster v. Florida, 537 U.S. 990, 123 S.Ct. 470 2002[450]

Foucha v. Louisiana, 504 U.S. 71, 112 S.Ct. 1780 (1992).[451]

Garlotte v. Fordice, 515 U.S. 39, 115 S.Ct. 1948 (1995).[452]

General Dynamics Land Systems, Inc. v. Cline, 540 U.S. 581, 124 S.Ct. 1236 (2004)[453] .

Georgia v. Ashcroft, 539 U.S. 461, 123 S.Ct. 2498 (2003).[454]

Georgia v. McCollum, 505 U.S. 42, 112 S.Ct. 2348 (1992).[455]

Gitlitz v. Commissioner of Internal Revenue, 531 U.S. 206, 121 S.Ct. 701 (2001).[456]

Glickman v. Wileman Brothers & Elliott, Inc., 512 U.S. 457, 117 S.Ct. 2130 (1997).[457]

Godinez v. Moran, 509 U.S. 389, 113 S.Ct. 2680 (1993).[458]

Gonzales v. Raich, _U.S._, 125 S.Ct. 2195 (2005).[459]

Good News Club v. Milford Central School, 533 U.S. 98, 121 S.Ct. 2093 (2001).[460]

Grable & Sons Metal Products, Inc. v. Darue Engineering & Manufacturing, _U.S._, 125 S. Ct. 2363 (2005).[461]

Graham v. Collins, 506 U.S. 461, 113 S.Ct 892 (1993).[462]

Graham County Soil & Water Conservation District v. United States ex rel. Wilson, _U.S._, 125 S. Ct. 2444 (2005).[463]

Granholm v. Heald, _U.S._, 125 S. Ct. 1885 (2005).[464]

Gratz v. Bollinger, 539 U.S. 244, 123 S.Ct. 2411 (2003).[465]

Greater New Orleans Broadcasting Association, Inc. v. United States, 527 U.S. 173, 119 S.Ct. 1923 (1999)[466]

Green Tree Financial Corp. v. Bazzle, 539 U.S. 444, 123 S.Ct. 2402 (2003).[467]

Groh v. Ramirez, 540 U.S. 551, 124 S.Ct. 1284 (2004).[468]

Grutter v. Bollinger, 539 U.S. 306, 123 S.Ct. 2325 (2003).[469]

Gustafson v. Alloyd Company, Incorporated, 513 U.S. 561, 115 S.Ct. 1061 (1995).[470]

Haitian Refugee Center, Inc. v. Baker, 502 U.S.1122, 112 S.Ct.1245 (1992).[471]

Halbert v. Michigan, _U.S._, 125 S. Ct. 2582 (2005).

Hamdi v. Rumsfeld, 542 U.S. 507, 124 S.Ct. 2633 (2004).[472]

Harper v. Virgina Department of Taxation, 509 U.S. 86, 113 S.Ct. 2510 (1993).[473]

Harris v. United States, 536 U.S. 545, 122 S.Ct. 2406, 122 S.Ct. 2406 (2002).[474]

Harris Trust and Savings Bank v. Salomon Smith Barney, 530 U.S. 238, 120 S.Ct. 2180 (2000).[475]

Heck v. Humphrey, 512 U.S. 477, 114 S.Ct. 234 (1994).[476]

Helling v. McKinney, 509 U.S. 25, 113 S.Ct. 2475 (1993).[477]

Henderson v. United States, 517 U.S. 654, 116 S.Ct. 1638 (1996).[478]

Hillside Dairy, Inc. v. Lyons, 539 U.S. 59, 123 S.Ct. 2142 (2003).[479]

Hoffman v. Harris, 511 U.S. 1060, 114 S.Ct. 1631 (1994).[480]

Holder v. Hall, 512 U.S. 874, 114 S.Ct. 2581 (1994).[481]

Holloway v. United States, 526 U.S. 1, 119 S.Ct. 966 (1999).[482]

Hollywell Corp. v. Smith, 503 U.S. 47, 112 S.Ct. 1021 (1992).[483]

Hope v. Pelzer, 536 U.S. 730, 122 S.Ct. 2508 (2002).[484]

Hopkins v. Reeves, 524 U.S. 88, 118 S.Ct. 1895 (1998).[485]

Household Credit Services, Inc. v. Pfennig, 541 U.S. 232, 124 S.Ct. 1741 (2004).[486]

Howsam v. Dean Witter Reynolds, Inc., 537 U.S. 79, 123 S.Ct. 588 (2002).[487]

Hudson v. McMillian, 503 U.S. 1, 112 S.Ct. 995 (1992).[488]

Hughes Aircraft Company v. Jacobson, 525 U.S. 432, 119 S.Ct. 755 (1999).[489]

Hughes Aircraft Company v. United States ex rel. Schumer, 520 U.S. 939, 117 S.Ct. 1871 (1997).[490]

Hunt v. Cromartie, 526 U.S. 541, 119 S.Ct. 1545 (1999).[491]

Jackson v. Birmingham Board of Education, _U.S._, 125 S.Ct. 1497 (2005).[492]

J.E.M. AG Supply, Inc. v. Pioneer Hi-Bred International, 534 U.S. 124, 122 S.Ct. 592 (2001).[493]

Johanns v. Livestock Marketing Association, _U.S._, 125 S.Ct. 2055 (2005).[494]

John Hancock Mutual Insurance Co. v. Harris Trust and Savings Bank, 510 U.S. 86, 114 S.Ct. 517 (1993).[495]

Johnson v. California, _U.S._, 125 S.Ct. 1141 (2005).[496]

Johnson v. California, _U.S._, 125 S.Ct 2410 (2005).

Johnson v. De Grandy, 512 U.S. 997, 114 S.Ct 2647 (1994).[497]

Johnson v. Texas, 509 U.S. 350, 113 S.Ct. 2658 (1993).[498]

Johnson v. United States, 529 U.S. 694, 120 S.Ct. 1795 (2000).[499]

Jones v. United States, 527 U.S. 373, 119 S.Ct. 2090 (1999).[500]

Jones v. United States, 529 U.S. 848, 120 S.Ct. 1904 (2000).[501]

Kansas v. Colorado, _U.S._, 125 S. Ct. 526 (2004).[502]

Kansas v. Hendricks, 521 U.S. 346, 117 S.Ct. 2072 (1997).[503]

Kelly v. South Carolina, 534 U.S. 246, 122 S.Ct. 726 (2002).[504]

Kelo v. City of New London, 125 S.Ct. 2655 (2005).[505]

Kimel v. Florida Board of Regents, 528 U.S. 62, 120 S.Ct. 631 (2000).[506]

Knight v. Florida, 528 U.S. 990, 120 S.Ct. 458 (1999).[507]

Koons Buick Pontiac GMC, Inc. v. Nigh, _U.S._, 125 S.Ct. 460 (2004).[508]

Kowalski v. Tesmer, _U.S._, 125 S. Ct. 564 (2004).[509]

Lawrence v. Texas, 539 U.S. 558, 123 S.Ct. 2472 (2203).[510]

Lechmere, Inc.v. National Labor Relations Board, 507 U.S 527, 112 S.Ct. 841 (1992).[511]

Lewis v. Casey, 518 U.S. 343, 116 S.Ct. 2174 (1996).[512]

Lilly v.Virginia, 527 U.S. 116, 119 S.Ct. 1887 (1999).[513]

Locke v.Davey, 540 U.S. 712, 124 S.Ct. 1307 (2004).[514]

Lockhart v. Fretwell, 506 U.S. 364, 113 S.Ct. 838 (1993).[515]

Lockheed Corporation v. Spink, 517 U.S. 882, 116 S.Ct 1783 (1996).[516]

Lopez v. Monterey County, 525 U.S. 266, 119 S.Ct. 693 (1999).[517]

Lorillard Tobacco Co. v. Reilly, 533 U.S. 525, 121 S.Ct. 2404 (2001).[518]

Loving v. United States, 517 U.S. 748, 116 S.Ct. 1737 (1996).[519]

Lynce v. Mathis, 519 U.S. 433, 117 S.Ct. 891 (1997)[520]

Mastrobuono v. Shearson Lehman Hutton, Inc., 514 U.S. 52, 115 S.Ct 1212 (1995).[521]

Matsushita Electric Industrial Co., Ltd. v. Epstein, 516 U.S. 367, 116 S.Ct. 873 (1996).[522]

McConnell v. Federal Election Commission, 540 U.S. 93, 124 S.Ct. 619 (2003).[523]

McFarland v. Scott, 512 U.S. 849, 114 S.Ct. 2568 (1994).[524]

McIntyre v. Ohio Elections Commission, 514 U.S. 334, 115 S.Ct. 1511 (1995).[525]

Melendez v. United States, 518 U.S. 120, 116 S.Ct. 2057 (1996).[526]

Michaels v. McGrath, 531 U.S. 1118, 121 S.Ct. 873 (2001).[527]

Miller-El v. Cockrell, 537 U.S. 322, 123 S.Ct. 1029 (2003).[528]

Miller-El v. Dretke, _U.S._, 125 S. Ct. 2317 (2005).[529]

Minnesota v. Mille Lacs Band of Chippewa Indians, 526 U.S. 172, 119 S.Ct. 1187 (1999).[530]

Missouri v. Jenkins, 515 U.S. 70, 115 S.Ct. 2038 (1995).[531]

Mitchell v. Helms, 530 U.S. 793, 120 S.Ct. 2530 (2000).[532]

Mitchell v. United States, 526 U.S. 314, 119 S.Ct. 1307 (1999).[533]

M.L.B. v. S.L.J., 519 U.S. 102, 117 S.Ct. 555 (1996).[534]

Molzof v. United States, 502 U.S. 301, 112 S.Ct. 711 (1992).[535]

Morse v. Republican Party of Virginia, 517 U.S. 186, 116 S.Ct. 1186 (1996).[536]

Musick, Peeler & Garrett v. Employers Ins. of Wassau, 508 U.S. 286, 113 S.Ct. 2085 (1993).[537]

National Aeronautics and Space Administration v. Federal Labor Relations Authority, 527 U.S. 229, 119 S.Ct. 1979 (1999).[538]

National Cable & Telecommunications Association, Inc. v. Brand X Internet Services, 125 S.Ct. 2688 (2005).[539]

National Cable & Telecommunications Association, Inc. v. Gulf Power Co., 534 U.S. 327, 122 S.Ct. 782 (2002).[540]

National Credit Union Administration v. First National Bank & Trust Co., 522 U.S. 479, 118 S.Ct. 927 (1998).[541]

National Park Hospitality Association v. Department of the Interior, 538 U.S. 803, 123 S. Ct. 2026 (2003).[542]

National Passenger Railroad Corporation v. Morgan, 536 U.S. 101, 122 S.Ct. 2061 (2002).[543]

National Private Truck Council, Inc. v. Oklahoma Tax Commission, 515 U.S. 582, 115 S.Ct. 2351 (1995).[544]

Nebraska v. Wyoming, 515 U.S. 1, 115 S.Ct. 1933 (1995).[545]

Nebraska Department of Revenue v. Loewenstein, 513 U.S. 123, 115 S.Ct. 557 (1994).[546]

New York v. Federal Energy Regulatory Commission, 535 U.S. 1, 122 S.Ct. 1012 (2002).[547]

Nixon v. Shrink Missouri Government, 528 U.S. 377, 120 S.Ct. 897 (2000).[548]

Nobelman v. American Savings Bank, 508 U.S. 324, 113 S.Ct. 2106 (1993).[549]

Nordlinger v. Hahn, 505 U.S. 1, 112 S.Ct. 2326 (1992).[550]

Norfolk and Western Railway Company v. Hiles, 516 U.S. 400, 116 S.Ct. 890 (1996).[551]

Northeastern Florida Chapter of the Associated General Contractors of America v. City of Jacnksonville, Florida, 508 U.S. 656, 113 S.Ct. 2297 (1993).[552]

Northwest Airlines, Inc. v. County of Kent, Michigan, 510 U.S. 355, 114 S.Ct. 855 (1994).[553]

O'Dell v. Netherland, 521 U.S. 151, 117 S.Ct. 1969 (1997).[554]

Olmstead v. Zimring, 527 U.S. 581, 119 S.Ct. 2176 (1999).[555]

Olympic Airways v. Husain, 540 U.S. 644, 124 S.Ct. 1221 (2004).[556]

Oncale v. Sundowner Offshore Services, Incorporated, 523 U.S. 75, 118 S.Ct. 998 (1998).[557]

O'Neal v. McAnnich, 513 U.S. 432, 115 S.Ct. 992 (1995).[558]

Oregon Waste Systems, Inc. v. Department of Environmental Quality of the State of Oregon, 511 U.S. 93, 114 S.Ct 1345 (1994).[559]

Orff v. United States, _U.S._, 125 S. Ct. 2606 (2005).[560]

Oubre v. Entergy Operations, Inc., 522 U.S. 422, 118 S.Ct. 838 (1998).[561]

Overton v. Bazzetta, 539 U.S. 126, 123 S.Ct. 2162 (2003).[562]

Pasaquantino v. United States, 125 S.Ct. 1766 (2005).[563]

Peacock v. Thomas, 516 U.S. 349, 116 S.Ct. 862 (1996).[564]

Pennsylvania Bd. of Probation and Parole v. Scott, 524 U.S. 357, 118 S.Ct. 2014 (1998).[565]

Pennsylvania State Police v. Suders, 542 U.S. 129, 124 S.Ct. 2342 (2004).[566]

Penry v. Johnson, 532 U.S. 782, 121 S.Ct. 1910 (2001).[567]

Pharmaceutical Research & Manufacturers of America v. Walsh, 538 U.S. 644, 123 S.Ct. 1855 (2003).[568]

Pierce County, Washington v. Guillen, 537 U.S. 129, 123 S.Ct. 720 (2003).[569]

Pliler v. Ford, 542 U.S. 225, 124 S. Ct. 2441 (2004).[570]

Pollard v. E.I. du Pont de Nemours & Company v. 532 U.S. 843, 121 S.Ct.1946 (2001).[571]

Powell v. Nevada, 5121 U.S. 79, 114 S.Ct. 1280 (1994).[572]

Printz v. United States, 521 U.S. 898, 117 S.Ct. 2367 (1997).[573]

Professional Real Investors, Inc. v. Columbia Pictures Industries, Inc., 508 U.S. 49, 113 S.Ct. 1920 (1993).[574]

PUD No. 1 of Jefferson County v. Washington Department of Ecology, 511 U.S. 700, 114 S.Ct. 1900 (1994).[575]

Rainey v. Chever, 527 U.S. 1044, 119 S.Ct. 2411 (1999).[576]

Randall v. Illinois, 502 U.S. 346, 112 S.Ct 736 (1992).[577]

Rake v. Wade, 508 U.S. 464, 113 S.Ct. 2187 (1993).[578]

Raymond B. Yates, M.D., P.C. Profit Sharing Plan v. Hendon, 541 U.S. 1, 124 S.Ct. 1330 (2004).[579]

Raytheon Company v. Hernandez, 540 U.S. 44, 124 S.Ct. 513 (2003).[580]

Reno v. Bossier Parish School Board, 520 U.S. 471, 117 S.Ct. 1491 (1997).[581]

Reno v. Bossier Parish School Board, 528 U.S. 320, 120 S.Ct. 866 (2000).[582]

Republic National Bank of Miami v. United States, 506 U.S. 80, 113 S.Ct. 554 (1992).[583]

Richmond v. Lewis, 506 U.S. 40, 113 S.Ct. 528 (1992).[584]

Riggins v. Nevada, 504 U.S. 127, 112 S.Ct. 1810 (1992).[585]

Robertson v. Seattle Audubon Society, 503 U.S. 429, 112 S.Ct. 1407 (1992).[586]

Robinson v. Shell Oil Company, 519 U.S. 337, 117 S.Ct. 843 (1997).[587]

Roell v. Withrow, 538 U.S. 580, 123 S.Ct. 1696 (2003).[588]

Rosenberger v. Rector and Visitors of University of Virginia, 515 U.S. 819, 115 S.Ct. 2510 (1995).[589]

Rousey v. Jacoway, 125 S.Ct. 1561 (2005).[590]

Rowland v. California Men's Colony, 506 U.S. 194, 113 S.Ct. 716 (1993).[591]

Rubin v. Coors Brewing Company, 514 U.S. 476, 115 S.Ct 1585 (1995).[592]

Rush Prudential HMO, Inc. v. Moran, 536 U.S. 355, 122 S.Ct. 2151 (2002).[593]

Sabri v. United States, 541 U.S. 600, 124 S.Ct. 1941 (2004).[594]

Saenz v. Roe, 526 U.S. 489, 119 S.Ct. 1518 (1999).[595]

Scarborough v. Principi, 541 U.S. 401, 124 S.Ct. 1856 (2004).

Shalala v. Illinois Council on Long Term Care, Inc., 529 U.S. 1, 120 S.Ct. 1084 (2000).[596]

Shaw v. Murphy, 532 U.S. 223, 121 S.Ct.1475 (2001).[597]

Security Services, Inc. v. K Mart Corp., 511 U.S. 431, 114 S.Ct. 1702 (1994).[598]

Seling v. Young, 531 U.S. 250, 121 S.Ct. 727 (2001).[599]

Shafer v. South Carolina, 532 U.S. 36, 121 S.Ct. 1263 (2001).[600]

Shannon v. United States, 512 U.S. 573, 114 S.Ct. 2419 (1994).[601]

Shepard v. United States, _U.S._, 125 S. Ct. 1254 (2205).[602]

Sims v. Apfel, 530U.S. 103, 120 S.Ct. 2080 (2000).[603]

Small v. United States, _U.S._, 125 S.Ct. 1752 (2005).[604]

Smith v. Doe, 538 U.S. 84, 123 S.Ct. 1140 (2003).[605]

Smith v. Robbins, 528 U.S.259, 120 S.Ct. 746 (2000).[606]

South Central Bell Telephone Company v. Alabama, 526 U.S. 160, 119 S.Ct. 1180 (1999).[607]

South Dakota v. Bourland, 508 U.S. 679, 113 S.Ct 2309 (1993).[608]

Spector v. Norwegian Cruise Line Ltd., _U.S._, 125 S. Ct. 2169 (2005).[609]

State Farm Mutual Automobile Insurance Company v. Campbell, 538 U.S. 408, 123 S.Ct. 1513 (2003).[610]

Staples v. United States, 511 U.S. 600, 114 S.Ct. 1793 (1994).[611]

Stenberg v. Carhart, 530 U.S. 914, 120 S.Ct. 2597 (2000).[612]

Stewart v. Dutra Construction Company, 125 S.Ct. 1118 (2005).[613]

Stewart v. Martinez-Villareal, 523 U.S. 637, 118 S.Ct 1618 (1998).[614]

Swanner v. Anchorage Equal Rights Commission, 513 U.S. 979, 115 S.Ct. 460 (1994).[615]

Swierkiewicz v. Sorema N.A., 534 U.S. 506, 122 S.Ct. 992 (2002).[616]

Taylor v. Freeland & Kronz, 503 U.S. 638, 112 S.Ct. 1644 (1992).[617]

Tennard v. Dretke, 542 U.S. 274, 124 S. Ct. 2562 (2004).[618]

Tennessee Student Assistance Corporation v. Hood, 541 U.S. 440; 124 S.Ct. 1905 (2004).[619]

Things Remembered, Inc. v. Petrarca, 516 U.S. 124, 116 S.Ct. 494 (1995).[620]

Thomas Jefferson University v. Shalala, 512 U.S. 504, 114 S.Ct. 2381 (1994).[621]

Thompson v. Keohane, 516 U.S. 99, 116 S.Ct. 457 (1995).[622]

Thompson v. Western States Medical Center, 535 U.S. 357, 122 S.Ct. 1497 (2002).[623]

Till v. SCS Credit Corporation, 541 U.S. 465, 124 S.Ct. 1951 (2004).[624]

Tory v. Cochran, _U.S._, 125 S.Ct. 2108 (2005).[625]

Troxel v. Granville, 530 U.S. 57, 120 S.Ct. 2054 (2000).[626]

Two Pesos, Inc. v. Taco Cabana, Inc., 505 U.S. 763, 112 S.Ct. 2753 (1992).[627]

Tyler v. Cain, 533 U.S. 656, 121 S.Ct. 2478 (2001).[628]

United Dominion Industries, Inc. v. United States, 532 U.S. 822, 121 S.Ct. 1934 (2001).[629]

United States v. Alaska, 521 U.S. 1, 117 S.Ct. 1888 (1997).[630]

United States v. Alvarez-Sanchez, 511 U.S. 350, 114 S.Ct. 1599 (1994).[631]

United States v. Bakajakjian, 524 U.S. 321, 118 S.Ct. 2028 (1998).[632]

United States v. Bean, 537 U.S. 71, 123 S.Ct. 584 (2002).[633]

United States v. Booker, _U.S._, 125 S. Ct. 738 (2005).[634]

United States v. Craft, 535 U.S. 274, 122 S.Ct. 1414 (2002).[635]

United States v. Fordice, 505 U.S. 717, 112 S.Ct. 2727 (1992).[636]

United States v. Galletti, 541 U.S. 114, 124 S.Ct. 1548 (2004).[637]

United States v. Hatter, 532 U.S. 557, 121 S.Ct. 1782 (2001).[638]

United States v. Hubbell, 530 U.S. 27, 120 S.Ct. 2037 (2000).[639]

United States v. International Business Machines Corporation, 517 U.S. 843, 116 S.Ct. 1793 (1996).[640]

United States v. James Daniel Good Real Property, 510 U.S. 43, 114 S.Ct. 492 (1993).[641]

United States v. LaBonte, 520 U.S. 1673, 117 S.Ct. 1673 (1997).[642]

United States v. Lara, 541 U.S. 193, 124 S.Ct. 1628 (2004).[643]

United States v. Lopez, 514 U.S. 549, 115 S.Ct 1624 (1995).[644]

United States v. McDermott, 507 U.S. 447, 113 S.Ct. 1526 (1993).[645]

United States v. Mezzanatto, 513 U.S. 196, 115 S.Ct. 797 (1995).[646]

United States v. Morrison, 529 U.S. 598, 120 S.Ct. 1740 (2000).[647]

United States v. Oakland Cannabis Buyers' Cooperative, 532 U.S. 483, 121 S.Ct. 1711 (2001).[648]

United States v. O'Hagan, 521 U.S. 642, 117 S.Ct. 2199 (1997).[649]

United States v. Patane, 542 U.S. 630, 124 S.Ct. 2620 (2004).[650]

United States v. Playboy Entertainment Group, Inc., 529 U.S. 803, 120 S.Ct. 1878 (2000).[651]

United States v. Reorganized CF & I Fabricators of Utah, Inc., 518 U.S. 213, 116 S.Ct. 2106 (1996).[652]

United States v. R.L.C., 503 U.S. 291, 112 S.Ct. 1329 (1992).[653]

United States v. Rodriguez-Moreno, 526 U.S. 275, 119 S.Ct. 1239 (1999).[654]

United States v. Ruiz, 536 U.S. 622, 122 S.Ct. 2450 (2002).[655]

United States v. Salerno, 505 U.S. 317, 112 S.Ct. 2503 (1992).[656]

United States v. Scheffer, 523 U.S. 303, 118 S.Ct. 1261 (1998).[657]

United States v. United Foods, Inc., 533 U.S. 405, 121 S.Ct. 2334 (2001).[658]

United States v. White Mountain Apache Tribe, 537 U.S. 465, 123 S.Ct. 1126 (2003).[659]

United States v. Wilson, 503 U.S. 329, 112 S.Ct. 1351 (1992).[660]

United States Department of Defense v. Federal Labor Relations Authority, 510 U.S. 487, 114 S.Ct. 1006 (1994).[661]

United States Postal Service v. Gregory, 534 U.S. 1, 122 S.Ct. 431 (2001).[662]

U.S. By and Through I.R.S. v. McDermott, 507 U.S. 447, 113 S.Ct. 1526 (1993).[663]

U.S. Term Limits, Inc. v. Thornton, 514 U.S. 779, 115 S.Ct. 1842 (1995).[664]

Utah v. Evans, 536 U.S. 452, 122 S.Ct. 2190 (2002).[665]

Van Orden v. Perry, _U.S._, 125 S.Ct. 2854 (2005).[666]

Varity Corporation v. Howe, 516 U.S. 489, 116 S.Ct. 1065 (1996).[667]

Warner-Jenkinson Company, Inc. v. Hilton Davis Chemical Co., 520 U.S. 17, 117 S.Ct. 1040 (1997).[668]

Whitman v. American Trucking Associations, 531 U.S. 457, 121 S.Ct. 903 (2001).[669]

Wilson v. Arkansas, 514 U.S. 927, 115 S.Ct.1914 (1995).[670]

Woodford v. Garceau, 538 U.S. 202, 123 S.Ct. 1398 (2003).[671]

Wright v. West, 505 U.S. 277, 112 S.Ct. 2482 (1992).[672]

Wyoming v. Oklahoma, 502 U.S. 437, 112 S.Ct. 789 (1992).[673]

Young v. Harper, 520 U.S. 117 S.Ct.1148 (1997).[674]

Zelman v. Simmons-Harris, 536 U.S. 639, 122 S.Ct. 2460 (2002).[675]

---

[349] Concurring opinion.

[350] Majority opinion.

[351] Majority opinion.

[352] Concurring opinion.

[353] Dissenting opinion.

[354] Concurring opinion.

[355] Majority opinion.

[356] Concurring opinion.

[357] Dissenting opinion.

[358] Majority opinion.

[359] Majority opinion.

[360] Concurring opinion.

[361] Majority opinion.

[362] Concurring/dissenting opinion.

[363] Concurring/dissenting opinion.

[364] Majority opinion.

[365] Dissenting opinion.

[366] Majority opinion.

[367] Concurring/dissenting opinion.

[368] Majority opinion.

[369] Majority opinion.

[370] Concurring opinion.

[371] Dissenting statement in denial of certiorari.

[372] Concurring opinion.

[373] Majority opinion.

[374] Dissenting opinion.

[375] Majority opinion.

[376] Dissenting statement in denial of certiorari.

[377] Dissenting opinion.

[378] Concurring opinion.

[379] Dissenting opinion.

[380] Concurring opinion.

[381] Majority opinion.

[382] Majority opinion.

[383] Dissenting opinion.

[384] Dissenting opinion.

[385] Concurring opinion.

[386] Dissenting statement in denial of certiorari.

[387] Dissenting opinion.

[388] Majority opinion.

[389] Majority opinion.

[390] Dissenting opinion.

[391] Majority opinion.

[392] Dissenting statement in denial of certiorari.

[393] Concurring/dissenting opinion.

[394] Majority opinion.

[395] Concurring opinion.

[396] Dissenting opinion.

[397] Dissenting opinion.

[398] Dissenting opinion.

[399] Concurring opinion.

[400] Dissenting opinion.

[401] Majority opinion.

[402] Concurring/dissenting opinion.

[403] Dissenting statement in denial of certiorari.

[404] Dissenting opinion.

[405] Concurring opinion.

[406] Concurring opinion.

[407] Majority opinion.

[408] Majority opinion.

[409] Concurring opinion.

[410] Majority opinion.

[411] Concurring opinion.

[412] Concurring opinion.

[413] Majority opinion.

[414] Concurring opinion.

[415] Dissenting opinion.

[416] Dissenting opinion.

[417] Majority opinion.

[418] Concurring/dissenting opinion.

[419] Majority opinion.

[420] Majority opinion.

[421] Majority opinion.

[422] Majority opinion.

[423] Dissenting opinion.

[424] Dissenting opinion.

425 Majority opinion.

426 Majority opinion.

427 Dissenting opinion.

428 Concurring opinion.

429 Concurring opinion.

430 Majority opinion.

431 Concurring opinion.

432 Majority opinion.

433 Dissenting opinion.

434 Dissenting opinion.

435 Concurring opinion.

436 Majority opinion.

437 Dissenting opinion.

438 Concurring opinion.

439 Majority opinion.

440 Majority opinion.

441 Majority opinion.

442 Dissenting opinion.

443 Dissenting opinion.

[444] Majority opinion.

[445] Majority opinion.

[446] Dissenting opinion.

[447] Majority opinion.

[448] Majority opinion.

[449] Concurring opinion.

[450] Concurring opinion in denial of certiorari.

[451] Dissenting opinion.

[452] Dissenting opinion.

[453] Dissenting opinion.

[454] Concurring opinion.

[455] Concurring opinion.

[456] Majority opinion.

[457] Dissenting opinion.

[458] Majority opinion.

[459] Dissenting opinion.

[460] Majority opinion.

[461] Concurring opinion.

[462] Concurring opinion.

[463] Majority opinion.

[464] Dissenting opinion.

[465] Concurring opinion.

[466] Concurring opinion.

[467] Dissenting opinion.

[468] Dissenting opinion.

[469] Concurring/dissenting opinion.

[470] Dissenting opinion.

[471] Concurring statement in denial of certiorari.

[472] Dissenting opinion.

[473] Majority opinion.

[474] Dissenting opinion.

[475] Majority opinion.

[476] Concurring opinion.

[477] Dissenting opinion.

[478] Dissenting opinion.

[479] Concurring/dissenting opinion.

[480] Dissenting statement in denial of certiorari.

[481] Concurring opinion.

[482] Dissenting opinion.

[483] Majority opinion.

[484] Dissenting opinion.

[485] Majority opinion.

[486] Majority opinion.

[487] Concurring opinion.

[488] Dissenting opinion.

[489] Majority opinion.

[490] Majority opinion.

[491] Majority opinion.

[492] Dissenting opinion.

[493] Majority opinion.

[494] Concurring opinion.

[495] Dissenting opinion.

[496] Dissenting opinion.

[497] Dissenting opinion.

[498] Concurring opinion.

[499] Concurring opinion.

[500] Majority opinion.

[501] Concurring opinion.

[502] Concurring opinion.

[503] Majority opinion.

[504] Dissenting opinion.

[505] Dissenting opinion.

[506] Concurring opinion.

[507] Concurring statement in denial of certiorari.

[508] Concurring opinion.

[509] Concurring opinion.

[510] Dissenting opinion.

[511] Majority opinion.

[512] Concurring opinion.

[513] Concurring opinion.

[514] Dissenting opinion.

[515] Concurring opinion.

[516] Majority opinion.

[517] Dissenting opinion.

[518] Concurring opinion.

[519] Concurring opinion.

[520] Concurring opinion.

[521] Dissenting opinion.

[522] Majority opinion.

[523] Concurring/dissenting opinion.

[524] Dissenting opinion.

[525] Concurring opinion.

[526] Majority opinion.

[527] Dissenting statement in denial of certiorari.

[528] Dissenting opinion.

[529] Dissenting opinion.

[530] Dissenting opinion.

[531] Concurring opinion.

[532] Majority opinion.

[533] Dissenting opinion.

[534] Dissenting opinion.

[535] Majority opinion.

[536] Dissenting opinion.

[537] Dissenting opinion.

[538] Dissenting opinion.

[539] Majority Opinion.

[540] Concurring/dissenting opinion.

[541] Majority opinion.

[542] Majority opinion.

[543] Majority opinion.

[544] Majority opinion.

[545] Dissenting opinion.

[546] Majority opinion.

[547] Concurring/dissenting opinion.

[548] Dissenting opinion.

[549] Majority opinion.

[550] Concurring opinion.

[551] Majority opinion.

[552] Majority opinion.

[553] Dissenting opinion.

[554] Majority opinion.

[555] Dissenting opinion.

[556] Majority opinion.

[557] Concurring opinion.

[558] Dissenting opinion.

[559] Majority opinion.

[560] Majority opinion.

[561] Dissenting opinion.

[562] Concurring opinion.

[563] Majority opinion.

[564] Majority opinion.

[565] Majority opinion.

[566] Dissenting opinion.

[567] Concurring/dissenting opinion.

[568] Concurring opinion.

[569] Majority opinion.

[570] Majority opinion.

[571] Majority opinion.

[572] Dissenting opinion.

[573] Concurring opinion.

[574] Majority opinion.

[575] Dissenting opinion.

[576] Dissenting statement in denial of certiorari.

[577] Concurring opinion.

[578] Majority opinion.

[579] Concurring opinion.

[580] Majority opinion.

[581] Concurring opinion.

[582] Concurring opinion.

[583] Concurring opinion.

[584] Concurring opinion.

[585] Dissenting opinion.

[586] Majority opinion.

[587] Majority opinion.

[588] Dissenting opinion.

[589] Concurring opinion.

[590] Majority opinion.

[591] Dissenting opinion.

[592] Majority opinion.

[593] Dissenting opinion.

[594] Concurring opinion.

[595] Dissenting opinion.

[596] Dissenting opinion.

[597] Majority opinion.

[598] Dissenting opinion.

[599] Concurring opinion.

[600] Dissenting opinion.

[601] Majority opinion.

[602] Concurring opinion.

[603] Majority opinion.

[604] Dissenting opinion.

[605] Concurring opinion.

[606] Majority opinion.

[607] Concurring opinion.

[608] Majority opinion.

[609] Concurring/dissenting opinion.

[610] Dissenting opinion.

[611] Majority opinion.

[612] Dissenting opinion.

[613] Majority opinion.

[614] Dissenting opinion.

[615] Dissenting statement in denial of certiorari.

[616] Majority opinion.

[617] Majority opinion.

[618] Dissenting opinion.

[619] Dissenting opinion.

[620] Majority opinion.

[621] Dissenting opinion.

[622] Dissenting opinion.

[623] Concurring opinion.

[624] Concurring opinion.

[625] Dissenting opinion.

[626] Majority opinion.

[627] Concurring opinion.

[628] Majority opinion.

[629] Concurring opinion.

[630] Concurring opinion.

[631] Majority opinion.

[632] Majority opinion.

[633] Majority opinion.

[634] Dissenting opinion (in part).

[635] Dissenting opinion.

[636] Concurring opinion.

[637] Majority opinion.

[638] Concurring opinion.

[639] Concurring opinion.

[640] Majority opinion.

[641] Concurring/dissenting opinion.

[642] Majority opinion.

[643] Concurring opinion.

[644] Concurring opinion.

[645] Dissenting opinion.

[646] Majority opinion.

[647] Concurring opinion.

[648] Majority opinion.

[649] Concurring/ dissenting opinion.

[650] Majority opinion.

[651] Concurring opinion.

[652] Concurring/dissenting opinion.

[653] Dissenting opinion.

[654] Majority opinion.

[655] Concurring opinion.

[656] Majority opinion.

[657] Majority opinion.

[658] Concurring opinion.

[659] Dissenting opinion.

[660] Majority opinion.

[661] Majority opinion.

[662] Concurring opinion.

[663] Dissenting opinion.

[664] Dissenting opinion.

[665] Concurring/dissenting opinion.

[666] Concurring opinion.

[667] Dissenting opinion.

[668] Majority Opinion.

[669] Concurring opinion.

[670] Majority opinion.

[671] Majority Opinion.

[672] Majority opinion.

[673] Dissenting opinion.

[674] Majority opinion.

[675] Concurring opinion.

APPENDIX "B"
STATUTORY INTERPRETATION OPINION OF
JUSTICE THOMAS

Allied-Bruce Terminix Companies, Inc. v. Dobson, 513 U.S. 265, 115 S.Ct 834 (1995). ". . . we should resolve the uncertainty in light of core principles of federalism. * * * To the extent federal statutes are ambiguous, we do not read them to displace state law. Rather, we must be absolutely certain that Congress intended such displacement before we give preemptive effect to a federal statute.")

Archer v. Warner, 538 U.S. 314, 123 S.Ct. 1462 (2003). ("The Court today ignores the plain intent of the parties, as evidenced by a properly executed settlement agreement and general release . . . . I find no support for the Court's conclusion in the text of the Bankruptcy Code, or in the agreements of the parties . . . .")

AT&T Corporation v. Iowa Utilities Board, 525 U.S. 366, 119 S.Ct. 721 (1999). ("In my view, the Act does not unambiguously indicate that Congress intended for such a transfer to occur. Indeed, it specifically reserves for the States the primary responsibility to conduct mediations and arbitrations and to approve agreements between carriers.")

Baral v. United States, 528 U.S. 431, 120 S.Ct. 1006 (2000). ("The plain language of a nearby Code section . . . provides the answer: These remittances are 'paid' on the due date of the taxpayer;s income tax return.")

Barnhart v. Peabody Coal Co., 537 U.S. 149, 123 S.Ct. 748 (2003). ("Unless Congress explicitly states otherwise, 'we construe a statutory term in accordance with its ordinary meaning.' * * * Thus, absent a congressional directive to the contrary, 'shall' must be construed as a mandatory command . . . . * * * If Congress desires for this Court to give 'shall' a nonmandatory meaning, it must say so explicity by specifying the consequences for noncompliance or explicitly define the term 'shall' to mean something other than a mandatory directive. Indeed Congress is perfectly free to signify the hortatory nature of its wishes by choosing among a wide array of words that do, in fact, carry such meaning; 'should,' preferably, and 'if possible' readily come to mind. * * * I fail to see any reason for eviscerating the clear meaning of 'shall,' other than the impermissible goal of saving Congress from its own choices in the name of achieving better policy. But Article III does not vest judges with the authority to rectify those congressional decisions that we view as imprudent.")

Barnhart v. Sigmon Coal Company, Inc., 534 U.S. 438, 122 S.Ct. 941 (2002). ("As in all statutory construction cases, we begin with the language of the statute. The first step is to determine whether the language at issue has a plain and unambiguous meaning with regard to the particular dispute in the case. * * * The inquiry ceases if the statutory language is unambiguous and the statutory scheme is coherent and consistent. * * * With respect to the question presented in this case, this statute is unambiguous.")

Bates v. Dow Agrosciences LLC, _U.S._, 125 S. Ct. 1788 (2005).

Beck v. Prupis, 529 U.S. 494, 120 S.Ct. 1609 (2000). ("To determine what it means to be 'injured . . . by reason of' a 'conspir[acy],' we turn to the well-established common law of civil conspiracy.")

California Division of Labor Standards Enforcement v. Dillingham Construction, N.A., Inc., 519 U.S. 316, 117 U.S. 832 (1997).

Caron v. United States, 524 U.S. 308, 118 S.Ct. 2007 (1998). ("The plain meaning of Section 921(a)(20) thus resolves this case. [The ambiguity seen by the majority] exists because of an interpretation that . . . both accords with a natural reading of the statutory language and is consistent with the statutory purpose.")

Carter v. United States, 530 U.S. 255, 120 U.S. 2159 (2000).

Cedar Rapids Community School District v. Garret F., 526 U.S. 66, 119 S.Ct. 992 (1999). ("If the intent of Congress is clear, that is the end of the matter; for the court, as well as the agency, must give effect to the unambiguously expressed intent of Congress.")

Christensen v. Harris County, 529 U.S. 576, 120 S.Ct. 1655 (2000).

City of Edmonds v. Oxford House, Inc., 514 U.S. 725, 115 S.Ct. 1776 (1995). (". . . I do not agree with the majority's interpretive premise that 'this case [is] an instance in which an exception to "a general statement of policy" is sensibly read "narrowly in order to preserve the primary operation of the [policy].'" * * * Why *this* case? [Emphasis in original] Surely it is not because the FHA has a 'policy'; every statute has that. * * * We do Congress no service . . . by giving that congressional enactment an artificially narrow reading.")

City of Indianapolis v. Edmond, 531 U.S. 32, 121 S.Ct. 447 (2000). ("Because the Code's plain text permits the taxpayers here to receive these benefits, we need not address this policy concern.")

Commissioner of Internal Revenue v. Lundy, 516 U.S. 235, 116 S.Ct. 647 (1996). ("Congress's intent on this issue is difficult to discern. There is reason to think that Congress simply did not consider how not being delinquent in filing a return would affect a taxpayer's right to recover a refund—in any forum. * * * Nevertheless, in light of the language of Section 6511(a), the absence of any reason to think that Congress affirmatively intended to prevent taxpayers who file their returns more than two years late (but less than three years late) from collecting refunds, and the [Internal Revenue] Service's 20-year interpretation of Section 6511 in its Revenue Ruling, I would interpret Section 6511 in conformity with the Revenue Ruling.")

Commissioner of Internal Revenue v. Soliman, 506 U.S. 168, 113 S.Ct. 701 (1993).

Concrete Pipe and Products of California, Inc. v. Construction Laborers Pension Trust for Southern California, 508 U.S. 602, 113 S.Ct. 2264 (1993). ("I decline to participate in this redrafting of a federal law. * * * To me, the public interest is plain on the face of the statute.")

Connecticut National Bank, v. German, 503 U.S. 249, 112 S.Ct. 1146 (1992) ("In interpreting a statute a court should always turn first to one, cardinal canon [of construction] before all others. We have stated time and time again that courts must presume that a legislature says in a statute what it means and means in a statute what it says . . . .")

Consolidated Rail Corporation v. Gottshall, 512 U.S. 532, 114 S.Ct. 2396 (1994). ("First, as in other cases involving the scope of the statute, we must look to [the Federal Employers' Liability Act] itself, its purposes and background, and the construction we have given it over the years. Second, because 'FELA jurisprudence gleans guidance from common-law developments' . . . we must consider the common law's treatment of the right of recovery asserted by [plaintiffs].")

Cooper Industries, Inc. v. Aviall Services, Inc., _U.S._, 125 S. Ct. 577 (2004).

Desert Palace, Inc. dba Caesars Palace Hotel & Casino v. Costa, 539 U.S. 90, 123 S. Ct. 2148 (2003). ("Our precedents make clear that the starting point for our analysis is the statutory text. * * * And where, as here, the words of the statute are unambiguous, the judicial inquiry is complete. * * * Absent some congressional indication to the contrary, we decline to give the same term in the same Act a different meaning depending on whether the rights of the plaintiff or the defendant are at issue.")

District of Columbia v. Greater Washington Board of Trade, 506 U.S. 125, 113 St.Ct. 580 (1992). ("This reading is true to the ordinary meaning of 'relate to' . . . and thus gives effect to the 'deliberately expansive' language chosen by Congress.")

Dooley v. Korean Air Lines Co., Ltd., 524 U.S. 116, 118 S.Ct. 1890 (1998). ("Because Congress has already decided these issues, it has precluded the judiciary from enlarging either the class of beneficiaries or the recoverable damages").

Farrar v. Hobby, 506 U.S. 103, 113 U.S. 566 (1992).

Federal Deposit Insurance Corporation v. Meyer, 510 U.S. 471, 114 S.Ct. 996 (1994).

Federal Maritime Commission v. South Carolina State Ports Authority, 535 U.S. 743, 122 S. Ct. 1864 (2002). ("To decide . . . we must . . . decide whether they are the type of proceedings from which the Framers would have thought the States possessed immunity when the agreed to enter the Union.")

Fischer v. United States, 529 U.S. 667, 120 S.Ct. 1780 (2000). ("I think that the plain language . . . reflects a congressional intent to reach only those organizations that are themselves [emphasis in original] the beneficiaries of 'useful aid' or 'financial aid in time of sickness, old age, or unemployment,' rather than organizations that merely receive funds as part of a market transaction for goods or services.")

Fogerty v. Fantasy, Inc., 510 U.S. 517, 114 S.Ct. 1023 (1994). ("It is difficult to see how the Court, when faced with 'virtually identical' language in two provisions, can hold that a given interpretation is required by the 'plain language' in one instance, but reject that same interpretation as 'mechanical' and 'untenable' in the other)."

General Dynamics Land Systems, Inc. v. Cline, 540 U.S. 581, 124 S.Ct. 1236 (2004). ("This should have been an easy case. The plain language of 29 U.S.C. § 623(a)(1) . . . mandates a particular outcome: that the respondents are able to sue for discrimination against them in favor of older workers. The agency charged with enforcing the statute has adopted a regulation and issued an opinion as an adjudicator, both of which adopt this natural interpretation of the provision. And the only portion of legislative history relevant to the question before us is consistent with this outcome. Despite the fact that these traditional tools of statutory interpretation lead inexorably to the conclusion that respondents can state a claim for discrimination against the relatively young, the Court, apparently disappointed by this result, today adopts a different interpretation. In doing so, the Court, of necessity, creates a new tool of statutory interpretation, and then proceeds to give this newly created 'social history' analysis dispositive weight. Because I cannot agree with the Court's new approach to interpreting anti-discrimination statutes, I respectfully dissent.")

Gitlitz v. Commissioner of Internal Revenue, 531 U.S. 206, 121 S.Ct. 701 (2001).

Gustafson v. Alloyd Company, Incorporated, 513 U.S. 561, 115 S.Ct. 1061 (1995). ("In contrast to the majority's approach of interpreting the statute, I believe the proper method is to begin with the provision actually involved in this case . . . and then turn to the . . . Act's definitional section . . . before consulting the structure of the Act as a whole.")

Henderson v. United States, 517 U.S. 654, 116 S.Ct. 1638 (1996). ("As always, the starting point in interpreting the waiver of sovereign immunity is the text of the statute. * * * The text and structure of the SAA lead me to conclude that Congress intended to allow admiralty suits to proceed against the United States only in cases in which process is served 'forthwith'.")

Holder v. Hall, 512 U.S. 874, 114 S.Ct. 2581 (1994). ("I can no longer adhere to a reading of the Act that does not comport with the terms of the statute and that has produced such a disastrous misadventure in judicial policy-making.")

Holloway v. United States, 526 U.S. 1, 119 S.Ct. 966 (1999). ("I cannot accept the majority's interpretation of the term 'intent' in [the statute] to include the concept of conditional intent. The central difficulty in this case is that the text [of the statute] is silent as to the meaning of 'intent' . . . . * * * As the majority notes . . . there is some authority to support its view that the specific intent to commit an act may be conditional. In my view, that authority does not demonstrate that such a usage was part of a well established historical tradition. Absent a more settled tradition, it cannot be presumed that Congress was familiar with this usage when it enacted the statute. For these reasons . . . the statute cannot be read to include the concept of conditional intent . . . .")

Hollywell Corp. v. Smith, 503 U.S. 47, 112 S.Ct. 1021 (1992).

Hughes Aircraft Company v. Jacobson, 525 U.S. 432, 119 U.S. 755 (1999). ("Our review of the six claims recognized by the Ninth Circuit [Court of Appeals] requires us to interpret a number of ERISA's provisions. As in any case of statutory construction, our analysis begins with 'the language of the statute.' * * * And where the statutory language provides a clear answer, it ends there as well.")

J.E.M. AG Supply, Inc. v. Pioneer Hi-Bred International, 534 U.S. 124, 122 U.S. 592 (2001).

John Hancock Mutual Insurance Co. v. Harris Trust and Savings Bank, 510 U.S. 86, 114 S.Ct. 517 (1993). (". . . the Court . . . proposes a new test that bears little relation to the statute Congress enacted.")

Jackson v. Birmingham Board of Education, 125 S. Ct. 1497 (2005). ("The Court holds that the private right of action under Title IX of the Education Amendments of 1972, for sex discrimination . . . extends to claims of retaliation. Its holding is contrary to the plain terms of Title IX. . . . ")

Johnson v. De Grandy, 512 U.S. 997, 114 S.Ct 2647 (1994).

Kimel v. Florida Board of Regents, 528 U.S. 62, 120 S.Ct. 631 (2000). ("It is natural to begin the . . . inquiry by examining those provisions that reside within the four corners of the Act in question.")

Koons Buick Pontiac GMC, Inc. v. Nigh, 125 S. Ct. 460 (2004).

Lechmere, Inc. v. National Labor Relations Board, 507 U.S 527, 112 S.Ct. 841 (1992).

Lockheed Corporation v. Spink, 517 U.S. 882, 116 S.Ct 1783 (1996).

McConnell v. Federal Election Commission, 540 U.S. 93, 124 S.Ct. 619 (2003).

Melendez v. United States, 518 U.S. 120, 116 S.Ct. 2057 (1996).

Morse v. Republican Party of Virginia, 517 U.S. 186, 116 S.Ct. 1186 (1996). ("The Voting Rights Act provides no definition of the term 'State.' When words in a statute are not otherwise defined, it is fundamental that they will be interpreted as taking their ordinary, contemporary, common meaning. * * * That the statutory term 'State' should be applied in light of its ordinary meaning is reinforced by the Act's definition of the term 'political subdivision.' * * * There is further statutory evidence to support this interpretation of 'State.' * * * In light of the plain meaning of the phrase 'State or political subdivision,' I see no reason to defer to the Attorney General's regulation interpreting that statute to cover political parties.")

Matsushita Electric Industrial Co., Ltd. v. Epstein, 516 U.S. 367, 116 S.Ct. 873 (1996).

Nebraska Department of Revenue v. Loewenstein, 513 U.S. 123, 115 S.Ct. 557 (1994).

Norfolk and Western Railway Company v. Hiles, 516 U.S. 400, 116 S.Ct. 890 (1996). (". . . Congress legislated working automatic [railroad car] couplers for employee safety, not employee safety by whatever method a court might deem appropriate.")

Northwest Airlines, Inc. v. County of Kent, Michigan, 510 U.S. 355, 114 S.Ct. 855 (1994).

Olmstead v. Zimring, 527 U.S. 581, 119 S.Ct. 2176 (1999).

O'Neal v. McAnnich, 513 U.S. 432, 115 S.Ct. 992 (1995).

Orff v. United States, 125 S.Ct. 2606 (2005).

Oubre v. Entergy Operations, Inc., 522 U.S. 422, 118 S.Ct. 838 (1998). ("Not only does the text of the [Older Workers Benefit Protection Act] make no mention of ratification, but it also cannot be said that the doctrine is inconsistent with the statute.")

Pasaquantino v. United States, _U.S._, 125 S. Ct. 1766 (2005). ("The question presented in this case is whether a plot to defraud a foreign government of tax revenue violates the federal wire fraud statute . . . . Because the plain terms of §1343 criminalize such a scheme, and because this construction of the wire fraud statute does not derogate from the common-law revenue rule, we hold that it does.")

Pharmaceutical Research & Manufacturers of America v. Walsh, 538 U.S. 644, 123 S.Ct. 1855 (2003).

Pierce County, Washington v. Guillen, 537 U.S. 129, 123 S.Ct. 720 (2003).

Pollard v. E.I. du Pont de Nemours & Company v. 532 U.S. 843, 121 S.Ct. 1946 (2001).

Professional Real Investors, Inc. v. Columbia Pictures Industries, Inc., 508 U.S. 49, 113 S.Ct. 1920 (1993).

PUD No. 1 of Jefferson County v. Washington Department of Ecology, 511 U.S. 700, 114 S.Ct. 1900 (1994). ("The Court today fundamentally alters the federal-state balance Congress carefully crafted in the [Clean Water Act], and . . . such a result is neither mandated nor supported by the text of Section 401 . . . .")

Raymond B. Yates, M.D., P.C. Profit Sharing Plan v. Hendon, 541 U.S. 1, 124 S.Ct. 1330 (2004). ("Since the text is inconclusive, we must turn to the common-law understanding of the term "employee.")

Robinson v. Shell Oil Company, 519 U.S. 337, 117 S.Ct. 843 (1997). ("Our first step in interpreting a statute is to determine whether the language at issue has a plain and unambiguous meaning with regard to the particular dispute in the case. Our inquiry must cease if the statutory language is unambiguous and 'the statutory scheme is coherent and consistent'.")

Roell v. Withrow, 538 U.S. 580, 123 S.Ct. 1696 (2003). ("In my view, this interpretation of Section 636(c)(1) is contrary to its text, fails to respect the statutory scheme, and raises serious constitutional concerns").

Rosenberger v. Rector and Visitors of University of Virginia, 515 U.S. 819, 115 S.Ct. 2510 (1995). ("Thus, history provides an answer for the constitutional question posed by this case, but, it is not the one given by the dissent. The dissent identifies no evidence that the Framers intended to disable religious entities from participating on neutral terms in evenhanded government programs. The evidence that does exist points in the opposite direction and provides ample support for today's decision.")

Rousey v. Jacoway, _U.S._, 125 S.Ct. 1561 (2005).

Rush Prudential HMO, Inc. v. Moran, 536 U.S. 355, 122 S.Ct. 2151 (2002).

Saenz v. Roe, 526 U.S. 489, 119 S.Ct. 1518 (1999). ("Unlike the majority, I would look to history to ascertain the original meaning of the [Privileges or Immunities] Clause.")

Security Services, Inc. v. K Mart Corp., 511 U.S. 431, 114 S.Ct. 1702 (1994).

Shannon v. United States, 512 U.S. 573, 114 S.Ct. 2419 (1994). ("We are not aware of any case . . . in which we have given authoritative weight to a single passage of legislative history that is in no way anchored in the text of the statute. * * * To give effect to this snippet of legislative history, we would have to abandon altogether the text of the statute as a guide in the interpretation process.")

Small v. United States, 125 S. Ct. 1752 (2005) ("In concluding that 'any' means not what it says, but rather 'a subset of any,' the Court distorts the plain meaning of the statute and departs from established principles of statutory construction.")

South Dakota v. Bourland, 508 U.S. 679, 113 S.Ct 2309 (1993).

Staples v. United States, 511 U.S. 600, 114 S.Ct. 1793 (1994). ("The language of the statute, the starting place in our inquiry . . . provides little explicit guidance . . . . * * * [Accordingly] we must construe the statute in light of the background rules of the common law . . . .")

Stenberg v. Carhart, 530 U.S. 914, 120 S.Ct. 2597 (2000). ("In their brief analyses, the majority and Justice O'Connor disregard all of the statutory language except for the final definitional sentence, thereby violating the fundamental canon of construction that statutes are to be read as a whole.")

Stewart v. Dutra Construction Company, 125 S. Ct. 1118 (2005) ("Although the statute is silent on who is a 'seaman,' both the maritime law backdrop against which Congress enacted the Jones Act and Congress' subsequent enactments provide some guidance.")

Stewart v. Martinez-Villareal, 523 U.S. 637, 118 S.Ct 1618 (1998). ("Unlike the Court, I begin with the plain words of the statute. * * * Ultimately, the Court's holding is driven by what it sees as the 'far reaching and seemingly pervasive' implications for federal habeas [corpus] practice of a literal reading of the statute. * * * Such concerns are not, in my view, sufficient to override the statute's plain meaning.")

Taylor v. Freeland & Kronz, 503 U.S. 638, 112 U.S. 1644 (1992).

Things Remembered, Inc. v. Petrarca, 516 U.S. 124, 116 S.Ct. 494 (1995).

Thomas Jefferson University v. Shalala, 512 U.S. 504, 114 S.Ct. 2381 (1994).

Tyler v. Cain, 533 U.S. 656, 121 S.Ct. 2478 (2001).

United Dominion Industries, Inc. v. United States, 532 U.S. 822, 121 S.Ct. 1934 (2001). ("At a bare minimum, in cases such as this one, in which the complex statutory and regulatory scheme lends itself to any number of interpretations, we should be inclined to rely on the traditional canon that construes revenue-raising laws against their drafter.")

United States v. Alvarez-Sanchez, 511 U.S. 350, 114 S.Ct.1599 (1994). ("When interpreting a statute, we look first and foremost to its text. * * * Because 'delay' is not defined in the statute, we must construe the term in accordance with its ordinary or natural meaning.")

United States v. Hubbell, 530 U.S. 27, 120 S.Ct. 2037 (2000). ("None of this Court's cases . . . has undertaken an analysis of the meaning of the term at the time of the founding. A review of that period reveals substantial support for the view that the term 'witness' meant a person who gives or furnishes evidence, a broader meaning than that which our case law currently ascribes to that term.")

United States v. LaBonte, 520 U.S. 1673, 117 S.Ct. 1673 (1997). ("We conclude that the Commission's interpretation is inconsistent with [the statute's] plain language, and therefore hold that 'maximum term authorized' must be read to include all applicable statutory sentencing enhancements.")

United States v. R.L.C., 503 U.S. 291, 112 S.Ct. 1329 (1992).

United States v. Rodriguez-Moreno, 526 U.S. 275, 119 S.Ct. 1239 (1999). ("The Third Circuit . . . looked to the verbs of the statute to determine the nature of the substantive offense. But we have never before held, and decline to do so here, that verbs are the sole consideration in identifying the conduct that constitutes and offense. While the 'verb test' certainly has value as an interpretive tool, it cannot be applied rigidly, to the exclusion of other relevant statutory language. The test unduly limits the inquiry and thereby creates a danger that certain conduct prohibited by statute will be missed.")

United States v. Salerno, 505 U.S. 317, 112 S.Ct. 2503 (1992) ("Thus, history provides an answer for the constitutional question posed by this case, but, it is not the one given by the dissent. The dissent identifies no evidence that the Framers intended to disable religious entities from participating on neutral terms in evenhanded government programs. The evidence that does exist points in the opposite direction and provides ample support for today's decision.")

United States v. Wilson, 503 U.S. 329, 112 S.Ct. 1351 (1992).

United States Department of Defense v. Federal Labor Relations Authority, 510 U.S. 487, 114 S.Ct. 1006 (1994). ("We decline to accept respondents' ambitious invitation to rewrite the statutes before us . . . .")

U.S. Term Limits, Inc. v. Thornton, 514 U.S. 779, 115 S.Ct. 1842 (1995). ("Nothing in the Constitution deprives the people of each State of the power to prescribe eligibility requirements for the candidates who seek to represent them in Congress. The Constitution is simply silent on this question. And where the Constitution is silent, it raises no bar to action by the States or the people.")

Utah v. Evans, 536 U.S. 452, 122 S.Ct. 2190 (2002). ("Mindful of the importance of calculating the population, the Framers chose their language with precision, requiring an 'actual Enumeration,' . . . . They opted for this language even though they were well aware that estimation methods and inferences could be used to calculate population. If the language of the Census Clause any room for doubt, the historical context, debates accompanying ratification, and subsequent early Census Acts confirm that the use of estimation techniques . . . do not comply with the Constitution.")

Varity Corporation v. Howe, 516 U.S. 489, 116 S.Ct. 1065 (1996). ("If Congress had intended to allow individual plan participants to secure equitable relief for fiduciary breaches, I presume it would have made that clear in . . . the provisions specifically enacted to address breach of fiduciary duty. * * * With only passing reference to the relevant statutory text, the majority discards the limits that Congress imposed on fiduciary status and replaces them with a far broader standard plucked from the common law of trusts.")

ABOUT THE AUTHOR

Henry Mark Holzer received his B.A. degree from New York University, where he studied Russian and political science.

He then served in Korea with military intelligence, holding top-secret security clearance, and was Chief Order of Battle Analyst (Chinese Communist Forces) for the Eighth Army.

Professor Holzer received his Juris Doctor degree from New York University School of Law. For over forty-six years, he has practiced constitutional and appellate law.

In addition to his law practice, for over two decades Professor Holzer was a full-time tenured professor of law at Brooklyn Law School, where he is now professor emeritus. His courses included Constitutional Law, First Amendment, National Security, and Appellate Advocacy.

Professor Holzer is the author of nearly two hundred articles, essays, and reviews. He frequently publishes commentary on current legal and political events on the Internet at www.henrymarkholzer.com, www.frontpagemag.com, www.theconservativevoice.com, and other websites.

Professor Holzer's six out-of-print books—*The Gold Clause; Government's Money Monopoly; Sweet Land of Liberty? The Supreme Court and Individual Rights; The Layman's Guide to Tax Evasion; Speaking Freely: The Case Against Speech Codes*; and *Why* Not *Call It Treason?Korea, Vietnam, Afghanistan and Today*—are available from various Internet booksellers, including www.amazon.com.

Professor Holzer is co-author—with his wife, lawyer and novelist Erika Holzer—of "*Aid and Comfort*": *Jane Fonda in North Vietnam*, which answers the question of whether Fonda's trip to Hanoi during the Vietnam War, and her activities there, constituted treason. With Erika Holzer, he also co-authored *Fake Warriors: Identifying, Exposing, and Punishing Those Who Falsify Their Military Service.* Each of these books are available at www.amazon.com.

Henry Mark Holzer's legal practice is limited to consulting with other lawyers in constitutional and appellate cases.

Further information concerning Professor Holzer may be obtained at his website, www.henrymarkholzer.com. He may be contacted at hank@henrymarkholzer.com.

Printed in the United States
52349LVS00004B/145-165